Praise for *Loved Egyptian Night*

'This is a superbly constructed compilation of Hugh Roberts's writings that marries his key, near-contemporaneous writings about the uprisings in Libya, Egypt, and Syria with his more recent reflections on those events. Chapter 4, "What Was the Arab Spring?", is a must-read.'
Helena Cobban, president of Just World Educational, author of *The Palestinian Liberation Organisation* and *The Making of Modern Lebanon*

'The old adage "without fear or favour" came to mind when reading Hugh Roberts's incisive and insightful analysis of the Arab Spring. Roberts draws on his intimate knowledge and careful tracing of events in Libya, Egypt and Syria to subvert the myths and falsehoods that led to political and policy mistakes. But it is the book's offer of a constructive alternative – what could have been, but never was – that makes it, more than anything, essential reading for the future.'
Katerina Dalacoura, London School of Economics, author of *Islamist Terrorism and Democracy in the Middle East*

'Roberts's insight-laden book unravels multilayered legacies, temporalities and dynamics that are at the heart of understanding the Arab uprisings and their far-reaching consequences.'
Tamirace Fakhoury, Aalborg University, co-author of *Resisting Sectarianism*

Loved Egyptian Night

The Meaning of the Arab Spring

Hugh Roberts

VERSO

London • New York

First published by Verso 2024
© Hugh Roberts 2024

Author and publisher are grateful to the *London Review of Books* for permitting
the republication of articles that appear herein in expanded form as chapters 1–3.

1 3 5 7 9 10 8 6 4 2

Verso
UK: 6 Meard Street, London W1F 0EG
US: 388 Atlantic Avenue, Brooklyn, NY 11217
versobooks.com

Verso is the imprint of New Left Books

ISBN-13: 978-1-83976-883-5
ISBN-13: 978-1-83976-882-8 (US EBK)
ISBN-13: 978-1-83976-881-1 (UK EBK)

British Library Cataloguing in Publication Data
A catalogue record for this book is available from the British Library

Library of Congress Cataloging-in-Publication Data

Names: Roberts, Hugh, 1950– author.
Title: Loved Egyptian night : the meaning of the Arab Spring / Hugh
  Roberts.
Description: Brooklyn, NY : Verso Books, 2024. | Includes bibliographical
  references and index.
Identifiers: LCCN 2023036504 (print) | LCCN 2023036505 (ebook) | ISBN
  9781839768835 (hardback) | ISBN 9781839768828 (ebk)
Subjects: LCSH: Arab Spring, 2010– | Egypt—Politics and government—21st
  century. | Libya—Politics and government—21st century. |
  Syria—Politics and government—2000-
Classification: LCC JQ1850.A91 R62 2024 (print) | LCC JQ1850.A91 (ebook)
  | DDC 909/.097492708312—dc23/eng/20230812
LC record available at https://lccn.loc.gov/2023036504
LC ebook record available at https://lccn.loc.gov/2023036505

Typeset in Sabon by Hewer Text UK Ltd, Edinburgh
Printed and bound by CPI Group (UK) Ltd, Croydon CR0 4YY

FSC
www.fsc.org
MIX
Paper | Supporting
responsible forestry
FSC® C171272

For Leila

and in memory of
Dr David Goldey, late Fellow of Lincoln College, Oxford,
and lecturer in politics at Trinity College, Oxford,
an inspiring teacher

Take up the White Man's burden –
And reap his old reward:
The blame of those ye better
The hate of those ye guard –
The cry of hosts ye humour
(Ah, slowly!) towards the light:
'Why brought ye us from bondage,
'Our loved Egyptian night?'

Rudyard Kipling, *The White Man's Burden* (1899)

Contents

Preface

This book addresses the political history of the uprisings in Egypt, Libya and Syria that began in early 2011 and offers an explanation of the course of each of them. These explanations are grounded in a critical understanding of the general character of the Arab Spring that oriented my thinking from the outset.

If politics – in the sense of the practice of politics – is, as Bismarck declared, an art, not a science, the study of politics must be a branch of criticism. Like other branches – literary criticism, theatre criticism, and so on – it must obey certain standards of intellectual rigour if it is to be of any worth. These requirements include respect for the evidence and for the rules of reasoning and a commitment to objectivity. An additional but essential element of a critical analysis is that the author takes responsibility for his or her own judgments. A feature of international commentary on the Arab Spring has been the degree of uniformity of its main elements, the extent to which it has resembled a chorus. I am suspicious of choruses where understandings of political history are at stake. I have made my own judgments and defend them here.

In this book I examine the three episodes of regime change – successful, at least in achieving the downfall of the autocrat, in Egypt and Libya; attempted but unsuccessful in Syria – that were at the heart of the Arab Spring. A central issue is the validity or invalidity of the label of 'revolution' when affixed to these events. That the Arab Spring was a series of revolutions became the orthodoxy of international academic as well as media coverage very quickly. I was in no doubt that what had occurred in Tunisia was a revolution. But I was strongly inclined to scepticism where Egypt was concerned, not to mention Libya and Syria.

The uprising in Tunisia had gone beyond merely overthrowing President Zine el-Abidine Ben Ali; it had ended the political monopoly of the ruling party, on which Ben Ali's dictatorship had been premised, and had then charted a course towards democracy with the legalising of numerous political parties and the organising of elections to a Constituent Assembly. The rising did not merely eject an autocrat, it transcended and left behind the system that had made his dictatorship possible, and so had every right to call itself a revolution. The subsequent uprisings in Egypt, Libya, Syria and elsewhere were all inspired in part by the Tunisian example and claimed comparable revolutionary credentials. But, having devoted my life to the study of North Africa and having lived in Egypt since 2001, I was keenly aware of the differences between Tunisia and its putative emulators.

Tunisia was the only one of these countries to have been governed by a political party; where, that is, a political party did not merely 'rule' in name but was the source of power, the orchestrater of the state–society relationship and the maker of laws. This primacy of a modern political institution, the ruling party, was exceptional. In neither Egypt nor Algeria did the nominally ruling parties play a similar role;[1] while in both cases the form of government was presidential, the president derived his power from the army commanders, not the party, and the party was in reality a façade for the power structure, the source neither of power nor policy nor law. Syria might be said to have been ruled by the Ba'th Party since 1963, but in fact this was a militarised hybrid, the Ba'th Party as remade by its 'military committee', in which it was no longer the party as such but the armed forces and security organs that were the principal sources of power. Tunisia's experience of being governed by a political party for over fifty years (1956–2011) was, in the Middle East and North Africa, quite unique.[2]

This experience of party rule had several corollaries that would prove extremely useful from the point of view of an aspiration to refashion the state along democratic lines. It confined the army to a modest role as the loyal servant of the state; it kept official Islam subordinate to *raison d'État*; and it enabled the state to promote an exceptionally advanced view of the rights and status of women. To these widely overlooked benefits of party rule should be added two other factors: the character of the Tunisian General Labour Union (Union Générale Tunisienne du Travail, UGTT) and the importance of the constitutionalist tradition.

The standard practice of governments in the MENA region has been to impose some form of corporatism on national labour organisations, except in those monarchies (Saudi Arabia, UAE) that do not allow any form of labour organisation at all. In Algeria, the General Union of Algerian Workers (Union Générale des Travailleurs Algériens, UGTA) was founded in 1956, during the war of independence, as an extension of the FLN's social presence and under its aegis, drawing Algerian Muslim workers out of the French unions they had been enrolled in up to that point, and this relationship was consolidated after independence when the Party of the FLN imposed its control on the UGTA at the expense of the latter's aspirations for autonomy. In Egypt, the Free Officers' state imposed a corporatist formula on the previously more loosely organised trade unions there with the formation of the Egyptian Trade Union Federation (ETUF) in 1957.[3] In Syria, where the General Federation of Trade Unions (GFTU) had been founded in 1948, a corporatist formula was imposed by the Ba'thist government in 1968, obliging all trade unions to affiliate to the GFTU while ensuring that the latter's leadership was controlled by the Arab Ba'th Socialist Party.[4]

In Tunisia it has been a different story. The UGTT was founded in 1946 and functioned for its first decade as a free trade union, while also participating in the struggle against French rule. Its leaders being committed nationalists as well as trade unionists, the UGTT played a key role as an ally of Habib Bourguiba's Néo-Destour Party and acquired considerable political legitimacy of its own within the party, a development promoted and reinforced by the striking personality and later martyrdom of its founder and first general secretary, Farhat Hached, assassinated by the ultra-colonialist Main Rouge in 1952. Obliged after Tunisia's independence in 1956 to accept subordination to the party in exchange for representation in the party's leadership and a say in government policy, it was never fully reduced to a corporatist instrument of the state and the hegemony of the party was conditional and incomplete, the regime never daring to restructure let alone replace the UGTT at any point. For its part, the UGTT, even under 'collaborationist' national leaderships, preserved fundamental trade union rights and practices and was capable of rebelling against the government on occasion, notably in the general strike of 1978. Thus it was that the UGTT proved to have both the organisational capacity and the political will to play a crucial and leading role in the uprising of December 2010. It was the UGTT that developed the initially localised demonstrations over the fate of Mohamed Bouazizi into a national movement of protest that increasingly targeted President Ben Ali while moving from the periphery to the core of the Tunisian state. The UGTT continued to guide the development of the revolution and subsequently that of the fledgling democracy thereafter, and crucially came to the rescue in 2013, as the leader of the 'Quartet' of four civil society organisations, by brokering the compromise between Ennahda, the Islamist party dominating the government since the elections of October 2011, and the other political parties that headed off a political breakdown when this was very much in prospect. It did this by making possible the adoption of a new constitution on the basis of a large consensus as the *quid pro quo* of early elections leading to a transfer of power between Ennahda and its main rival, the newly formed secularist party Nidaa Tounes (The Call of Tunisia), that respected the rules of the fledgling democratic order.

Nothing like this was available to the uprising in Egypt, let alone to those in Libya and Syria. The comprehensively corporatist nature of the ETUF meant that Egyptian workers were able to join and support the rising only as individuals and 'played no political role in determining the political contours of the post-Mubarak era'.[5]

Finally, party rule from 1956 to 2010 contributed decisively to preserving the collective memory of constitutionalism as a founding tradition of the Tunisian polity and thus as an important element – guidepost, yardstick, compass – in the social consciousness of the Tunisian people. This tradition had given rise to the first expression of modernist anti-colonialism in Tunisia, the Constitutional Liberal Party – al-Ḥizb al-Ḥurr al-Dustūrī – founded in 1920, from which Bourguiba's Néo-Destour was derived as a more radical breakaway in 1934, and had been carried by every successive incarnation of Tunisian nationalism as a thread running through Tunisia's political history and development thereafter. These things cannot be measured with precision but there is no doubt that this tradition contributed substantially to the ability displayed by Tunisia's political elite to envisage, negotiate and carry through a constitutional revolution. Although constitutionalism had featured in Egypt's political life in the early twentieth century, it had not survived as an effective tradition into the twenty-first; outside a certain, rather intellectual, element of the Muslim Brothers, Nasserist ideology and the successive dictatorial governments of the Free Officers' state had wiped it out.[6]

Being familiar with these features of the Tunisian case, I always doubted the possibility of a comparable revolution in Egypt, let alone Libya. Moreover, I also doubted that the Egyptian revolutionaries were even aware of these remarkable aspects of the revolution they aspired to emulate. During my time in Cairo, I had been repeatedly struck by the indifference of secular Egyptian intellectuals to developments in the Maghreb; they were interested exclusively in the Mashreq (Middle East) – Israel–Palestine, the Levant in general, the Gulf – and not at all in the Maghreb. In her recent book on Tahrir Square, Rusha Latif describes what the Egyptian would-be revolutionaries learned from the Tunisians,

> whose unexpected revolt in December 2010 demonstrated what was possible for Egyptians if they tapped into their people power. If Tunisians could rise up in the streets and take down their dogged dictator and his regime in a matter of weeks, what was to stop Egyptians – whose numbers were after all far greater – from doing the same?

This suggests that the Egyptians learned next to nothing from the Tunisian events, of which they had an entirely superficial view, reducing the Tunisian revolution – and accordingly the Egyptian project of emulating it – to 'taking down the dictator and his regime'. And the only significant difference between Tunisia and Egypt as far as they could see was that there were more Egyptians. Latif's brisk summary may be unfair to the Egyptian revolutionaries but, if there were some among them who had appreciated the specificity of Tunisia and the particular logic of events there, it cannot be said that they had any influence over how events unfolded in Egypt.

In early 2011, when I was due to return to my old post as director of the International Crisis Group's North Africa Project, I was invited to have breakfast with a delegation from the Open Society Foundation at the Semiramis Hotel on 24 January. Ben Ali had fallen ten days earlier and my hosts wanted to know whether comparable upheavals were in prospect elsewhere. I told them that we could certainly expect uprisings encouraged by the Tunisians' success and to their question, 'Where next?', I replied, 'Here.' I explained that, while Egypt was a very different country, with a different form of government and state–society relationship from Tunisia, it resembled Tunisia superficially at that juncture in that it too had an aged autocrat whose legitimacy was challenged by the charge that he was subordinating the presidency to the interest of his family by trying to ensure his son, Gamal Mubarak, succeeded him (as Ben Ali had let his office be damaged by the ruthlessly self-aggrandising activities of his second wife, Leila Trabelsi). Moreover, this was happening just a few weeks since the brazenly rigged legislative elections of November–December 2010, calamitously mismanaged by the president's son and his cronies, and at a time of widespread distress over the decline of living standards for millions of Egyptians in the wake of the 2007–8 global financial crisis. I told them the eventual outcome would be determined by the differences between Egypt and Tunisia but that the short term would be shaped by the superficial similarities. I did not know that demonstrations had been planned for the following day but, aware of Gamal's limitations, the army's hostility to his succession and the deteriorating economy, I had been expecting serious unrest in any case since long before the uprising in Tunisia got under way.[8]

That Egypt, Libya and Syria could not really emulate Tunisia did not mean that they could not have revolutions of their own, each with its own dynamics and trajectory. But the fact that the uprisings in these countries resembled past revolutions in formal terms, displaying some of the sound and fury and spectacular street theatre so often associated with the idea of revolution, did not signify much to my eyes, despite my sympathy for the protesters and my admiration for their courage. In assessing these uprisings, the question I asked concerned not their form but their substance, and it was this: are they really on course to transcend the political and constitutional framework of the authoritarian rule they are denouncing? This was the litmus test in my opinion. While wholly opposed to the military intervention in Libya, I was at first open-minded about the secretive and accordingly difficult to appraise leadership of the so-called Transitional National Council and adopted a wait-and-see attitude to it. Where Egypt was concerned, the question was whether the rising would put paid to the underlying premise of Mubarak's autocratic presidency, the Free Officers' state. It became clear within days that this was not in prospect and that, whatever the 'revolutionaries' thought they were doing, they were in fact facilitating a renewal of the Free Officers' state by complementing the generals' manœuvres to recover the controlling role that Mubarak had long denied them.

In view of the extent to which international media coverage of these episodes had personalised the issue, reducing what was at stake to the ejection of the ruler, thoroughly demonised by Western commentary in particular every time, my contrary opinion risked being mistaken for support for the ruler, and was so misinterpreted by some in the Libyan case. I took it that the emphasis placed by Western and Arab media on the business of securing the downfall of the autocrat, whether Mubarak or Qadhafi or Asad, indicated the lack of Western or Arab interest in these risings leading to any deeper change. This did not surprise me; I have watched the policies of the Western powers towards the MENA region and the behaviour of the Gulf monarchies for decades, and it has long been evident to me that they have always been and are still wholly opposed to any genuine development of democracy in the region.

In the essays published in edited form in the *London Review of Books* in 2011, 2013 and 2015, and republished here in slightly fuller versions as chapters 1–3, my criticism went so far as to disapprove of all three of the episodes in question. These essays were written in the wake of watershed events: the killing of Qadhafi; the coup deposing President Morsi; the dramatic complication of the Syrian situation by the emergence of Islamic State. I have no reason to take back now what I wrote then. Who today can, in the name of democracy or human rights, seriously approve of or rejoice in what has become of Egypt, or Libya, or Syria?

In the second half of the book, written much more recently and previously unpublished, I consider the general character of the Arab Spring and then revisit the Libyan and Egyptian cases in depth, in the light of the additional evidence available. In opposition to the convenient myths that the outcomes of these 'revolutions' should be blamed on counter-revolutionary 'deep states' (Egypt, Syria), or 'mission creep' plus 'militias' (Libya), I show how the bitter ends of these risings were in their beginnings. Approving of these beginnings by calling them revolutions is a kind of intellectual complicity in their failure to be real revolutions, and expresses the conformism required by a cult rather than a truly revolutionary outlook.

I did not criticise these episodes because they were revolutions, but because, seeing how far – and why – they fell short of being the genuine revolutions they were hailed as and claimed to be, I expected them to have disastrous consequences, as they have done. These outcomes have owed a lot to the real nature of Western policy and action in these events, as I explain and document in this book.

When Kipling wrote 'The White Man's Burden', he took it for granted that the British Empire was a force for progress and exhorted the United States, then demonstrating new ambition in the Philippines, to follow the British example and carry on promoting progress in the world, no matter how unappreciative its supposed beneficiaries. These notions have had a new currency since the end of the Cold War with the resurgence of Western imperialism in the shape of the globalisation agenda and its rider, 'democracy promotion'. *Wherefore by their fruits ye shall know them.* Whatever grounds may once have existed for reading into Western neo-imperialism a promise of real progress benefiting the peoples in its thrall, let alone of genuine support for democratic aspirations, those grounds have vanished as far as the peoples of the Middle East and North Africa are concerned. What remains is the debris of a cynical pretension. In the course of the Arab Spring, the Western powers did not vainly strive to free the Egyptians or anyone else from authoritarian rule, they contrived to seal them up in it. The 'loved Egyptian night' Kipling talked of is not going to be ended by Western power; it is guaranteed by it.

Acknowledgements

I wish to thank Adam Shatz, Daniel Soar and Alice Spawls for supporting and assisting the publication of my original articles on Libya, Egypt and Syria in the *London Review of Books* (on 17 November 2011, 12 September 2013 and 16 July 2015 respectively), and the editors of *LRB* and Alice Spawls in particular for their permission to republish these, in slightly expanded versions, as Chapters 1–3 of this book.

At the International Crisis Group, I greatly appreciated Rob Malley's support for my work and his willingness to back my view of the Libyan drama in 2011; I wish also to thank for their support the two presidents of ICG I worked under, Gareth Evans in 2002–7 and Louise Arbour in 2011, and, among my other colleagues, Rob Blecher, Alain Deletroz, Comfort Ero, Romain Grandjean, Joost Hiltermann, Mouin Rabbani and Andrew Stroehlein.

More generally, my thinking about the Middle East has benefited from conversations over the years with numerous other observers, scholars and colleagues. These have included Christopher Alexander, Michaël Ayari, Paul Beran, Peter Brooke, Jack Brown, Ken Brown, Terry Burke, Edouard Bustin, Melani Cammett, John Chalcraft, Laryssa Chomiak, Helena Cobban, Patrick Cockburn, Sylvain Cypel, Katerina Dalacoura, Daikha Dridi, Issandr ElAmrani, Jean-Noël Ferrié, Mansouria Mokhefi Geist, Michael Gilsenan, Maria Golia, Amr Hamzawy, Clement Henry, Fahmy Howeidy, Hisham Kassem, Laleh Khalili, Philip Khoury, Eberhard Kienle, Joshua Landis, Fred Lawson, Jean Leca, Ann Lesch, Paul Lubeck, David Morrison, Hassan Nafaa, Ronald Neumann, the late Augustus Richard Norton, Robin Ostle, the late Roger Owen, Alison Pargeter, Robert Parks,

William Quandt, Hilary Rantisi, Dia Rashwan, Max Rodenbeck, Paul Saba, Heba Saleh, the late Mohamed El-Sayed Said, Mustafa Kamal al-Sayed, the late Patrick Seale, David Seddon, Hilmy Shaaraoui, Emad Shahin, the late Mohamed Sid Ahmed, Robert Springborg, Joshua Stacher, Yassine Temlali, Dirk Vandewalle, I. William Zartman and Sami Zubaida.

I should also like to thank Tariq Ali and Andrew Hsiao for their support for this project, Robert Brenner and Perry Anderson for their invitation to address a seminar on Egypt at UCLA in 2014 and for their hospitality on that occasion, and my editor at Verso, Tom Hazeldine, for his shrewd advice, assistance and encouragement.

None of the above bear any responsibility for the opinions and judgments expressed in this book.

Finally, I should like to thank my partner, Elizabeth, my daughter Leila, and all the members of my families in England and Egypt for their support while I have been completing this book.

A Note on Transliteration

I have adopted the transliteration employed by Hans Wehr's authoritative *Dictionary of Modern Written Arabic*. Where authors I am quoting use other transliteration formulas, I quote the Arabic words they use as they spell them, while adhering to Wehr's spelling in my own writing.

1

Delivering Libya

I

So Qadhafi is dead and NATO has fought a war in North Africa for the first time since the FLN defeated France in 1962. The Arab world's one and only 'State of the Masses', the Socialist People's Libyan Arab Jamahiriyya, has ended badly, as Dirk Vandewalle, one of the rare Western specialists on the country, suggested it might at a conference I attended several years ago. In contrast to the bloodless coup of 1 September 1969 that deposed King Idris and brought Qadhafi and his colleagues to power, the combined rebellion/civil war/NATO bombing campaign to protect civilians has occasioned several thousand (5,000? 10,000? 25,000?) deaths, many thousands of injured and hundreds of thousands of displaced persons, as well as massive damage to infrastructure. What if anything has Libya got in exchange for all the death and destruction that have been visited on it over the past seven and a half months?

The overthrow of Qadhafi & co. was far from being a straightforward revolution against tyranny. Presented by the National Transitional Council (NTC) and cheered on by the Western media as an integral part of the Arab Spring, and thus supposedly of a kind with the upheavals in Tunisia and Egypt, the Libyan drama is rather an addition to the list of Western or Western-backed wars against hostile, 'defiant', insufficiently 'compliant', or 'rogue' regimes: Afghanistan I and II (1979–92; 2001), Iraq I and II (1990–1; 2003) and the Federal Republic of

Yugoslavia (1999); to which we might, with qualifications, add the military interventions in Panama (1989–90), Sierra Leone (2000) and the Ivory Coast (2011). An older series we might bear in mind includes the Bay of Pigs (1961), the intervention by Western mercenaries in the Congo (1964), the British-assisted palace coup in Oman in 1970 and – last but not least – three abortive plots, farmed out to David Stirling and sundry other mercenaries under the initially benevolent eye of Western intelligence services, to overthrow the Qadhafi regime between 1971 and 1973 in an episode known as the Hilton Assignment.[1]

At the same time, the story of Libya in 2011 stands at the intersection of several different debates. The first of these, over the pros and cons of the military intervention, has tended to eclipse the others. But numerous states in Africa and Asia and no doubt Latin America as well (Cuba and Venezuela spring to mind) may wish to consider why the Jamahiriyya, despite mending its fences with Washington and London in 2003–4 and dealing reasonably with Paris and Rome, should have proved so vulnerable to their sudden hostility. And the Libyan war should also give those of us in Europe and North America who value our democratic heritage a renewed interest in examining what the Western powers are doing to democratic principles and the idea of the rule of law in the process of doing what they are doing to the rest of the world, and the Arab and Muslim world in particular.

The Afghans who rebelled against the Communist regimes of Nur Mohammed Taraki, Hafizullah Amin and the Soviet-backed Babrak Karmal, and in 1992 overthrew Mohammed Najibullah before laying waste to Kabul in protracted factional warfare, called themselves *mujahidin*, 'fighters for the faith'. They were conducting a jihad against godless Marxists and saw no need to be coy about it, in view of the enthusiastic media coverage as well as logistical support the West was giving them. But the Libyans who took up arms against Qadhafi's Jamahiriyya have sedulously avoided this label, at least when near Western microphones. Religion had little to do with the upheavals in Tunisia and Egypt: Islamists were almost entirely absent from the stage in Tunisia until the fall of Ben Ali; in Egypt the Muslim Brothers had not instigated the protest movement (in which Coptic Christians also took part) and tactfully made sure their support for it, while important, remained discreet. And so the irrelevance of Islamism to the popular revolt against despotic regimes was part of the way the Arab Spring came to be read in the West, and the rhetorical strategies of Libyan rebels and Qadhafi loyalists alike tacitly recognised this fact.

The Western media generally endorsed the rebels' description of themselves as forward-looking liberal democrats, and dismissed Qadhafi's exaggerated claim that al-Qaida was behind the revolt. But the evidence that the rebellion has mobilised Islamists and acquired an Islamist coloration that significantly qualifies its liberal-democratic pretensions has become impossible to ignore. On his first visit to Tripoli, Mustafa Abdul Jalil, the chairman of the NTC, then still based in Benghazi, declared that all legislation of the future Libyan state would be grounded in the Sharī'a, pre-empting any future elected body on this cardinal point. And Abdul Hakim Belhaj, whom the NTC appointed to the newly created post of military commander of Tripoli, is a former leader of the Libyan Islamic Fighting Group, a movement which conducted a campaign of terrorism against the Libyan state in the 1990s and went on to provide recruits to al-Qaida. The democratic revolutionaries in Tunisia are now concerned that the re-emergence of the Islamist movement there has diverted political debate from constitutional questions to toxic identity issues and may derail the country's nascent democracy; so the Islamist aspect of the Libyan rebellion should put us on our guard and is one among several reasons to ask whether what we have been witnessing is a revolution or a counter-revolution.

The rebels have gone through several name changes in the Western media's serviceable lexicon: peaceful demonstrators, democracy protesters, civilians; then (a belated admission) rebels and, finally, revolutionaries. Revolutionaries – in Arabic, *thuwwār* (singular: *thā'ir*) – has been their preferred label at least since the fall of Tripoli. *Thā'ir* can simply mean 'agitated' or 'excited'. The young men who spent much of the period between April and July careering up and down the coastal highway in Toyota pick-ups (and the whole of September running backwards and forwards around Bani Walid), while firing as much of their ammunition into the air as at the enemy, have certainly been excited. But how many veterans of revolutions elsewhere, as distinct from Western journalists, would recognise them as their counterparts?

In their subjective aspect the events in both Tunisia and Egypt have merited the 'revolutionary' label. The change that has occurred in Egypt falls well short of a genuine revolution, because the army's return to power means that the country's political life has yet to transcend the logic of the Free Officers' state established in 1952. But the way hundreds of thousands stood up against Hosni Mubarak last winter was a historic event Egyptians will never forget. The same is true of Tunisia, except that events have gone much further, amounting to a revolution in their objective as well as subjective aspects, not merely toppling Ben Ali but also ending the monopoly of the old ruling party. With the demise of the *parti-État*, the Tunisians have entered the unknown. Whether they have the resources to cope with the Islamist movement may be their greatest test. The recent elections suggest they are coping pretty well. But, whether or not their revolution proves a success in the longer term, it is certainly a revolution.

Libya is another matter. The events of mid-February were part of the wider 'Arab awakening' in two respects. The unrest began on 15 February, three days after the fall of Mubarak: so there was a contagion effect and clearly many of the Libyans who took to the streets over the next few days were animated by some of the same sentiments as their counterparts elsewhere. But the Libyan uprising diverged from the Tunisian and Egyptian templates in two ways: the rapidity with which it took on a violent aspect – the destruction of state buildings and xenophobic attacks on Egyptians, Serbs, Koreans and, above all, black Africans;[2] and the extent to which, brandishing the old Libyan flag of the 1951–69 era, the protesters identified their cause with the monarchy Qadhafi & co. overthrew.[3] This divergence owed a lot to external influences. But it also owed much to the character of Qadhafi's state and regime.

II

Widely ridiculed as the bizarre creation of its eccentric if not lunatic 'Guide', the Socialist People's Libyan Arab Jamahiriyya in fact shared many features with other Arab states. With the massive increase in oil revenues following the nationalisations and the rise of OPEC in the early 1970s, Libya became not only a 'hydrocarbon society', as the English anthropologist John Davis remarked in a penetrating study,[4] but one that resembled the states of the Gulf more than its North African neighbours. Contrary to the thesis put about as part of the war effort, Libya's oil revenues were distributed very widely, the new regime laying on a welfare state from which virtually all Libyans benefited, while also relying on oil wealth, as the Gulf states do, to buy in whatever it lacked in terms of technology and consumer goods, not to mention foreign workers. To the emerging 'hydrocarbon society' corresponded the new Jamahiriyya as a 'distributive state', and it is fairly clear that, for Qadhafi and his colleagues, the state's distributive role quickly became the central element in their strategy for governing the country, given the dilemma they faced over the question of political institutions.

The 1969 coup belonged to the series of upheavals that challenged the arrangements made by Britain and France to dominate the Arab world after the destruction of the Ottoman Empire at the end of the First World War. These challenges took on a new vigour in the wake of the defeats of France and Italy during the Second World War and the supersession of British by American hegemony in the Middle East. A key feature of these arrangements was the sponsoring, safeguarding and manipulation of newly confected monarchies in Saudi Arabia, Jordan, Iraq, Egypt, Libya and the Gulf statelets, and in most cases the challenges were precipitated by abrupt – and for the Arabs, catastrophic – developments in the Arab–Israeli conflict. Just as the Free Officers who deposed King Farouq in Egypt in 1952 were outraged at the incompetent way Egypt's armed forces were led in 1948, and the 1958 revolution in Iraq owed much to the increased hostility of the officer corps as well as public opinion to the pro-British monarchy in the wake of the Suez affair, so the Arab defeat in 1967 and, crucially, frustration at Libya's absence from the Arab struggle prompted Qadhafi and his colleagues to overthrow the Libyan monarchy. The problem was that, beyond closing the US base at Wheelus Field and nationalising the oil, they didn't know what to do next.

Unlike his Hashemite counterparts, who came from Mecca and were foreigners in Jordan and Iraq, King Idris was at least a Libyan. He also had legitimacy as the head of the Sanussiyya religious order, which in the course of the nineteenth and early twentieth centuries had established itself the length and breadth of eastern Libya and had distinguished itself in the resistance to the Italian conquest from 1911 onwards. But, like the Hashemites, Idris came to the throne as a protégé of the British, who fished him out of Cairo, where he had spent more than twenty years in exile, to make him king and thereby recast Libya as a monarchy when the UN in 1951 finally decided what should be done with the former Italian colony.

The Sanussiyya, originally an Islamic revivalist order, was set up in north-eastern Libya, the province the Italians called Cyrenaica, by an immigrant divine from Mostaganem in western Algeria, Sayyid Mohammed ben Ali al-Sanussi al-Idrisi,* who founded his order in Mecca in 1837 but moved it to Libya in 1843. It took root throughout the eastern province in the interstices of Bedouin tribal society and spread south along the trade routes that crossed the Sahara into Sudan, Chad and Niger. It had less of a presence in western Libya: in Tripolitania in the north-west, which had its own religious and political traditions based on the Ottoman connection, and Fezzan in the south-west. The two western provinces have always been considered part of the Maghreb (the Arab west), linked primarily to Tunisia and Algeria, while eastern Libya has always been part of the Mashreq (the Arab east) and oriented to Egypt and the rest of the Arab Levant. And there is a case for saying that the rise of the Sanussiyya aggravated the gulf between western and eastern

---

* 'Al-Sanussi' denoted his ancestors' origins in the Beni Snous tribe south of Tlemcen; 'Al-Idrisi' claimed descent from the first dynasty to rule Morocco.

Libya; the headquarters of the order were located, not near Cyrenaica's border with Tripolitania, but at Al-Bayda in north-central Cyrenaica and then far to the east at Jaghbub, on the border with Egypt, where Idris himself was born. The new monarchy's internal social basis was thus markedly uneven, and Idris was badly placed to promote a genuine process of national integration. He opted instead for a federal constitution that, politically speaking, left Libyan society much as he found it while, out of deference to his Western sponsors as well as alarm at the rise of radical Arab nationalism and Nasserism in particular, he insulated the country as far as possible from developments in the rest of the Arab world. Qadhafi's coup was a revolt against this state of affairs, and the key to understanding the otherwise baffling flamboyance of his foreign policy thereafter is that it was grounded in his determination that Libya should no longer be a backwater. But the sense of mission that this foreign policy expressed was also connected to his internal strategy.

The new regime's inner circle was drawn from a small number of tribes, above all the Qadhadhfa, the Magarha and the Warfalla. The Qadhadhfa have historically occupied a band of territory extending from near Sebha in the eastern Fezzan up to Sirte on the coast, close to where Tripolitania ends and Cyrenaica begins. The Magarha, the tribe of Qadhafi's long-time deputy, Abdessalam Jalloud, are located to the west of the Qadhadhfa, straddling the north-eastern Fezzan and south-eastern Tripolitania. The Warfalla, Libya's largest tribe, said to number over a million, are based in south-eastern Tripolitania with their capital at Bani Walid. This background did not dispose Qadhafi and his associates to identify with the political and cultural traditions of the Tripoli elites or those of Benghazi and the other coastal towns. As the elites saw it, the 1969 coup had been made by 'Bedouin' – that is, country bumpkins. For Qadhafi & co., neither the traditions of Tripoli nor those of Benghazi offered a satisfactory recipe for governing Libya, but rather recipes for perpetuating its disunity.

The Mediterranean and the Middle East are not short of examples of lands made painfully into nations by states based, not on the more advanced and sophisticated societies of the seaboards, but on the backward, bleak and hard regions of the interior. It was the austere society and sombre towns of the Castilian plateau, not cosmopolitan Barcelona or sunny Valencia or Granada, that brought forth the kingdom which, once joined to Aragon, united the rest of Spain around it, at the expense of the rich culture of Andalusia in particular. In much the same way, Abdelaziz Ibn Sa'ūd, ruler of Arabia's Castile, the unforgiving plateau of the Nejd, united Arabia under his sword while forcing the far more cultured townsmen of the Hijaz, nourished on the traditions of all four *maḍāhib* (legal schools) of Sunni Islam and well acquainted with the various Shī'a traditions, to bend the knee to the Al-Sa'ūd and to the Hanbali dogmatism of the Wahhabi Ikhwān. Bearing these precedents in mind, we can see that the great problem for Qadhafi & co., once they had made their coup, was the simulta-neous imperative and difficulty of emulating the Spanish and Saudi templates. *Los Reyes Catolicos* could act as the local secu-lar arm of the international church militant in forcibly uniting Spain and putting those who resisted in the name of its cultural diversity to the question and the stake. Ibn Sa'ūd had the Muwahhidūn, the militant disciples of the Nejdi religious reformer Muhammad Ibn Abd al-Wahhāb, behind him in his drive to unify Arabia by conquest. Even the mainly modernist revolutionaries of the FLN had religion going for them in confronting a Christian colonial power, and as heirs to the reform movement (*al-iṣlāḥ*) conducted by the Association of the '*ulama* (religious scholars) from the 1930s onwards. But Qadhafi & co. had no militant and serviceable religious banner available to them, and what existed in the way of organised Islam in Libya was disposed to resist them.

Pre-empted in the religious sphere by both the Sanūssiyya in the east and the pan-Islamic tradition, dating from the Ottoman era, of the Tripolitanian '*ulama*, they desperately needed a doctrinal source of some sort for the kind of ideological enthu-siasm required to mobilise and reorder Libyan society. At the outset, they thought they had this in pan-Arabism, which, espe-cially in its Nasserist version, had from 1952 onwards inspired enthusiasm across North Africa, putting the champions of

Islamic enthusiasm on the back foot. But Qadhafi & co. were latecomers to the Arab-nationalist revolutionary ball and, little more than a year after their seizure of power, Nasser was dead. For some time Qadhafi persisted with the idea of a strategic relationship with Egypt, which would have helped to solve several of the new Libya's problems, providing both the much-needed sense of belonging to a powerful alliance and facilitating the regime's efforts to deal with refractory currents in Cyrenaica. But, as Egypt under Anwar Sadat veered away from pan-Arabism, the premises of this perspective dissolved. Plans for an Egyptian–Libyan union, belatedly announced in August 1972, led nowhere and relations deteriorated. In late 1973 an anti-Egyptian campaign was launched in the Libyan press and Libya's embassy in Cairo was closed.

Qadhafi now tried to contract a – very different – alliance with his western neighbour, in the joint declaration of a new 'Arab-Islamic Republic' with Tunisia's Habib Bourguiba in January 1974. This too proved stillborn, as numerous onlookers – particularly Tunisians – wondered *what on earth* the worldly, Francophile, secular and moderate Bourguiba could have been thinking and Algeria's President Houari Boumediène weighed in to remind Tunis that there could be no shift in the geopolitical balance of the Maghreb without Algeria's agreement. Following the logic of this, Qadhafi sought and secured an alliance with Algeria, and in 1975 Boumediène and Qadhafi signed a treaty of mutual friendship and solidarity. It appeared that Libya had at last entered an alliance it could rely on and be steadied by. Two years later, following Sadat's visit to Jerusalem, Libya joined Algeria, Syria, South Yemen and the PLO in the 'Steadfastness Front' opposed to any rapprochement with Israel. But Boumediène unexpectedly fell ill and died in late 1978; his successor, Chadli Bendjedid, emulating Sadat, abandoned Algeria's revolutionary commitments and the protective alliance with Tripoli among them, and Libya was alone again. A measure of Qadhafi's desperation was evident in the – again, short-lived – treaty he signed with Morocco's King Hassan in 1984. It was his last attempt to fit in with fellow North African and Arab states. Instead, he now looked with increased interest to sub-Saharan Africa, where the Jamahiriyya, having much to offer African states, could play the benevolent patron.

All the states of North Africa have had African policies of a kind. And all but Tunisia have strategic hinterlands consisting of the countries to their south: for Egypt, the Sudan; for Algeria, the Sahel states (Niger, Mali and Mauritania); for Morocco, Mauritania also, a permanent bone of contention with Algeria. In pursuing their African policies, the North African states often compete with one another, but they have also been in competition with Western powers keen to preserve or, in the case of the US, to contract patron–client relations with these states. What distinguished Qadhafi's Libya from its North African neighbours was the extent of its investment in this southern strategy and the degree to which this became central to Tripoli's conception of Libya's mission in the world.

The Jamahiriyya's African policy had a darker side, as seen in Qadhafi's support for fellow Muslim Idi Amin (though that seems less grotesque when weighed against the support of Western governments for Mobutu Sese Seko or Jean-Bedel Bokassa). There was also Libya's involvement in Chad's civil war and attempted annexation of the Aouzou Strip and its sustained involvement in the Tuareg question in Niger and Mali. At the same time, it gave strong financial and practical support to the African Union, opposed the installation of the US military's 'Africom' on the soil of any African country and funded a wide range of development projects in sub-Saharan countries. According to the Egyptian political economist Samir Amin, an instance of this was Qadhafi's plan, as part of his project of exploiting the immense water reserves under Libya's Sahara, to make available to the Sahel countries a substantial amount of this water, which could have transformed their economic prospects.[5] This possibility has now almost certainly been killed off by NATO's intervention, since Western (and perhaps particularly French) water companies are lining up alongside Western oil firms for their slices of the Libyan pie.

Qadhafi's African policy gave Libya a firm geopolitical position and consolidated its strategic hinterland while also benefiting Africa. That many African countries appreciated Libya's contribution to the continent's affairs was made clear by the AU's opposition to NATO's intervention and its sustained efforts to broker a ceasefire and negotiations between the two sides of the civil war. These efforts were dismissed with scorn by Western governments and press, with African opposition to the military intervention derided as Libya's clients merely doing their duty to their patron, a judgment that was outrageously disrespectful and unfair to South Africa in particular. That the Arab League's support for a no-fly zone, trumpeted by London, Paris and Washington as implying Arab endorsement and legitimation of NATO's intervention, was almost entirely the affair of client states which, dependent upon Western protection and favour, had demonstrated their subservience to Western policy years ago, was of course never mentioned.

The irony in this state of affairs appears to have escaped notice. Saif al-Islam's contemptuous comment on the Arab League's resolution – 'El-Arab? Toz fi el-Arab!' ('The Arabs? To hell with the Arabs!')[6] – expressed the family's bitter recognition that the pan-Arabism behind the 1969 revolution had long ago become obsolete as the majority of Arab states subsided into shamefaced submission to the Western powers. The problem for Qadhafi & co. was that the African perspective they had diligently pursued as a *solution de rechange* for defunct pan-Arabism consistent with their original anti-imperialist world-view meant little to the many Libyans who wanted Libya to approximate to Dubai, or, worse, stirred virulent resentment against the regime and black Africans alike. And so, in taking Libya into Africa while tending to remove it from, or constitute it into a lonely and embarrassingly unwanted presence in, Arab regional affairs, the foreign policy of the Jamahiriyya ended up resembling in one key respect that of Idris's monarchy before it, relegating Libya into a backwater in relation to the rest of the Middle East and cutting the Libyans off from other Arabs, especially the well-heeled Gulf Arabs to whose lifestyle many middle-class Libyans aspired. In this way, the regime's foreign policy made it vulnerable to a revolt inspired by events elsewhere in the Arab world. But it was also vulnerable for a more important reason.

The authors of the 1969 coup initially took Nasser's Egypt for their model, imitating its institutions and terminology – Free Officers, Revolutionary Command Council – and equipping themselves with a single 'party', the [Libyan] Arab Socialist Union (ASU), like Nasser's prototype essentially a state apparatus providing a façade for the new regime. But within two years, Sadat's de-Nasserisation purges were under way and he was mending fences with the Muslim Brothers, while the beginning of *infitāḥ* – his policy of opening up the economy – announced the retreat from 'Arab socialism', and the rift with Moscow presaged the turn to America. Thus the Egyptian model evolved rapidly into an anti-model, while the experiment with the ASU proved an instructive failure. The idea of a single party seemed to make sense in Libya as it had originally made sense in Egypt and also Algeria. Leaders of military regimes needed to set up a civilian façade so that they could offer a degree of controlled representation and socialise the politically ambitious into the new dispensation. But in Egypt and Algeria the architects of the new single party were dealing with comparatively politicised populations. Qadhafi & co. were confronting something else, a politically inert society, with little in the way of a state tradition, that had been pulverised by a brutal colonial conquest, and a population reduced to onlookers as the country became a battleground in the Second World War, then liberated from colonial rule by external forces and finally tranquillised by the Sanussi monarchy. In trying to launch the ASU, the new regime found little to work with in terms of political talent or energy in the wider population; instead, it was the old elites of Tripoli and Benghazi who invested in the party, which accordingly not only failed to mobilise popular enthusiasm but became a focus of resistance to the revolution Qadhafi had in mind.

This was the context in which Qadhafi began to develop an idea he had first voiced within weeks of seizing power in 1969: that representative democracy was unsuited to Libya. Other leaders in North Africa and the Middle East privately took the same view of their own countries, and in pretending to allow and provide for representation they were acknowledging their vice in tacitly paying homage to virtue. But, in eventually erecting, in his *Third Universal Theory* (a.k.a. the *Green Book*), his rejection of representation into an explicit constitutive principle of the 'State of the Masses', Qadhafi scandalised people by refusing to be a hypocrite.[7] The real problem, however, was that his new course ultimately engaged Libya in a historic impasse.

Dispensing with the ASU and the very idea of a single ruling party, he promoted instead the tandem of 'People's Congresses' and 'Revolutionary Committees' as the key political institutions of the Jamahiriyya, which was eventually proclaimed in 1977. The former were to assume responsibility for public administration and secure popular participation, the latter to keep the flame of the Revolution alive. The members of the People's Congresses were elected, and these elections were taken seriously, at least at the local level and for a while.[8] But voters were not, in theory, choosing representatives, merely deciding whom among the candidates on offer they trusted to assume the mainly administrative responsibilities of the bodies in question. The system encouraged political and ideological unanimity, allowing no voice for dissident opinion except on trivial or at best secondary matters. It drew many ordinary Libyans into a sort of participation in public affairs, although this was waning by the mid-1990s, but it did not educate them in other aspects of the political art and did not work well on its own terms either.

Widely described as the bizarre product of an eccentric ideology, Qadhafi's State of the Masses actually drew on ideas developed elsewhere. The championing of direct over representative democracy was a prominent feature of the utopian outlook of young Western leftists in the 1960s. And the strategic decision to mobilise the 'revolutionary' energies of the young to outflank conservative party apparatuses was central to Mao's Cultural Revolution and a feature of Boumediène's 'Révolution socialiste' as well. Where Qadhafi went further was in abolishing the ASU and outlawing parties altogether, but in this he could claim a doctrinal warrant. The notion that there should be no political parties in a Muslim country has long been advocated by some currents of Sunni Islamism, on the grounds that 'party' connotes *fitna*, division of the community of the faithful, the supreme danger. Kuwait, Oman, Saudi Arabia and the United Arab Emirates allow no political parties to this day.

This was not a minor consideration. Qadhafi's rule had a definite Islamic aspect that was more pronounced than that of the regimes in Cairo and Algiers. That this went together with intolerance of Islamists owed everything to the fact that he was the source of radicalism, intent on remaining so and unwilling to allow rivals to infringe his monopoly. In 1978, he announced that the Qur'ân was the sole source of scriptural authority for Islamic government and law, thereby promoting a radically egalitarian national Islam, in that all Libyans had equal access to the Qur'ân – given the general literacy that the regime made real efforts to promote – but, above all, depriving at a stroke the *'ulama* of their claim to influence as the authorities in matters of scriptural exegesis and interpretation, in so far as this claim relied on their specialist erudition regarding the Sunna, the hadith and the legal and theological commentaries, all of which Qadhafi effectively decreed to be henceforth irrelevant.

Finally, the idea of direct popular participation in public administration could claim a local origin in the tradition of the Bedouin tribes known as *hukuma 'arabiyya* (meaning here 'people's government', not 'Arab government'), in which every adult male can have his say, a tradition that has its counterpart among Libya's Berbers as well as the Bedouin and Berbers of Algeria and Morocco. Libyan tribesmen were apt to counterpose their understanding of *hukuma 'arabiyya* to the use Qadhafi made of it in the workings of the Jamahiriyya,[9] but that the co-opting of this tradition (like Julius Nyerere's co-opting of *ujamaa* in Tanzania) was an element of his edifice seems clear.

III

The Jamahiriyya lasted thirty-four years (forty-two if backdated to 1969), a respectable innings by any contemporary yardstick. It did not work for foreign businessmen, diplomats and journalists, who found it more exasperating to deal with than the run of Arab and African states, and their views shaped the country's image abroad. But the regime was not designed to work for foreigners, and seems to have worked fairly well for many Libyans much of the time. It achieved more than a tripling of the total population (6.5 million in 2011, up from 1.8 million in 1968), high standards of healthcare, high rates of schooling for girls as well as boys, a literacy rate of 88 per cent, a degree of social and occupational promotion for women that women in many other Arab countries might well envy and an annual per capita income of $12,000, the highest in Africa. But the point about these indices, routinely cited, naturally enough, by critics of the West's intervention in reply to the propaganda that has relentlessly blackened the Qadhafi regime, is that they are in one crucial sense beside the point.

The socio-economic achievements of the regime can be attributed very largely to the distributive state: that is, to the success of the hydrocarbons sector and of the mechanisms put in place early on to distribute the petrodollars. But the central institutions of the Jamahiriyya, the tandem of People's Congresses and Revolutionary Committees, did not make for effective government at all, in part because they involved a tension between two distinct notions and sources of legitimacy. The Congresses embodied the idea of the people as the source of legitimacy and the agent of legitimation. But the Committees embodied the very different idea of the Revolution as possessing a legitimacy that trumped all others. The apex of this element of the edifice was Qadhafi himself, which is why it was entirely logical for him to locate his position outside the structure of Congresses and hence of the formal institutions of government, neither prime minister nor president but simply *Murshid*, 'Guide', 'Brother Leader'. This position enabled him to mediate in free-wheeling fashion between the various components of the system and broader public opinion, criticising the government (and thereby articulating public restiveness) or deploring the ineffectiveness and correcting the mistakes of People's Congresses and doing so always from the standpoint of 'the Revolution', whatever this was understood to signify. The tradition of an Arab ruler making a virtue of siding with public opinion against his own ministers goes back to Hārūn al-Rashīd. But the way revolutionary legitimacy could override popular legitimacy in Qadhafi's system also resembles Khomeini's insistence that the interests of Iran's revolution could override the precepts of the Sharī'a – i.e. that political considerations could trump Islamic dogma – and that he was the arbiter of when this was necessary. It is striking that Qadhafi considered that the interest of the Revolution required the hydrocarbons sector to be spared the ministrations of People's Congresses and Revolutionary Committees alike.

Despite the work of a small number of Libya specialists, notably Davis and Vanderwalle,[10] prevailing Western discourses on authoritarianism, tyranny and dictatorship have never really captured the character of this set-up but have caricatured it instead. Most dictators have controlled their states from their occupancy of a formal office possessing commanding prerogatives ruthlessly exercised. As a result, people have at least known who is in charge and roughly what they can expect and what is expected of them. But Qadhafi, unlike any other head of state, stood at the apex not of the pyramid of governing institutions but of the *informal sector* of the polity which, dominated by him, exercised a degree of hegemony over the formal sector that has had no contemporary counterparts. And what this meant was that the great problem of the Jamahiriyya was the extreme weakness of its institutions, including eventually the army itself, which Qadhafi mistrusted and kept weak.

Davis indicated this problem by talking of 'statelessness' and 'the non-state'.[11] One is tempted to say of Qadhafi that *l'État, c'était lui*. But unlike the *Roi Soleil* and the other absolutist monarchs who did so much to lay the foundations of Europe's nation-states, it was the mystical idea of the Revolution, not heredity and divine right, that legitimated his power. And the imprecise content of this revolution, what Ruth First called its elusiveness,[12] was closely connected to the fact that 'the Revolution' was never over.

A clear distinction between revolutionary and constitutional government was made in 1793 by Robespierre, when he wrote: 'The aim of constitutional government is to preserve the Republic; that of revolutionary government is to lay its foundation.'[13] The effective historical function of the revolutionary government Qadhafi gave his country was to ensure that, while Libya was modernised in important respects, it did not and could not become a republic. The Libyan Revolution turned out to be permanent because its objects were imprecise; its architects had no form of law-bound, constitutional government in view as a final destination and no conception of a political role for themselves or anyone else *after* the Revolution, which they therefore had an interest in perpetuating while taking it nowhere in particular. The State of the Masses, al-Jamahiriyya, was presented as far superior to a mere republic – *jumhuriyya* – but in fact fell far short of one. And, unlike all those states that call themselves republics but fail to live up to the name, its pretensions signalled that its rulers had no intention of establishing a real republic in which government would truly be the affair of the people and that the 'State of the Masses' was in reality little more than a side-show, a game to occupy and contain ordinary Libyans, while the grown-up business of political decision-making was conducted behind the scenes, the affair of a mysterious and unaccountable elite.

The mobilisation of society in the French Revolution threw up several independent-minded leaders – Danton, Marat, Hébert et al., as well as Robespierre – which made it psychologically possible for fellow Jacobins to rebel against Robespierre eventually and effect, with Thermidor, the historical punctuation mark that set in train the tortuous process of superseding revolutionary by constitutional government. Something similar, up to a point, can be said of Algeria (where the independence struggle threw up a superabundance of strong-minded revolutionaries), although, forty-nine years on, the winding road to the democratic republic still stretches far ahead, as it did in France. But the politically inert condition of Libyan society meant that its revolution had one and only one leader. Qadhafi's closest colleagues no doubt had personal influence but only Abdessalam Jalloud had it in him to disagree openly with Qadhafi on major issues (and finally quit on his own terms in 1995). And so Qadhafi's rule can be seen as an extreme instance of what Rosa Luxemburg called 'substitutionism' and the informal government that was the real government of Libya was a one-man show. Incarnating the nebulous revolution, the imprecise interest of the nation and the inarticulate will of the people at the same time, Qadhafi clearly considered he needed to make the show interesting. His flamboyance had a political purpose. But how long could colourfulness command consent, let alone loyalty? A political Pied Piper leading Libyans – mostly well fed, housed and schooled, it is true, but maintained in perpetual political infancy – to no destination in particular: the wonder of it is that the show had such a long run.

IV

Qadhafi seems to have realised years ago what he had done – the quasi-utopian dead end he had got Libya and himself into – and tried to escape its implications. As early as 1987 he was experimenting with liberalisation: allowing private trading, reining in the Revolutionary Committees, allowing Libyans to travel to neighbouring countries, returning confiscated passports, releasing hundreds of political prisoners, inviting exiles to return with assurances that they would not be persecuted, and even meeting opposition leaders to explore the possibility of reconciliation, while acknowledging that serious abuses had occurred and that Libya lacked the rule of law. These reforms and the discourse accompanying them represented a striking change of direction and the beginning of the supersession of the earlier revolutionary outlook by elements of a constitutionalist one, notably in Qadhafi's proposals for the codification of citizens' rights and punishable crimes, in order to end the syndrome of arbitrary arrests for unspecified offences.[14] But this line of development was cut short by the imposition of international sanctions in 1992 in the wake of the Lockerbie bombing, a national emergency that reinforced the regime's conservative wing and ruled out risky reform for more than a decade. It was only in 2003–4, after Tripoli had paid a massive sum in compensation to the bereaved families in 2002 (having already surrendered Abdelbaset Ali al-Megrahi and Al Amin Khalifa Fhima for trial in 1999), that sanctions were lifted, at which point a new reforming current headed by Qadhafi's son Saif al-Islam emerged within the regime.

It was the fashion some years ago in British academic and media circles close to the Blair government to talk up Saif al-Islam's commitment to reform and it is the fashion now to heap opprobrium on him as his awful father's son. Both these judgments have been self-serving; neither is accurate. A relevant yardstick is provided by Egypt, where Gamal Mubarak did little other than surround himself with tycoons and US-educated whizz-kids, make vacuous speeches about 'New Thought', take over the National Democratic Party apparatus as a launching pad for his presidential ambitions, and rig the presidential election in 2005 and the legislative elections in 2010. In contrast, Saif al-Islam had begun to play a serious and constructive role in Libyan affairs of state, persuading the Libyan Islamic Fighting Group to end its terrorist campaign in return for the release of LIFG prisoners in 2008, promoting a range of practical reforms and broaching the idea that the regime should formally recognise the country's Berbers.[15] While it was always unrealistic to suppose that he could have remade Libya into a liberal democracy had he succeeded his father, he certainly recognised the problems of the Jamahiriyya and the need for substantial reform. The prospect of a reformist path under Saif was ruled out by this spring's events. Is there a parallel with the way international sanctions in the wake of Lockerbie put paid to the earlier reform initiative?

Since February, it has been relentlessly asserted that the Libyan government was responsible both for the bombing of a Berlin discotheque on 5 April 1986 and the Lockerbie bombing on 21 December 1988. News of Qadhafi's violent end was greeted with satisfaction by the families of the American victims of Lockerbie, understandably full of bitterness towards the man they have been assured by the US government and media ordered the bombing of Pan Am 103. But many informed observers have long wondered about these two stories, especially Lockerbie. Jim Swire, the spokesman of *UK Families Flight 103*, whose daughter was killed in the bombing, has repeatedly expressed dissatisfaction with the official version. Hans Köchler, an Austrian jurist appointed by the UN as an independent observer at the trial, expressed concern about the way it was conducted (notably about the role of two US Justice Department officials who sat next to the Scottish prosecuting counsel throughout and appeared to be giving them instructions) and described al-Megrahi's conviction as 'a spectacular miscarriage of justice'. Swire, who also sat through the trial and fainted when the verdict was announced, subsequently launched the *Justice for Megrahi* campaign.[16] In giving a characteristically stylish resumé of Qadhafi's career on BBC World Service Television on the night of 20 October 2011, the veteran reporter John Simpson stopped well short of endorsing either charge, noting of the Berlin bombing that 'it may or may not have been Colonel Qadhafi's work', an honest formula that acknowledged the room for doubt, and that Libya subsequently 'got the full blame for the Lockerbie bombing', a statement that is quite true, since Libya certainly got the blame and paid for it dearly, whether it deserved it or not.

It is often claimed by British and American government personnel and the Western press that Libya admitted responsibility for Lockerbie in 2003–4. This is untrue. As part of the deal with Washington and London, which included Libya paying $2.7 billion to the 270 victims' families, the Libyan government in a letter to the president of the UN Security Council stated that Libya 'has facilitated the bringing to justice of the two suspects charged with the bombing of Pan Am 103, and accepts responsibility for the actions of its officials'. That this formula was agreed in negotiations between the Libyan and British (if not also American) governments was made clear when it was echoed word for word by Jack Straw in the House of Commons. The formula allowed the government to give the public the impression that Libya was indeed guilty, while also allowing Tripoli to say that it had admitted nothing of the kind. The statement does not even mention al-Megrahi by name, much less acknowledge his guilt or that of the Libyan government, and any self-respecting government would sign up to the general principle that it is responsible for the actions of its officials. The prime minister, Shukri Ghanem, confirmed that this was Tripoli's position on 24 February 2004 on the *Today* programme, explaining that the payment of compensation did not imply an admission of guilt and that the Libyan government had 'bought peace'.[17]

The standards of proof underpinning Western judgments of Qadhafi's Libya have not been high. The doubt over the Lockerbie trial verdict has encouraged rival theories about who really ordered the bombing, which have predictably been dubbed 'conspiracy theories'. But the prosecution case in the Lockerbie trial was itself a conspiracy theory. And the meagre evidence adduced would have warranted acquittal on grounds of reasonable doubt, or, at most, the 'not proven' verdict that Scottish law allows for, rather than the unequivocally 'guilty' verdict brought in, oddly, on one defendant but not the other. I do not pretend to know the truth of the Lockerbie affair, but the British rarely forgive the authors of atrocities committed against them and their friends. So I find it hard to believe that a British government would have fallen over itself as it did in 2003–5 to welcome Libya back into the fold had it really held Qadhafi responsible. And in view of the number of Scottish victims of the bombing, it is equally hard to believe that representative Scottish politicians would have countenanced al-Megrahi's release if they believed the guilty verdict had been sound. In the light of these considerations, I submit that the hypothesis that Libya and Qadhafi and al-Megrahi were framed can be taken very seriously indeed.[18] And, if so, it would follow that the greatly diminished prospect of reform from 1989 onwards as the regime battened down the hatches to weather international sanctions, the material suffering of the Libyan people during this period, and the aggravation of internal conflict (notably the Islamist terrorist campaign waged by the LIFG between 1995 and 1998) can all in some measure be laid at the West's door.

But, wherever the blame lies, the fact remains that the Jamahiriyya survived up to 2011 unchanged in its key features: the absence of political parties and of independent associations, newspapers and publishing houses and the corresponding weakness of civil society; the dysfunctional character of the formal institutions of government; the weakness of the armed forces; and the indispensability of the 'Brother leader', bestriding Libya at the apex of the informal sector as the architect of the revolution that constituted the state and authoritative guide of its fortunes thereafter. And what this meant is that, after forty-two years of Qadhafi's rule, the people of Libya were, politically speaking, not much further forward than they were on 31 August 1969, yet to acquire the substance of citizenship, let alone that precious asset, the political experience that comes from exercising, or even simply trying to exercise, the rights of citizens in relation to their governments. And so the Jamahiriyya was bound to prove vulnerable to internal challenge the moment that mass movements making an issue of human dignity and citizens' rights got going in Libya's neighbourhood. The tragic irony is that the features of the Jamahiriyya that made it vulnerable to the Arab Spring also, in their combination, ruled out any emulation of the Tunisian and Egyptian scenarios.

The factors that enabled a positive evolution to occur in these countries once the protest movement started were absent from Libya. In both Tunisia and Egypt, the population's greater experience of political action gave the protests a degree of sophistication, coherence and organisational flair. The fact that neither president had been a founding figure allowed for a distinction to be made between a protest against the president and his cronies and a rebellion against the state. And in both cases the role of the armed forces was crucial: being loyal to the state and the nation rather than to a particular leader, they were disposed to act as arbiters and facilitate a resolution without the existence of the state being put in jeopardy. None of this applied to Libya. Qadhafi was the founder of the Jamahiriyya and the guarantor of its continued existence. The regular armed forces were incapable of playing an independent political role. The absence of any tradition of non-violent opposition and independent organisation ensured that the revolt at the popular level was a raw affair, incapable of formulating any demands that the regime might be able to negotiate over but, on the contrary, clearly challenging Qadhafi and the Jamahiriyya (and thus the state) *en bloc*, and doing so with considerable violence.

V

The situation that developed over the weekend following the initial unrest on 15 February admitted of three possible scenarios: a rapid collapse of the regime as the uprising spread; the crushing of the revolt as the regime got its act together; or – instead of an early resolution – the onset of civil war. Had the revolt been crushed straightaway, the implications for the Arab Spring would have been serious, but not more damaging than events in Bahrain, Yemen or Syria; Arab public opinion, long used to the idea that Libya was a place apart, was insulated against the demonstration effect of events there. Had the revolt precipitated the rapid collapse of the regime, Libya might well have tumbled into anarchy, since it is clear the rebels had neither a developed political organisation nor leadership, let alone a serious army, and were incapable of establishing a new state in place of the old in the short term. Moreover, the collapse of Libya into a zone of anarchy, an oil-rich Somalistan on the Mediterranean, would have had destabilising repercussions for all its neighbours and prejudiced the prospects for democratic development in Tunisia in particular. A protracted civil war, while costly in terms of human life, might have given the rebellion time to cohere as a rival centre of state formation, and thus prepared it for the task of establishing a functional Libyan state in the event of victory. And, even if defeated, such a rebellion would have undermined the premises of the Jamahiriyya and ensured its eventual demise.

None of these scenarios took place. A military intervention by the Western powers under the cloak of NATO and the authority of the United Nations happened instead. A fourth scenario turned out to be in the cards.

How should we evaluate this fourth scenario in terms of the democratic principles that have been invoked to justify the military intervention? There is no doubt that many Libyans consider NATO their saviour and that some of them genuinely aspire to a democratic future for their country. But I nonetheless felt great alarm at the emergence of the fourth scenario and opposed it from the outset, and remain opposed to it despite its recent apparent triumph, because I have not doubted that the balance of the argument from democratic principles favoured an entirely different policy and course of action.

The claim that the 'international community' had no choice but to intervene militarily and that the alternative was to do nothing is false. An active, practical, non-violent alternative was proposed, and deliberately rejected.

The argument for a no-fly zone and then for a military intervention employing 'all necessary measures' was that only this could stop the regime's repression and protect civilians. In opposition to this, a range of serious actors argued that the way to protect civilians in what was becoming a civil war was not to intensify the conflict by intervening on one side or the other, but to end it by securing a ceasefire followed by negotiations. Several proposals were put forward. The International Crisis Group published a statement on 10 March arguing for a three-point initiative: (i) securing an immediate ceasefire should be the priority, with military intervention a last resort; (ii) the ceasefire should be followed by 'direct talks between the two sides to secure a transition to a post-Qadhafi regime that has legitimacy in the eyes of the Libyan people'; (iii) the UN should appoint a contact group consisting of leading figures from Arab and African states acceptable to both sides to broker the necessary agreements to the ceasefire and the subsequent negotiations. This proposal was echoed by the African Union and was consistent with the views of many major non-African states – Russia, China, Brazil and India, not to mention Germany and Turkey. It was restated by the ICG in more detail (adding provision for the deployment under a UN mandate of an international peacekeeping force) in an open letter to the UN Security Council on 16 March, the eve of the debate which concluded with the adoption of UNSC Resolution 1973.[19]

In short, before the Security Council voted to approve the military intervention, a worked-out proposal had been put forward which addressed the need to protect civilians by seeking a rapid end to the fighting, and set out the main elements of an orderly transition to a more legitimate form of government, one that would avoid the danger of a collapse into anarchy, with all this might mean for Tunisia's revolution, the security of Libya's other neighbours and the wider region. The imposition of a no-fly zone would be an act of war; as the US defense secretary, Robert Gates, told Congress on 2 March, it required the disabling of Libya's air defences as an indispensable preliminary. In authorising this and 'all necessary measures', the Security Council was choosing war when no other policy had even been tried, but also when a non-violent, political approach that was far more likely to achieve the objectives of protecting civilians and securing the desired political change was available to it. Why?

Many critics of NATO's intervention have complained that it departed from the terms of Resolution 1973 and was therefore illegal, and that the resolution authorised neither regime change nor the introduction of troops on the ground. This is a misreading. Article 4 ruled out the introduction of an occupying force. But Article 42 of the 1907 Hague Regulations states that 'territory is considered occupied when it is actually placed under the authority of the hostile army', a definition conserved by the 1949 Geneva Conventions.[20] What Resolution 1973 ruled out was the introduction of a force intended to take full political and legal responsibility for the place, but that was never the intention; ground forces were indeed eventually introduced, but they have at no point accepted political or legal responsibility for anything and so fall short of the conventional definition of an occupying force. It may be that this misreading of the resolution was connived at by the governments that drafted it in order to secure the best (or least bad) tally of votes in favour on 17 March; this would of course be only one instance of the sophistry to which the *metteurs en scène* of intervention have resorted. And regime change was tacitly covered by the phrase 'all necessary measures'. That this was the right way to read the resolution had already been made clear by the stentorian rhetoric of Cameron and Hague, Sarkozy and Juppé, and Obama and Clinton in advance of the Security Council vote. Since the issue was defined from the outset as protecting civilians from Qadhafi's murderous onslaught 'on his own people', it followed that effective protection required the elimination of the threat, which was Qadhafi himself for as long as he was in power (subsequently revised to 'for as long as he is in Libya' before finally becoming 'for as long as he is alive'). From the attitudes struck by the Western powers in the run-up to the Security Council debate, it was evident that the cunningly drafted resolution tacitly authorised a war to effect regime change. Those who subsequently said that they did not know that regime change had been authorised either did not understand the logic of events or were pretending to misunderstand in order to excuse their failure to oppose it. By inserting 'all necessary measures' into the resolution, London, Paris and Washington licensed themselves, with NATO as their proxy, to do whatever they wanted whenever they wanted in the full knowledge that they would never be held to account, since as permanent veto-holding members of the Security Council they are above all laws.[*]

In two respects, however, the conduct of the Western powers and NATO did indeed appear explicitly to violate the terms of Security Council resolutions. The first instance was the repeated supply of arms to the rebellion by France, Qatar, Egypt (according to the *Wall Street Journal*), and no doubt various other members of the 'coalition of the willing', in what seemed a clear breach of the arms embargo imposed by the Security Council in Articles 9, 10 and 11 of Resolution 1970 passed on 26 February and reiterated in Articles 13, 14 and 15 of Resolution 1973.[21] It was later explained that Resolution 1973 superseded 1970 in this respect and that the magic phrase 'all necessary measures' licensed the violation of the arms embargo; thus Article 4 of

---

[*] Alan J. Kuperman claims that I stated that Resolution 1973 was drafted to authorise regime change 'because NATO had always viewed this as necessary to protect Libya's civilians'. (Alan J. Kuperman, 'A model humanitarian intervention', *International Security*, 38, 1, Summer 2013, 105–136, at 113, fn. 30.) This misreading of a passage – reproduced unchanged here – of my 2011 *LRB* article mistakes my account of the public rationale of the policy for my view of its purpose. My view has always been that the overthrow of Qadhafi was the objective of London, Washington and Paris from the outset: that protecting civilians was merely the pretext for intervening and NATO merely the instrument of this policy.

Resolution 1973 trumped Articles 13 to 15 of the same resolution. In this way it was arranged that any state might supply arms to the rebels while none might do so to the Libyan government, which by that time had been decreed illegitimate by London, Paris and Washington.

The second violation was another matter, for it was not merely apparent but real. Yet, most curiously, scarcely anyone has drawn attention to it.

The efforts of the ICG and others seeking an alternative to war did not go entirely unnoticed. Apparently their proposals made some impression on the less gung-ho members of the Security Council and a left-handed homage was paid them by the drafters of Resolution 1973. In the final version – unlike any earlier ones – the idea of a peaceful solution was incorporated in the first two articles, which read:

[The Security Council . . .]

(1) *Demands* the immediate establishment of a ceasefire and a complete end to violence and all attacks against, and abuses of, civilians.

(2) *Stresses* the need to intensify efforts to find a solution to the crisis which responds to the legitimate demands of the Libyan people and *notes* the decisions of the Secretary-General to send his Special Envoy to Libya and of the Peace and Security Council of the African Union to send its ad hoc High Level Committee to Libya with the aim of facilitating dialogue to lead to the political reforms necessary to find a peaceful and sustainable solution[22]

In this way, Resolution 1973 formally took on board the concerns of those who favoured an alternative to war and, in demanding a ceasefire and mentioning the idea of 'facilitating dialogue to lead to . . . political reforms' *in its first and second articles* (while authorising the military intervention option as a fallback if a ceasefire was refused), seemed to be actively envisaging this peaceful alternative as its first preference. In reality, nothing could have been further from the truth.

Resolution 1973 was passed in New York late in the evening of 17 March. The next day, Qadhafi, whose forces were camped on the southern edge of Benghazi, announced a ceasefire in conformity with Article 1 and proposed a political dialogue in line with Article 2. What the Security Council demanded and suggested, he provided in a matter of hours. His ceasefire was immediately rejected on behalf of the NTC by a senior rebel commander, Khalifa Haftar, and dismissed by Western governments. 'We will judge him by his actions not his words,' David Cameron declared, implying that Qadhafi was expected to deliver a complete ceasefire by himself: that is, not only order his troops to cease fire but ensure this ceasefire was maintained indefinitely despite the fact that the NTC was refusing to reciprocate. Cameron's comment also ignored the fact that Article 1 of Resolution 1973 did not place the burden of a ceasefire exclusively on Qadhafi at all, for it would have been absurd for it to do so, as would undoubtedly have been pointed out in the Security Council debate. No sooner had Cameron covered for the NTC's unmistakable violation of Resolution 1973 than Obama weighed in, insisting that for Qadhafi's ceasefire to count for anything he would – in addition to sustaining it indefinitely, single-handed, irrespective of the NTC – have to withdraw his forces not only from Benghazi but also from Misrata *and* from the most important towns his troops had retaken from the rebellion, Ajdabiya in the east and Zawiya in the west, that is, accept strategic defeat in advance, conditions that were impossible for Qadhafi to accept and which were absent from Article 1.[23]

In this way, Cameron and Obama made it clear that the last thing they wanted was a ceasefire, that the NTC could violate Article 1 of the resolution with impunity and that in doing so it would be acting with the agreement of its Security Council sponsors. So Qadhafi's first ceasefire offer came to nothing, as did his second offer of 20 March. A week later, Turkey, which had been working within the NATO framework to help organise the provision of humanitarian aid to Benghazi, announced that it had been talking to both sides and offered to broker a ceasefire. The offer was given what Ernest Bevin would have called 'a complete ignoral' and nothing came of it either, as nothing came of a later initiative, seeking a ceasefire and negotiations, to which Qadhafi explicitly agreed, undertaken by the African Union in April; this too was rejected out of hand by the NTC, which demanded Qadhafi's resignation as a condition of any ceasefire.[24] This demand went beyond even Obama's earlier list of conditions, none of which had figured in Resolution 1973. More to the point, it was a demand that made a ceasefire impossible, since securing a ceasefire requires commanders with decisive authority over their armies, and removing Qadhafi would have meant that no one any longer had overall authority over the regime's forces.[25]

A position paper outlining how a ceasefire might work to the benefit of the rebellion and further the prospect of a democratic outcome was drafted in late May, when the military position appeared stalemated, and was made available by ICG staff to Libyans sympathetic to the rebellion who were in touch with members of the NTC.[26] It was received with interest by the former, who said they would transmit it to the NTC leaders then about to meet in Doha. Nothing whatever came of it.

And so it was shown, again and again, that in incorporating the alternative non-violent policy proposals in its text, the Western war party had simply been pulling a confidence trick, stringing along a few undecided states to get them to vote for the resolution on 17 March. A war to the finish, violent regime change and the end of Qadhafi had been the policy from the outset. In line with this, all subsequent offers of a ceasefire by Qadhafi – on 30 April, 26 May and 9 June – were treated with the same contempt.[27]

Those who believe in 'international law' and are happy with wars they consider 'legal' may wish to make something of this. But the crucial point here is how these considerations reveal the true logic of events and of the policy choices associated with them. In incorporating the peace party's suggestions into the revised text of Resolution 1973, London, Paris and Washington headed off a real debate in the Security Council, one that would have considered alternatives, at the price of making their own resolution incoherent. They were accordingly bound to consider the part they liked (no-fly zone, all necessary measures, etc.) as the operative part, ignore the other bits and defy critics in the UNSC to raise the issue, which they were generally unwilling to do to any effect beyond complaints about 'mission creep'. But there was no mission creep.

London, Paris and Washington could not allow a ceasefire because it would have involved negotiations, first about peace lines, peacekeepers and so forth, and then about fundamental political differences, a line of development that would have subverted the possibility of the kind of regime change that interested the Western powers. The sight of representatives of the rebellion sitting down to talks with representatives of Qadhafi's regime, Libyans talking to Libyans, would have undone the demonisation of Qadhafi. The moment he became once more someone people talked to and negotiated with, he would in effect have been rehabilitated. And, while that could have allowed serious reform to occur, it would, by ruling out violent regime change, have denied the Western powers their chance of a major intervention in North Africa's Spring, and the whole interventionist scheme would have flopped. The demonisation of Qadhafi in late February, crowned by the referral, by Resolution 1970, of his alleged crimes against humanity to the International Criminal Court and then by France's decision on 10 March to recognise the NTC as the sole legitimate representative of the Libyan people, meant that Qadhafi was banished forever from the realm of international political discourse, never to be negotiated with, not even about the surrender of Tripoli when in August he offered to talk terms to spare the city further destruction, an offer once more dismissed with contempt.[28] And this logic was preserved all the way, as the death toll of civilians in Tripoli and above all Sirte proves beyond doubt. The thesis of mission creep is a mystification of what happened and why it happened. The mission was one of violent regime change from the very outset.

That this is the truth of the matter has been obscured by the hullabaloo over the supposedly threatened massacre at Benghazi. The official version is that it was the prospect of a 'second Srebrenica' or even 'another Rwanda' in Benghazi were Qadhafi allowed to retake the city that forced the 'international community' (minus Russia, China, India, Brazil, Germany, Turkey et al.) to act. What grounds were there for supposing that, once the regime's forces had retaken Benghazi, they would be ordered to embark on a general massacre?

Qadhafi dealt with many revolts over the years. He invariably quashed them by force and usually executed the ringleaders. The NTC and other rebel leaders had reason to fear that, once Benghazi had fallen to government troops, they would be rounded up and made to pay the price. So it was natural that they should try to convince the 'international community' that it was not only their lives that were at stake, but those of thousands of ordinary civilians. But, in retaking the towns that the uprising had briefly wrested from the government's control, Qadhafi's forces had committed no massacres at all; the fighting had been bitter and bloody, but there had been nothing remotely resembling the slaughter at Srebrenica, let alone in Rwanda. The only known massacre carried out during Qadhafi's rule was the killing of some 1,200 Islamist prisoners at Abu Salim prison in 1996. This was a very dark affair, and whether or not Qadhafi ordered it, it is fair to hold him responsible for it. It was therefore reasonable to be concerned about what the regime might do and how its forces would behave in Benghazi once they had retaken it, and to deter Qadhafi from ordering or allowing any excesses. But that is not what was decided. What was decided was to declare Qadhafi guilty in advance of a massacre of defenceless civilians on a vast scale and instigate the process of destroying his regime and him (and his family), by way of punishment of a crime he was yet to commit, and was actually unlikely to commit, and to persist with this process despite his repeated offers to suspend military action.

There was no question of anything that could properly be described as ethnic cleansing or genocide in the Libyan context.[*] All Libyans are Muslims, the majority of Arab-Berber descent,

---

[*] This claim, which I made in ICG's internal debate in February–March 2011, referred to the regime's behaviour and did not take into account the attacks perpetrated by rebel forces on 'Africans' in the following weeks and months.

and while the small Berber-speaking minority had a grievance concerning recognition of its language and identity (its members are Ibadi, not Sunni, Muslims), this was not what the conflict was about. The conflict was not ethnic or racial but political, between defenders and opponents of the Qadhafi regime; whichever side won could be expected to deal roughly with its adversaries, but the premises for a large-scale massacre of civilians on grounds of their ethnic or racial identity were absent.* All the talk about another Srebrenica or Rwanda was extreme hyperbole, clearly intended to panic various governments into supporting the war party's project of a military intervention in order to save the rebellion from imminent defeat.

Why did the panic factor work so well with international, or at any rate Western, public opinion, and especially governments? It is reliably reported that it was Obama's fear of being accused of allowing another Srebrenica that tipped the scales in Washington, when not only Robert Gates but also, initially, Hillary Clinton had resisted US involvement in another military intervention in an Arab and Muslim country.[29] The answer is that Qadhafi had already been so thoroughly demonised that the wildest accusations about his likely (or, as many claimed, certain) future conduct would be believed whatever his actual behaviour. This demonisation took place on 21 February, the day all the important cards were dealt.

VI

On 21 February the world was shocked by the news that the Qadhafi regime was using its air force to slaughter peaceful demonstrators in Tripoli and other cities. The main purveyor of this story was Al Jazeera, but the story was quickly taken up by

---

* An exception to this was the township of Tawergha, near Misurata. Its black population, some 30,000–40,000, mainly of slave descent, had benefited from Qadhafi's benevolent treatment and stayed loyal to him, so were subjected to brutal ethnic cleansing by Misrata's militias in July–August 2011, and Tawergha reduced to a ghost town.

the Sky network, CNN, the BBC, ITN et al.[30] Before the day was over the idea of imposing a no-fly zone on Libya was widely accepted, as was the idea of a Security Council resolution imposing sanctions and an arms embargo, freezing Libya's assets and referring Qadhafi and his associates to the ICC on charges of crimes against humanity. Resolution 1970 was duly voted five days later and the no-fly zone proposal monopolised international discussion of the Libyan crisis from then on.

A lot of other things happened on 21 February. Zawiya was reported to be in chaos. The minister of justice, Mustafa Abdul Jalil, resigned. Fifty Serbian workers were attacked by looters. Canada condemned 'the violent crackdowns on innocent demonstrators'. Two air force pilots flew their fighters to Malta claiming they did so to avoid carrying out an order to bomb and strafe demonstrators. By late afternoon regime troops and snipers were reported to be firing on crowds in Tripoli. Eighteen Korean workers were wounded when their place of work was attacked by a hundred armed men. The European Union condemned the repression, followed by Ban Ki-moon, Nicolas Sarkozy and Silvio Berlusconi. Ten Egyptians were reported to have been killed by armed men in Tobruk. William Hague, who had condemned the repression the previous day (as had Hillary Clinton), announced at a press conference that he had information that Qadhafi had fled Libya and was *en route* to Venezuela. The Libyan ambassador to Poland stated that defections from the armed forces as well as the government could not be stopped and Qadhafi's days were numbered. Numerous media outlets carried the story that Libya's largest tribe, the Warfalla, had joined the rebellion. Libya's ambassadors to Washington, India, Bangladesh and Indonesia all resigned, and its deputy ambassador to the UN, Ibrahim Dabbashi, rounded off the day by calling a news conference at Libya's mission in New York and claimed that Qadhafi had 'already started the genocide against the Libyan people' and was flying in African mercenaries. It was Dabbashi more than anyone else who, having primed his audience in this way, launched the idea that the UN should impose a no-fly zone and the ICC should investigate Qadhafi's 'crimes against humanity and crimes of war'.[31]

At this point the total death toll since 15 February was 233, according to Human Rights Watch. The Fédération Internationale des Droits de l'Homme suggested it was between 300 and 400 (but it also announced the same day that Sirte had fallen to the rebels). We can compare these figures with the total death toll in Tunisia (300) and Egypt (at least 846).[32] We can also compare both HRW's and FIDH's figures with the death toll, plausibly estimated at between 500 and 600, of the seven days of rioting in Algeria in October 1988, when the French government rigorously refrained from making any comment on events.[33] But the figures were beside the point on 21 February; it was impressions that counted. The impression made by the story that Qadhafi's airforce was slaughtering peaceful protesters was huge, and it was natural to take the resignations of Abdul Jalil and the ambassadors, the flight of the two pilots, and especially Dabbashi's dramatic declaration about genocide as corroborating Al Jazeera's story.

And so ... *game on!* Qadhafi was irremediably demonised right then and there, goodies and baddies (to use Tony Blair's categories) clearly identified, the Western media's outraged attention totally engaged, the Security Council urgently seized of the matter, the ICC primed to stand by, and a fundamental shift towards intervention had been made – all in a matter of hours. And quite right too, many may say. Except that the Al Jazeera story was untrue, just as the story of the Warfalla's siding with the rebellion was untrue and Hague's story that Qadhafi was fleeing to Caracas was untrue. And, of course, Dabbashi's 'genocide' claim was histrionic rubbish which, curiously, none of the organisations with a serious interest in the proper use of this important term were moved to challenge.

These considerations raise awkward questions. If the reason cited by these ambassadors and other regime personnel for defecting on 21 February was false, what really prompted them to defect and make the declarations they did? What was Al Jazeera up to? And what was Hague up to? A serious history of this affair when more evidence comes to light will seek answers to these questions. But I don't find it hard to understand that Qadhafi and his son should suddenly have resorted to such fierce rhetoric. They clearly believed that, far from confronting merely 'innocent demonstrators', as the Canadians had it, they were being destabilised by forces acting to a plan with international ramifications. It is possible that they were mistaken and that everything was spontaneous and accidental and a chaotic muddle; I do not pretend to know for sure. But there had been attempts to destabilise their regime before, and they had grounds for thinking that they were being destabilised again. The partisan and slanted coverage in the British media in particular, notably the insistence that the regime was facing only peaceful demonstrators when, in addition to ordinary Libyans trying non-violently to make their voices heard, it was facing politically motivated as well as random violence (e.g. the lynching of fifty alleged mercenaries in Al-Bayda on 19 February), was consistent with the destabilisation theory. And on the evidence I have since been able to collect, I am inclined to think that destabilisation is exactly what was happening.

In the days that followed I made efforts to check the Al Jazeera story for myself. One source I consulted was the well-regarded blog Informed Comment, maintained and updated every day by Juan Cole, a Middle East specialist at the University of Michigan. This carried a post on 21 February entitled 'Qaddafi's bombardments recall Mussolini's', which made the point that 'in 1933–40, Italo Balbo championed aerial warfare as the best means to deal with uppity colonial populations'. The post began: 'The strafing and bombardment in Tripoli of civilian demonstrators by Muammar Gaddafi's fighter jets on Monday . . .', with the underlined words linking to an article by Sarah El Deeb and Maggie Michael for Associated Press, published at 9 p.m. on 21 February. This article provided no corroboration of Cole's claim that Qadhafi's fighter jets (or any other aircraft) had strafed or bombed anyone in Tripoli or anywhere else. The same is true of every source indicated in the other items on Libya relaying the aerial onslaught story which Cole posted that same day.

I was in Egypt for most of the time, but since many journalists visiting Libya were transiting through Cairo, I made a point of asking those I could get hold of what they had picked up in the field. None of them had found any corroboration of the story. I especially remember on 18 March asking the British North Africa expert Jon Marks, just back from an extended tour of Cyrenaica (taking in Ajdabiya, Benghazi, Brega, Derna and Ras Lanuf), what he had heard about the story. He told me that no one he had spoken to had mentioned it. Four days later, on 22 March, *USA Today* carried a striking article by Alan Kuperman, the author of *The Limits of Humanitarian Intervention* (2001) and co-editor of *Gambling on Humanitarian Intervention* (2006). The article, 'Five Things the US Should Consider in Libya', provided a powerful critique of the NATO intervention as violating the conditions that needed to be observed for a humanitarian intervention to be justified or successful. But what interested me most was his statement that 'despite ubiquitous cellphone cameras, there are no images of genocidal violence, a claim that smacks of rebel propaganda'. So, four weeks on, I was not alone in finding no evidence for the aerial slaughter story. I subsequently discovered that the issue had come up more than a fortnight earlier, on 2 March, in hearings in the US Congress when Gates and Admiral Mike Mullen, chairman of the Joint Chiefs of Staff, were testifying. They told Congress that they had no confirmation of reports of aircraft controlled by Qadhafi firing on citizens.[34]

The story was untrue, just as the story that went round the world in August 1990 that Iraqi troops were slaughtering Kuwaiti babies by turning off their incubators was untrue, and the claims in the sexed-up dossier on Saddam's WMD were untrue. But as Mohammed Khider, one of the founders of the FLN, once remarked, 'when everyone takes up a falsehood, it becomes a reality'. The rush to regime change by war was on and could not be stopped, as I knew in my bones when, at midnight in Cairo on 21 February, I decided I was going to try stopping it anyway and sat down to draft the first of a series of long notes on Libya for my ICG colleagues.

The intervention tarnished every one of the principles the war party invoked to justify it. It occasioned the deaths of thousands of civilians. It debased the idea of democracy. It debased the idea of law. And it passed off a counterfeit revolution as the real thing. In doing so, it relied heavily on two assertions that were in fact mystifications, endlessly reiterated because crucial to the Western powers' case for war: that Qadhafi was engaged in 'killing his own people';[35] and that he had 'lost all legitimacy', the latter presented as the corollary of the former.[36]

'Killing his own people' is a bit of cant, a hand-me-down line from the previous regime change war against Saddam Hussein. In both cases the phrase suggested two things: that the despot was a monster and that he represented nothing in the society he ruled. Qadhafi was not 'killing his own people' indiscriminately; he was killing those of his people who were rebelling. He was doing what every government in history has done when faced with a rebellion. We are free to prefer the rebels to the government in any given case. But the relative merits of the two sides in such situations are not the issue here: the issue is the right of a state to defend itself against violent subversion. That right, once taken for granted as the corollary of sovereignty, is now compromised. Theoretically, it is qualified by certain rules. But, as we have seen, the invocation of rules (e.g. *no genocide*) can go together with a cynical exaggeration and distortion of the facts by other states. There are in fact no reliable rules. A state may repress a revolt if the permanent veto-holding powers on the Security Council allow it to (e.g. Bahrain, but also Sri Lanka), and not otherwise. And if a state thinks it can take this informal authorisation to defend itself as read because it is on good terms with London, Paris and Washington, and is honouring its agreements with them, as Libya was, it had better beware. Terms can change without warning from one day to the next. The matter is now arbitrary, and arbitrariness is the opposite of law.

The idea that Qadhafi represented nothing in Libyan society, that he was taking on his entire people and that his people were all against him, was another distortion of the facts. As we now know from the length of the war, the huge pro-Qadhafi demonstration in Tripoli on 1 July, the spirited fight Qadhafi's forces put up, the month it took the rebels to get anywhere at Bani Walid and the further month at Sirte, Qadhafi's regime enjoyed a substantial measure of support, as the NTC did. Libyan society was divided and this political division was in itself a hopeful development since it signified the end of the old political unanimity enjoined and maintained by the Jamahiriyya. In this light, the Western governments' portrayal of 'the Libyan people' as uniformly ranged against Qadhafi had a sinister implication, because it insinuated a new Western-sponsored and correspondingly artificial and suspect unanimity back into Libyan life. This profoundly undemocratic idea followed naturally from the equally undemocratic idea that, in the absence of an electoral consultation or even an opinion poll to ascertain the Libyans' actual views, the British, French and American governments had the right and authority to determine who was part of the Libyan people and who wasn't. No one supporting the Qadhafi regime counted. Because they were not part of 'the Libyan people' they could not be among the civilians to be protected, even if they were civilians as a matter of mere fact. And they were not protected; they were killed with total impunity by NATO air strikes as well as by uncontrolled rebel units. The number of such civilian victims on the wrong side of the war must be many times the total death toll as of 21 February. But they don't count, any more than the thousands of young men in Qadhafi's army who innocently imagined that they too were part of 'the Libyan people' and were only doing their duty to the state counted when they were incinerated by NATO's planes or extra-judicially executed *en masse* after capture, as in Sirte. Thus were Qadhafi's forces and supporters dehumanised by decree of the Western powers so that we might not feel their death agonies.

The same contempt for democratic principle characterised the claim that Qadhafi had 'lost all legitimacy'. Every state needs international recognition, and to that extent depends on external sources of legitimation. But the democratic idea gives priority to national over international legitimacy. The Western powers' insistence that Qadhafi had lost all legitimacy pre-empted an eventual electoral consultation in Libya to ascertain the true balance of Libyan public opinion, but it also mimicked the Qadhafi regime. As we have seen, in the Jamahiriyya the People as a source of legitimacy were liable to be trumped by 'the Revolution' as a source of superior legitimacy. The way in which the Western powers have arrogated to themselves the authority to decide who is legitimate in Libya similarly pre-empts and trumps the Libyan people, with NATO's intervention, garnished by the antics of the rebel militias, constituting the new 'Revolution' that replaces Qadhafi's old Revolution as the source of the trump cards.

VII

'If you break it, you own it,' Colin Powell famously remarked, in order to alert the Beltway to the risks of a renewed war against Iraq. The lesson of the mess in Iraq has been learned, at least to the extent that the Western powers and NATO have repeatedly insisted that the Libyan people – the NTC and the revolutionary militias – own their revolution. So, not owning Libya after the fall of Qadhafi, NATO and London and Paris and Washington cannot be accused of breaking it, nor be held responsible for the debris. The result is a shadow play. The NTC occupies centre stage in Libya, but since February every key decision has been made in the Western capitals in consultation with the other, especially Arab, members of the 'contact group' meeting in London or Paris or Doha. It is unlikely that the structure of power and the system of decision-making which have guided the 'revolution' since March are going to change radically. And so unless something happens to upset the calculations that have brought NATO and the NTC this far, what will probably emerge is a system of dual power, in some ways analogous to that of the Jamahiriyya itself, and similarly inimical to democratic accountability: that is, a system of formal decision-making about secondary matters acting as a façade for a separate and independent, because offshore, system of decision-making about everything that really counts (oil, gas, water, finance, trade, security, geopolitics) behind the scenes, in which Libya's formal government will be a junior partner of the new Libya's Western sponsors. This will be more of a return to the old ways of the monarchy than to those of the Jamahiriyya.

2

Loved Egyptian Night

I

Western opinion has had difficulty working out what to think, or at any rate what to say, about Egypt. It now seems that the pedlars of hallucinations have been cowed and it is no longer fashionable to describe the events of 30 June to 3 July in Cairo, when demonstrations called on President Morsi to resign and the army commanders then deposed him, as a 'second revolution'. But to describe them as a counter-revolution, while indisputably more accurate, presupposes that there was a revolution in the first place. The bulk of Western media commentary seems still to be wedded to this notion. That what the media called 'the Arab spring' was a succession of revolutions became orthodoxy very quickly. Egypt was indispensable to the idea of an 'Arab spring' and so it had to have had a revolution too.

In part this was due to wishful thinking. The daring young Egyptians who organised the remarkable demonstrations in Tahrir Square and elsewhere from 25 January 2011 onwards were certainly revolutionary in spirit and when their demand that Mubarak should go was granted they couldn't help thinking that a revolution was what they had achieved. They were of course encouraged in this by the enthusiastic reporting of the Western media, disoriented as they have been since the rise of the 'journalism of attachment' during the Balkan wars. But it was also due to the influence of accomplished fact. The events in Tunisia were certainly a revolution. The role of the Tunisian army was a very modest one, essentially that of refusing, in its moment of truth, to slaughter the demonstrators to save Ben Ali. The role of the Egyptian army in January–February 2011, however, was not modest; it only seemed to be. Where the Tunisian army showed itself to be a genuinely apolitical servant of the state, the Egyptian army struck an attitude of neutrality and even sympathy for the demonstrators that masked its commanders' real outlook. That was good enough for reporters who could not tell the difference between appearances and realities. In outward form, both countries had had revolutions, and practically identical ones at that. So the 'Arab spring' was up and running, and the question was simply: 'Who's next?'

To think about the recent appalling turn of events in Egypt in terms of an original revolution, with 25 January 2011 as the start of Year One, is to amputate the drama of the last two and half years from its historical roots, the story of what the Egyptian state became during the later stages of Hosni Mubarak's protracted presidency. This is not a simple affair. It is the story of what the Mubarak presidency signified for the Egyptian state, for its various components, especially the army, and for its form of government, but also of what it signified for the various types of opposition his rule provoked or allowed. All this combined in the gathering crisis of the state itself, a crisis that was building long before the revolution in Tunisia got under way.

Hosni Mubarak ruled Egypt for nearly thirty years, longer than Gamal Abd el-Nasser and Anwar Sadat put together, and he made clear his intention to remain in office until he died, while simultaneously giving the impression that he intended his son Gamal to succeed him. His reign was thus an instance of both the wider phenomena that Roger Owen discusses in exemplary depth: the rise of 'presidents for life' in the Arab world and these leaders' tendency to try to secure the presidency for their families by instituting a dynastic succession.* Moreover, in the course of his rule, Mubarak concentrated power in the presidency to an arguably unprecedented degree, building on what

---

* Roger Owen, *The Rise and Fall of Arab Presidents for Life* (Cambridge, MA: Harvard University Press, 2012).

Sadat had done but taking it much further, which prompts the question of how his rule compared with the other presidencies-for-life that Owen examines.

In his detailed survey of the Arab 'republics', Owen distinguishes between two main categories: states where the central government was relatively strong (Tunisia, Syria, Egypt and Algeria) and those where it was weak (Sudan, Libya and Yemen). He thus treats Egypt and Syria as substantially similar. Focusing on the Egypt–Syria comparison, Joshua Stacher offers a different view, arguing that the two regimes were dissimilar in several critical ways: the Egyptian power structure was highly centralised, while the Syrian was and is comparatively decentralised, with Bashar al-Asad wielding nothing like the commanding authority over his regime that Mubarak had.* Arguably, Owen's perspective allows for such variation; in both cases – as also in Tunisia and Algeria – central government has clearly been far stronger in relation to society than in Libya, Sudan or Yemen, and Owen himself illustrates how, within each of his categories, there are various permutations. But because the uprisings in the Middle East and North Africa have primarily been focused on and seen elsewhere in terms of the toppling of autocratic presidents, and neither Syria nor Algeria's presidents have so far been toppled, the particular configurations have mattered a great deal. Stacher persuasively argues that the oligarchical rather than autocratic configuration in Syria has meant both that the regime has found it difficult to agree on a reformist course and that its various elements were bound to stick with Bashar against all comers, so Western expectations that it would unravel under pressure were misplaced. How then does the other part of his thesis – that Egypt's power structure has been extremely centralised – help explain the course of events there?

Long before the uprisings of late 2010 and early 2011, it seemed to me that the extreme accumulation of power that characterised the Mubarak regime – at any rate during the last third of his reign, which I observed while living in Cairo from

* Joshua Stacher, *Adaptable Autocrats: Regime Power in Egypt and Syria* (Stanford, CA: Stanford University Press, 2012).

2001 – had at least one definite implication for the future: it couldn't possibly be sustained after Mubarak's departure, whether or not his son succeeded him. There was bound to be a redistribution of power within the state away from the presidency, and the question would be how this redistribution was handled, and to whose benefit.

The matter of the succession was a central issue in Egyptian political debate from at least 2002, catalysed by the suspicion that a dynastic succession was planned, and problematised by some outspoken intellectuals' indignant rejection of this scenario as *tawrith al-sulta* – the inheritance of power. That the problematic succession was a major factor underlying the events of January and February 2011 is self-evident. But the sensational entry onto the political stage of young liberal and leftist activists and, above all, of hundreds of thousands of ordinary Egyptians, who found the courage to stand up and shout aloud their pent-up anger at years of despotic rule and their dream of freedom and justice, profoundly complicated the question of who would benefit from the redistribution of power.

The cheerleaders for what was transacted on 3 July have presented it as the renewal of 25 January – 11 February 2011. The revolution, hijacked and perverted by the Muslim Brothers, their Freedom and Justice Party and Mohamed Morsi, had been retrieved by the people and the army – *one hand!* – and put back on track. A feature of this story is that it elides what happened in Egypt in the months following Mubarak's fall. The early honeymoon between the revolutionaries and the Supreme Council of the Armed Forces (SCAF) didn't last long. Again and again, Tahrir Square and other public spaces were reoccupied by demonstrations expressing impatience with the SCAF's management of *l'après-Mubarak*, and, in the autumn of 2011, disappointment gave way to more radical sentiments.

A vivid illustration of the SCAF's true outlook was provided by the crushing of a demonstration by Copts at the Maspero building, the state broadcasting centre, on the Nile Corniche on 9 October 2011. Throughout the Mubarak era the Copts had become accustomed to being treated as second-class Egyptians, almost entirely excluded from what passed for political life. The legal but hopelessly small opposition parties, notably the New Wafd and El-Ghad, provided some scope for a few Copts to engage in a simulacrum of politics, but Mubarak's National Democratic Party scarcely ever fielded Copt candidates. The handful of Copts in Parliament were almost always there by presidential appointment; only three of the 444 members of the People's Assembly elected in 2000 were Copts. Instead, the government dealt with them as a politically undifferentiated religious community whose 'party' was the Coptic Church and whose political leader and representative was the Coptic Pope. But Copts took part in the demonstrations against Mubarak in Tahrir Square and were welcomed by the other demonstrators. The cry went up, 'Muslims, Copts, one hand!', and suddenly the transcending of the religious divide in the accession of all to an equal citizenship that at last meant something seemed to be part of the revolutionary promise. And that is why what happened at Maspero was so terrible. A group of Copts determined to take part in public life as free citizens had organised a demonstration to protest against the demolition of a church in Aswan by Salafis acting with the complicity of the regional governor. Before all of the entirely peaceful marchers had arrived at the Maspero building, they were attacked by army units firing live ammunition. Twenty-eight demonstrators were killed, at least two deliberately run over by army vehicles, and 212 others injured. The message was brutally clear: whatever the supposed 'revolution' had meant, the emancipation of the Copts was not part of it as far as the SCAF was concerned.

The sending of such messages went on and on. Between 19 and 24 November 2011, forty-five demonstrators demanding an end to military rule and the formation of a civilian government were killed in and around Mohamed Mahmoud Street. On 16 December a three-week-old sit-in near the Cabinet Office was violently dispersed and seventeen demonstrators were killed. Women who made clear their determination to take part in political life were also repeatedly victimised. In March 2011, within weeks of Mubarak's fall, the army was targeting female demonstrators and subjecting them to the appalling humiliation and intimidation of virginity tests carried out by male army doctors in the presence of other male soldiers. One of these women, Samira Ibrahim, had the courage to file a legal action against the government in order to make a public issue of this practice. But women demonstrators continued to be targeted, as was dramatically illustrated by images of six or seven military policemen savagely beating a young woman and stripping her upper body to her underwear. On 20 December 2011, thousands of Egyptian women demonstrated against these abuses. Seven days later, the army appeared to give ground when an administrative court pronounced virginity testing illegal. But the head of the judicial military authority promptly declared that this ruling couldn't be implemented because the court had no jurisdiction over what went on in military prisons.

On 31 December 2011 another large rally was held in Tahrir Square. The SCAF seemed to have realised it needed to take a step back, because there were no military or other police in evidence and the atmosphere was relaxed; people brought their children with them, as I did. It was a massive New Year's Eve party rather than a demonstration, but it had a political message all the same. A succession of speakers addressed the crowd, and Ramy Essam, whose song 'Irhal!' ('Clear Off!') had put Tahrir's message to Mubarak to music, came on stage with his guitar. But instead of 'Yasqut, yasqut, Hosni Mubarak' (Down, down with Hosni Mubarak), he and the crowd now sang 'Yasqut, yasqut, hukm al-'askar': 'Down, down with military rule.' And they seemed to mean it.

So how did Egypt travel from Tahrir Square on 31 December 2011 to Tahrir Square on 30 June 2013?

II

The air has been thick with partisan argument since 3 July. A blizzard of debating points has swirled around the actual events of the last two months and the thirty months that led up to them. For outsiders to take sides and add to the heat and dust serves no useful purpose. It should be obvious that Western opinion has been disabled where internal Egyptian politics is concerned, and that attempts by Western onlookers to pose as judges and pretend to the authority to arbitrate what has been at issue in Egypt are not only unlikely to succeed but increasingly fatuous. Let us instead consider two of the mysteries at the heart of this drama: the behaviour of the Tamarrud protest movement, which spearheaded the demonstrations of June this year in the name of 'the Revolution', and the behaviour of the Muslim Brothers' Freedom and Justice Party. Both have been widely misunderstood.

Tamarrud, which means disobedience, insubordination, revolt, rebellion and mutiny, is the name of the group that organised a nationwide petition against President Morsi and then the demonstrations of 30 June. It's a new group, founded last April. The petition stated that its signatories called on President Morsi to resign. The organisers announced their ambition to collect 15 million signatures and claim to have obtained 22 million, a figure I have never seen verified. But let us allow that they did obtain millions of signatures. To organise, let alone sign, such a petition is not an anti-democratic act: citizens have a right to call on an elected office-holder to resign, just as he or she may choose to stay in office until defeated at the polls. The petition said nothing about the army, let alone calling on it to act in the matter. The same was true of the mobilisation for the 30 June demonstrations. Several well-known groups that had played key roles in the demonstrations against Mubarak, notably the 6 April Youth Movement, the Revolutionary Socialists and the 'We Are All Khaled Sa'id' movement (formed to protest at the murder of a young man by the Alexandria police in 2010), did not hesitate to take part. They had reasons to dislike Morsi and his FJP and to want him out of office. But what happened at the demonstration itself was another matter, for many of those present did indeed call on the army to intervene. When the army deposed Morsi three days later, many of the demonstrators reacted as those on 11 February 2011 had reacted, triumphant that their point had been gained and inclined to see the army as the instrument of the people's will. As one Tamarrud activist, quoted by the *Observer* on 6 July, exulted:

Sisi and the army took their cue from the people. They had many previous chances to do what they did but they didn't take them. But once millions of people went out and started chanting for the army to step in, they took their orders from us. The army did not take over power. They were merely a partner in the democratic change we were seeking.[1]

The element of wishful thinking, if not sheer delusion, in this is a pointer to Tamarrud's real nature. But so is the statement of fact it contains. Why did the demand raised by Tamarrud's petition, that Morsi step down and early presidential elections be held, mutate into the demand that the army 'step in'? Clearly Tamarrud itself was happy with this development. Could it be that it was the Tamarrud activists themselves who, having got millions of Egyptians to sign a petition in support of one clear demand, then managed, during the demonstration itself, to convert this demand into something else? The organisers of demonstrations are usually the source of the slogans chanted by the participants and most demonstrators will happily chant the slogans they hear others chanting.

The target of 15 million signatories for the petition was chosen because it exceeded the number of Egyptians – 13.23 million – who voted for Morsi in the presidential election of June 2012. It was subsequently claimed that at least 14 million marched against him on 30 June. This figure was soon overtaken by others: 17 million, 22 million. The veteran Egyptian feminist Nawal el-Saadawi even claimed that 34 million had been there, a majority of the total electorate.[2] These figures were fairy tales, the tallest of tall stories. But the Egyptians who bombarded the world's media with such whoppers cannot seriously be faulted for trying it on; the West constituted itself into the gallery, so they played to it. For them, the stakes were immense and *c'est de bonne guerre*. The question we should confront is how and why our media swallowed this nonsense and then regurgitated it all over us.

The numbers question was investigated by Jack Brown, an American writer who has lived in Cairo for several years, and who on 11 July published a detailed article in *Maghreb*

Émergent, an indispensable source of serious coverage of North African developments, republished in English on the website *International Boulevard*. Brown worked out, from the actual area of Tahrir Square and the streets leading to it, that on the most generous estimate the demonstration cannot have exceeded 265,000 people.[3] If we assume for the sake of argument that the other big demonstration in Cairo, in Heliopolis, added a further 211,000, that gives at most 476,000. So where did the other 12.8 million needed to exceed Morsi's election tally come from? Cairo is home to nearly a quarter of Egypt's total population. Vague Western media references to 'hundreds of thousands' marching in other cities may authorise us to push up the overall tally, but we're still looking at maybe a million, or at the very most 2 million across the country as a whole, less than the 2.85 million Morsi polled in Cairo and Giza. The phantasmagorical figures quoted to the Western media may, as Brown observes, have exploited a confusion between attendance at the demonstrations and Tamarrud's claim for the number of petition signatories. But, however many millions really signed the petition, none of them signed a petition calling for the army to depose the president.

As the violence of the army's assault on Morsi's supporters grew and grew, some of the participants on 30 June had second thoughts. Ahmed Maher, the leader of the 6 April Youth Movement, supported the anti-Morsi campaign but later dissociated himself from the army's actions. The Revolutionary Socialists also eventually dissociated themselves.[4] But the Tamarrud leaders did not. They saw no significant difference between citizens calling on a president to resign and the minister of defence ordering him to be removed *manu militari*, and they were not only delighted with the outcome but claimed the credit for it. The Tamarrud activist quoted by the *Observer* was called Mohamed Khamis. On 16 August, two days after the massacres at Rabaa al-Adawiya mosque and Nahda Square, in which at least 628 protesters died, the *Guardian* quoted him again: 'We agree with what happened at Rabaa and at Nahda. We don't like what the Brotherhood did.'[5]

III

The activists who set up Tamarrud were veterans of an earlier protest movement, dating from 2004 and 2005, whose official name was Al-Haraka al-Masriyya min ajli 'l-Taghyir, 'the Egyptian Movement for Change', but which rapidly became known by its main slogan, 'Kifaya!' (Enough!). Kifaya was not an organised presence in the demonstrations of January and February 2011: it had petered out in 2006 and been superseded by more recently formed groupings. But, as I followed the drama in 2011, it became clear to me that the young revolutionaries, with the exception of the Trotskyist Revolutionary Socialists, were Kifaya's spiritual children and were bound to lose the initiative the moment their single, purely negative demand was conceded. I was a sceptic about the 'revolution' from that moment onwards.

A good account of Kifaya can be found in Holger Albrecht's timely study of the opposition movements that existed under Mubarak.* Contrary to the caricatures that became *de rigueur* once the balloon went up, Albrecht insists that Mubarak's rule was 'a liberalised authoritarian regime that provides [*sic*] limited – because entirely controlled from above – though surprisingly substantial degrees of pluralism'. This is more or less the way I saw it while living there. The press in particular was generally lively, with room for a wide spectrum of opinion, including plenty of criticism of the government. But there were definite 'red lines' and, as Albrecht explains, what was interesting about Kifaya is that it crossed two of them: the ban on unauthorised demonstrations under the Emergency Law; and the ban on explicit criticism of the president and his family.[6] Moreover, it did so with relative impunity; most of its demonstrations, while small (two or three hundred strong) and always massively outnumbered by riot police, were not suppressed or broken up but, strangely, tolerated, except when activists tried to

* Holger Albrecht, *Raging against the Machine: Political Opposition under Authoritarianism in Egypt* (Syracuse, NY: Syracuse University Press, 2013).

demonstrate outside Cairo. Kifaya was essentially an agitation conducted by a dissident wing of the Egyptian elite against Mubarak's 'monopoly of power' and the prospect of his son succeeding him. Although, under the very sober-sounding name of the Egyptian Movement for Change, it attracted a range of reformist viewpoints and published a lengthy shopping list of democratic-sounding aims and demands, the agitation it conducted was entirely negative in character.[7]

In investigating Kifaya in 2005 I found that it was dominated by secularist Arab nationalists and Nasserists. Its seven-man (later nine-man) steering committee included two liberals and the moderate Islamist Abu 'l-Ala Madi, the founder of the Wasat (Centre) Party, as well as two communists. But its co-ordinator and most prominent figure was George Ishaq, a Copt and a veteran Arab nationalist, and its other main spokesman was Abdel Halim Qandil, the editor-in-chief of the Nasserist paper *Al-Arabi*. Both men were impressive in their way: Ishaq, whom I interviewed, struck me as a combative and engagingly forthright person, and Qandil had shown admirable powers of resistance in enduring particularly thuggish harassment by the regime. In April 2005 I visited the offices of *Al-Arabi* and interviewed its other editor, Abdallah Senawi. In addition to telling me that 'Kifaya is the natural offspring of *Al-Arabi* and its slogans were first put forward by *Al-Arabi*; most Kifaya activists are Nasserists' – claims that may have been exaggerated but certainly weren't unfounded – he frankly outlined the Nasserists' true vision, which was to look to the army to resolve 'the Mubarak question', citing the recent military coup against President Ould Taya of Mauritania as a possible model.

In a report I wrote for the International Crisis Group in 2005, I argued that its exclusively negative message – the failure to agree on and agitate for a single positive demand or proposal – was a major reason for Kifaya's failure to gain a wider audience.[8] I came to the conclusion that, as Nasserists or at least Arab nationalists, their real objection to Mubarak was not his authoritarianism but his abandonment, like that of Sadat before him, of the pan-Arab vision that Nasser had proclaimed, and that they were not capable of organising a genuine democratic agitation. But it is possible that I got cause and effect at least partly back to front, and that the refusal to canvas a positive demand that might mobilise ordinary Egyptians reflected a concern to keep the challenge to the Mubaraks within the closed world of the Egyptian power elite, calling outsiders to witness the limits to the Mubaraks' dominion but not wanting to involve the public in the settling of scores that they dreamed about.

The demonstration on 25 January 2011 and the historic drama it inaugurated were made possible by the shockwave of the Tunisian revolution and the emergence since 2008 of a new generation of young middle-class activists enthused by the series of workers' strikes that began on 6 April that year (the *raison d'être* of Ahmed Maher's 6 April Youth Movement) and outraged by the thuggishness that the regime increasingly exhibited, culminating in the murder of Khaled Sa'id in June 2010, which prompted Wael Ghonim to launch his 'We are all Khaled Sa'id' page on Facebook.[9] But, while these developments supplied what had been so evidently absent in 2004 and 2005 – a substantial reservoir of politicised energies that made mass demonstrations feasible at last – the degree of politicisation was limited. The young activists knew and could agree on what they did not want, but that was all. Kifaya's negative agenda was what oriented them, whether they were conscious of its pedigree or not, and it was in these circumstances that the Nasserists' dream of the army resolving the Mubarak question came true.

We should not reduce 11 February 2011 to a coup. It was not a revolution, but it was not just a coup either. It was a popular rising that lost the initiative because it had no positive agenda or demand. 'Bread, freedom, social justice' are not political demands, just aspirations and slogans. A social movement might have made these slogans into demands by pressuring the government to take specific steps. But a movement that wants these desiderata provided by government and, at the same time, wants the government to clear off has a coherence problem. The only demand that mattered politically was 'Mubarak, irhal!' The army commanders captured the initiative by co-opting that demand to make it work for them. Almost certainly they did so because it had been their own undeclared objective for some time.

What happened on 11 February 2011 was a renewal of the Free Officers' state. Mubarak's fall did not in itself amount to a revolution because the fundamental framework of the state established by the Free Officers following their coup in 1952 was still in place, as the emergence of the SCAF as the dominant political actor should have made clear to everyone. In this respect, the outcome in Egypt fell far short of that in Tunisia. The Tunisians did not merely force the departure of Ben Ali, they went on immediately to abolish the ruling party, the Rassemblement Constitutionnel Démocratique (RCD). The RCD was the evolution of the nationalist party that, founded and led by Habib Bourguiba, had charted the course to independence. It was a genuine ruling party, the source of power and the principal instrument by which the state exercised its hegemony over society. It has had no counterpart in any other North African country. The abolition of the RCD signified the end of what Tunisia specialists called *le parti-État*.[10] It meant that Tunisian society was heading into *terra incognita*, constitutionally and politically. But when the Egyptian demonstrators destroyed the headquarters of Mubarak's National Democratic Party, they weren't attacking the source of political power in the state, merely the regime's façade. The army had been the source of political power since 1952. It had been marginalised by Mubarak and so took little part in the day-to-day business of government, but it had not been displaced by an alternative source of power. And so the events of January and February 2011 that brought it back to centre stage were not a revolution.

The Nasserist tradition of hailing coups as revolutions was inaugurated in July 1952. Some critics of the events of 3 July who have refused to endorse the 'second revolution' thesis have described what happened as a counter-revolution, a view for which I have some sympathy. Given that in June 2012 there was a real electoral contest in which people's votes really counted, such that a democratic line of development appeared to have got under way, one can certainly regard 3 July as having destroyed that and therefore as counter-revolutionary. But there is at least a germ of coherence in the claim made by General Sisi and by Tamarrud that 3 July 2013 restored the fundamental logic of 11 February 2011, as we can see once we accept, however reluctantly, that this logic was the reassertion and reclamation by the army of its historical political primacy and not a real revolution, let alone the revolutionary advent of democracy.

What, more than any other consideration, qualified the army commanders' success in surfing the wave of Tahrir Square to resolve the Mubarak question was the fact that the Muslim Brothers had been in Tahrir Square too, and had earned their share of the opening that ensued.

IV

In 1969, the Supreme Guide of the Muslim Brothers, Hassan al-Hodeibi, published from prison a text, *Du'āt, lā Quḍāt* (Missionaries, Not Judges), which dissociated the Brothers from the radical doctrines of Sayyid Qutb, in particular his condemnation of the Free Officers' state as not only *kufr* (infidel) but *jahili* (barbarous) and a licit object of jihad.[11] Thereafter the Brothers developed a reformist outlook and a gradualist strategy, which accepted the Islamic credentials of the existing state while seeking to enhance its Islamic character and that of society as a whole. Allowed, while still formally banned, to occupy a substantial amount of social space by both Sadat's regime (until they were briefly suppressed for opposing the Camp David agreement) and Mubarak's regime from 1981 onwards, the Brothers were able to build a large network of Islamic charitable, educational and cultural associations, as well as hospitals and clinics, giving them a social presence that none of the legal parties could rival. They were also able to participate in political life. Brothers were allowed to stand for election as independents or even occasionally on the list of a legal party such as the New Wafd, and some of them got elected, the number fluctuating depending on whether Mubarak was in liberalising or deliberalising mode. Throughout this period, the Brothers adhered to their non-violent strategy and behaved with prudence as well as stoicism, taking in their stride the intermittent clampdowns, when dozens and sometimes hundreds of Brothers would suddenly be arrested and imprisoned for months, and consoling themselves with the Quranic verse, 'God is with those who endure.'

A key if tacit element of the Brothers' gradualist approach was the determination to avoid a repetition of what had happened in 1954, when Nasser hanged six of their leaders and crushed their organisation. As a member of the Brothers' Guidance Bureau told me in 2004, 'We will never allow ourselves to be drawn into a confrontation with the army.'[12] So why has that happened now?

The reason so much emphasis has been placed on Morsi's mistakes and failures is that the preamble to Tamarrud's petition blamed everything on him so as to justify the call for his resignation.[13] This obscures the real reasons for the debacle that ensued. The great mistake that led to the confrontation the Brothers had sworn to avoid was their decision to contest the presidential election. They had originally announced that they would not do this. Their subsequent *volte-face* was naturally resented and criticised by their rivals and adversaries. They also initially suggested that they would seek to win only a third – and to that end contest only half – of the People's Assembly seats when the legislative elections took place, and then went back on this undertaking too, contesting two-thirds of them. They might have got away with changing their mind on the second point if they had not also changed it on the first.

Can it be that they had entirely failed to understand the implications of Mubarak's fall: that power was ineluctably being redistributed away from the presidency, that the first beneficiary of this was the army high command, and that the presidency was no longer so great a prize as to justify the costs and risks of contesting it? That may be part of the explanation, but only a secondary one. The key factor is the problem they had to confront when faced with the danger of serious defections and of being outflanked by Islamist rivals at the same time.

The Muslim Brothers had made clear as early as March 2011 that they would not run a candidate for the presidency. That

April they launched the Freedom and Justice Party (FJP). The next month, one of the Brothers' most prominent members, Abdul Moneim Aboul Fotouh, broke ranks by announcing that he would run for president as an independent, for which he was expelled in mid-June. Aboul Fotouh was on the liberal and progressive wing of the Brothers, well known for his commitment to democratic principles, his opposition to sectarian attitudes towards Christians and his support for women's participation in public life. He had a substantial reputation outside the Brothers and a strong following among the Brothers' younger members and took some of them with him when he left. The prospect of his running for president was an alarming one for the Brothers' leaders, threatening to cause major problems of discipline. And things were made much worse by the emergence of the Salafis as electoral competitors.

Originally a modernist, very political, anti-imperialist, pan-Islamic and non-sectarian movement when founded in the 1880s by the Persian Shiite agitator Jamal al-Din al-Afghani and his Egyptian Sunni deputy, Mohammed Abduh, the Salafiyya took a very conservative turn after the First World War, and since the 1970s has become synonymous with the Wahhabi tradition of Saudi Arabia and the United Arab Emirates and now stand for precisely the opposite of al-Afghani and Abduh's vision. The Salafis are the true fundamentalists in Sunni Islam, believing in the literal inerrancy of scripture. They are preoccupied with the opposition between *halal* (licit) and *haram* (forbidden) – that is, the dos and don'ts of correct Islamic conduct – and have generally been supportive of all Sunni regimes, offering a moralistic discourse on corruption but not a political challenge to governments. They are aggressively intolerant of Shiism and also of Christians and Jews, whom they call *kuffar* (infidels) instead of the traditional Ottoman view (to which the Brothers adhere) of respecting them as *Ahl al-Kitab* (People of the Book). Salafis have been hostile to political Islamists in general and the Muslim Brothers in particular, in part because they have opposed the very notion of political parties as divisive of the community of believers. The Salafi trend in Egypt has been growing for some years, as Arabian fashions have been brought back by Egyptian migrants returning from the Gulf, and as a reflection of the massive flow of Saudi and Emirati money into the country. But for the Salafis to launch their own political parties and enter the electoral arena was virtually unprecedented, and the Brothers' leaders were bound to see it as a major threat to their own electoral prospects. This explains their decision to contest more constituencies than originally envisaged in the legislative elections held between November 2011 and January 2012. Not to do so would have been to leave the field open to their conservative rivals.

The election results must have seemed to vindicate this decision: the Salafi Hizb al-Nour (Party of the Light) and its allies did astonishingly well, taking second place with 27.8 per cent of the vote and 123 seats, compared with the FJP-led alliance's 37.5 per cent and 235 seats; it would almost certainly have done even better if the Brothers had stuck to their original promise. The implications were ominous, however, presenting the Brothers with an appalling dilemma. While their leaders were broadly in the Islamic-modernist tradition, although on the conservative rather than the progressive wing, much of the rank-and-file membership would see little difference between the Salafis and themselves. This meant that the pressure from the Salafis on the Islamist flank would make it exceptionally difficult for the Brothers to seek alliances in Parliament with non-Islamist parties without putting their own internal unity under strain, and seeking instead to work with Hizb al-Nour would of course alienate the secular parties. As we now know, the Brothers proved unable to cope with this problem: they gave priority to maintaining their own cohesion at the expense of their relations with non-Islamists.

In the meantime, the movement faced a more immediate and perhaps even more excruciating problem: how to persist with its decision not to contest the presidential election when a still popular renegade from its most progressive wing, Aboul Fotouh, was going to run, and when the Salafis might put up a candidate as well. In the event, Hizb al-Nour didn't run a candidate and the main Salafi from another group was ruled ineligible. But the Brothers could not have known that in advance. What could they tell their members? Vote for a renegade whom conservative

Brothers didn't like? Vote for the Islamist you prefer, when this could split the Brothers down the middle if a Salafi entered the lists against Aboul Fotouh? Not vote at all, leaving the field open to all their rivals? They decided that the least bad option was to field their own candidate, a decision they made public in late March 2012 when they announced that this would be the Supreme Guide's deputy, Khairat al-Shater. Their U-turn was naturally attacked far and wide as just one more illustration of the Brothers' duplicity. In retrospect it was a terrible error – but a forced error. What remains to be explained is why the Brothers did not subsequently take avoiding action when it became clear that they were walking into a trap.

On 14 April 2012, Al-Shater was disqualified from standing on the grounds that he had been imprisoned under the Mubarak regime – further proof, if proof were needed, that no revolution had occurred.[14] Al-Shater was the Brothers' leading political brain and about as plausible a candidate as they could field. Denied this option, they fell back on the chairman of the FJP, the lacklustre and distinctly implausible Mohamed Morsi. In putting up their 'spare wheel', as he was immediately termed, the Brothers missed an opportunity to solve their dilemma in another way: indignantly to condemn the disqualification of their candidate and campaign for a boycott of the election as rigged, so putting the SCAF and the judges it was manipulating on the defensive, and delegitimising in advance whoever won. Instead, they soldiered on, limping. Two weeks later, al-Nour endorsed Aboul Fotouh's candidacy and the second part of the fix was in place. For the backward-looking and openly sectarian Salafis to endorse him may well have seemed to Aboul Fotouh the kiss of death, and who's to say it was not intended to be? For the Brothers, on the other hand, it may have seemed to raise rather than lower the stakes: whether Aboul Fotouh was embarrassed by Salafi support or not, it probably improved his chances of getting most of the Islamist vote and thereby considerably aggravated the Brothers' internal problem. If progressive and conservative Islamists were now united behind Aboul Fotouh, it would be harder than ever for the Brothers' leaders to forbid their members to vote for him.

They were given one more, very slight chance to extricate themselves from the quicksand in which they were floundering. Voting in the first round of the presidential election took place on 23 and 24 May and put Morsi ahead of the old regime's candidate, Ahmed Shafiq. The run-off between them was scheduled for 16–17 June. On 13 June, the SCAF announced a decree authorising soldiers to arrest civilians and stipulating that civilians could be tried in military courts.[15] This was a remarkable thing to do in the middle of a democratic presidential election but it was just the first, teasing, move in a three-part manœuvre. It was also the Brothers' last chance to pull out of the election, but the pretext it offered, while on the perfect issue – defending civilian rights against militarist bullying – was too slender, so they passed it up. The next day, 14 June – two days before the run-off vote – the Supreme Constitutional Court announced that the legislative elections held six months earlier that had given the FJP primacy in the People's Assembly were invalid, and the SCAF followed up with an administrative decree dissolving the Assembly forthwith. The pretext for this decision was that there had been procedural irregularities in a number of constituencies. The FJP acknowledged this but argued that the election results should be invalidated only in the constituencies concerned and that the proper solution was to hold by-elections in these places. This reasonable argument was rejected. At a stroke, the prospect that Morsi, if elected, could rely on the support of his party in Parliament was conjured away. I arrived in Cairo on 18 June and met a friend for dinner the following evening. As I sat down, his first words were: 'Welcome to our coup.' But the coup that removed the most democratically elected Parliament in Egyptian history was barely noticed in the Western media.

Can my readers, whatever their attitude to Islamism or the Muslim Brothers, imagine for a moment the impossible, agonising position in which this turn of events put Morsi's party? To soldier on was to condemn its candidate, if he won, to enter the presidency without any political support within the institutions of the state, since with the Assembly dissolved he would be facing the army, the police, the various intelligence services, the

vast unreformed bureaucracy and the unreformed and mani-
festly hostile judiciary entirely on his own.*[16] But to pull out
now would surely be to incur the undying reproaches of everyone else. Since his opponent was Shafiq, Mubarak's man, Morsi
was the last remaining option for all those who had been part of
or identified with Tahrir Square in 2011. Millions of Egyptians
– not least the members of the Brothers and the FJP – would feel
betrayed if Morsi let Shafiq win by default. Who among them
would begin to understand that it was the right thing to do?
How could they ever forgive the FJP and the Brothers? And so
Morsi and the FJP rolled with the killer punch and gamely
stayed in the ring, perhaps secretly hoping that the SCAF would
make Shafiq the winner and almost certainly knowing, the
moment they were awarded the poisoned chalice, that the fight
was irretrievably lost and all they could do was prolong it in a
gruelling last round that would end, calamitously, one year later.
And just to complete the business, on 17 June, the second day of
voting in the run-off, the SCAF issued a 'constitutional declaration' that arrogated key presidential powers, including the
power of appointment of army commanders, to the SCAF itself,
while giving other key powers of the president-to-be to the
SCAF or the judiciary.[17]

In seeking at all costs to avoid a confrontation with the army,
the Brothers helped to create the conditions for that very
confrontation. In trying above all else to negotiate an understanding with the SCAF, they allowed a wedge to be driven
between them and the 'revolutionaries', as when they refused to
support the Mohamed Mahmoud Street protests against the
SCAF in November 2011 because the legislative elections were
due to start a week later. In this way, the Brothers made a gift of
the young revolutionaries' volatile enthusiasms to the growing
alliance of their own implacable enemies. But the root of the

* The parliament's upper house, the Shura Council, was not
affected by the SCAF's decree. In the elections to it in January–February
2012, the FJP won 105 of the 270 seats and 'Islamic Bloc', dominated
by Hizb al-Nour, 45. But the council had very limited powers; elected
on a turn-out of only 10 per cent, with no claim to representativity, it
could offer President Morsi no real support.

Brothers' inability to navigate safely between Scylla and Charybdis lay in the continuing crisis within the organisation itself, of which Aboul Fotouh's behaviour had been a sign, and which dated back to the last years of Mubarak.

V

In charting with care the rise of Arab presidents for life, Roger Owen has pioneered a new strand in the academic debate on authoritarianism in the Middle East and North Africa. But his book relaunches that debate rather than closing it. He rightly emphasises the context of the permanent 'security state', the role of the army, of the other security services, the way leaders in the post-revolutionary era managed to adapt to 'the global waves of economic and political liberalisations', the correspondingly significant role of crony capitalists and so on.[18] But there are at least two further elements that need to be taken into account.

The first is the radical absence of republican political thought in the societies of the region. The Arab republics were mainly republics in the negative sense of not being monarchies. Beyond that, a kind of substitutionism – of paternalist rulers for the self-determining people – reigned for a while (Nasser, Bourguiba, Boumediène, Qadhafi, Hafez al-Asad), and then a degree of privatisation of the state set in, under their post-revolutionary or counter-revolutionary successors (Sadat, Chadli, Ben Ali) as the presidential autocracies came more and more to resemble the certified monarchies of the region. But when Egyptian intellectuals complained of *tawrith al-sulta* (inheritance of power) – the Mubaraks' apparent project of constituting themselves into a dynasty – it was not at all obvious that they were defending any positive republican principle, merely the (negative) fact that since 1952 the state had not been a monarchy. Government had long ceased to be *res publica*, if it ever had been.

The late Anouar Abdel-Malek, whose death in June 2012 spared him the sorrow he would surely have felt at the disaster which has overtaken his country, produced two books that could hardly be more relevant to this debate. *Egypt: Military*

Society (originally published in French in 1962) will help anyone understand the rejuvenated Free Officers' state that is now flexing its muscles.[19] *La Pensée politique arabe contemporaine* (1970), which he edited, bears witness to the lacuna I have mentioned.[20] Among all the essays by more than fifty Arab authors on the issues of the time – Islamism, national liberation, identity, Arab unity, socialism, Palestine – there is not one on the republican idea. And this absence points to one of the conditions of the phenomenon Owen describes.

The other element – undoubtedly linked to, indeed a supplementary illustration of, the first – is that the phenomenon of presidents for life is not limited to heads of state. In Cairo in the mid-2000s it was a matter for ironic comment that the leaders of the most prominent legal parties were all mini-Mubaraks, ageing autocrats like the *ra'is* himself, pocket pharaohs for their pocket pseudo-parties. They included No'man Gomaa, in his early seventies by then, whose self-centred leadership of the New Wafd drove Ayman Nour (the future founder of El-Ghad) out of the party and who was finally ejected himself only after a gun battle at the party headquarters; Rifaat al-Saïd, the seventy-three-year-old leader of Tagammu, who was notorious for ignoring his colleagues' opinions; Dia al-Din Dawoud, at seventy-nine the even older leader of the Nasserist Party, whose autocratic manner drove his most talented young recruit, Hamdeen Sabahi, to leave and found a new party of his own, Al-Karama (Dignity). But this is not just an Egyptian thing. The Kurdish Democratic Party in Iraq has been led by the Barzanis for generations, just as the Druze in Lebanon have been led by the Jumblatts. And what the Algerian press fondly refers to as the country's oldest opposition party, the Socialist Forces Front, has been led since its foundation in 1963 by Hocine Aït Ahmed, a president for life whose tenure (at fifty years) exceeds even Qadhafi's.

Another instance is provided by the Muslim Brothers themselves. Every Supreme Guide, from Hassan al-Banna onwards, has held office for life, except one. The exception is Mohamed Mahdi Akef, who took office in 2004 but was forced into retirement as a result of an internal power struggle in 2009.

Albrecht gives a concise account of this but does not fully explain it. But I believe future histories of this period will see this matter as crucial to an understanding of the behaviour of the Brothers since February 2011 and their eventual shipwreck.

When Akef took office in January 2004, the Brothers were virtually accepted participants in Egyptian public life. Seventeen Brothers had been elected as independents to the People's Assembly in 2000 and, while still liable to be reminded of their illegal status by occasional waves of arrests, their views were regularly reported in the press and leading Brothers were frequently invited to speak on non-Islamist public platforms. By this time, their political agenda had taken a markedly democratic direction: above all the demand for the end of the Emergency Law, followed by free and fair elections, freedom of speech and assembly and so forth. On 3 March 2004, two months after taking office, Akef added a major new policy when he announced that the Brothers were proposing a radical constitutional change to make the state a parliamentary republic.[21] This proposal directly addressed the problem of the authoritarian form of government, instead of personalising it by focusing on the Mubaraks, and could have allowed for a Gamal succession by institutionalising the redistribution of power towards the legislative branch, a precondition in any case of action to curb corruption and arbitrary rule. But, while one or two of the legal parties eventually adopted the policy, the proposal prompted no serious public debate and was soon eclipsed by Kifaya's agitation about 'the Mubarak question'. It continued to guide the Brothers' political activity, however. In the legislative elections of November and December 2005, they contested a third of the seats and won no fewer than eighty-eight, an unprecedented triumph which made them much the strongest opposition party, with a fifth of the Assembly seats. They began to use these to good effect, putting the NDP majority under pressure of a kind they had never experienced before.[22]

The regime's reaction wasn't long in coming. 'We're going after the Brothers,' a member of Gamal Mubarak's entourage in the NDP leadership told a colleague of mine, and over the next three years the regime not only rewrote most of the election rules to make it impossible for the Brothers to capitalise on their success, but also launched far and away the heaviest campaign of repression against them, imprisoning hundreds if not thousands and inflicting severe damage on the organisation.[23] The eventual result was that the pendulum swung towards the conservatives. The forward, outward-looking and very political strategy followed by Akef and incarnated in such figures as Aboul Fotouh and Issam el-Erian had cost the Brothers dear and the traditionalists, those largely content to sustain the Brothers' religious and social activities, rebelled against it. In January 2010 Akef stood down and was succeeded not by his deputy, another progressive, Mohammed Habib, but by a relatively obscure member of the Guidance Bureau from the conservative wing, Mohamed Badie. Passed over, Habib left the organisation, to be followed by Aboul Fotouh in 2011. From then on, it was the conservative and inward-looking wing of the Brothers that made policy. Less politically skilled and self-confident, clumsy and rigid in debate because less at ease with other points of view, inclined to be suspicious and invite suspicion in return and very much disposed to seek a deal of some kind with the regime as the precondition of everything else, the new leadership was to prove incapable of handling the endless challenges of the post-Mubarak era.

VI

Egypt is not Algeria. This truism and its corollary, 'we are not going to make the Algerians' mistake', were frequent themes in the discourse of the Mubarak regime and its media, used above all to justify the refusal to legalise the Brothers. The Algerians, who had largely copied (with certain important differences) the political template of the Free Officers' regime up until 1989, suddenly deviated from it when they let their Islamists off the leash by legalising the Islamic Salvation Front (FIS). The FIS's sensational election victories in June 1990 and December 1991, the crisis of the state in 1991–2 and the descent into nightmarish violence that ensued were all condemned in Cairo as folly, and cited as evidence of the wisdom of the Mubarak regime's handling of Egypt's Islamists. But what happened in November–December 2005 in fact anticipated what was to come six years later, a mini 'Algeria moment'. The reason the Brothers won eighty-eight seats (seventy-one more than in 2000) was that they had been tacitly encouraged by the regime to campaign as if they were entirely legal, and they did so with alacrity.[24] While registered as independents, their candidates openly ran as Brothers. Candidates' photographs posted on walls and lamp posts in every street carried the legends *Al-Ikhwān al-Muslimūn* (The Muslim Brothers) and *Al-Islām, huwa al-ḥall* (Islam is the solution); the Brothers were even allowed to hold mass meetings and marches in the constituencies they were contesting, and the press reported their campaigns just like those of the other parties.[*]

The reason the regime allowed all this was to get the Americans off its back. Under pressure from Washington to validate its claim that the destruction of Iraq had launched a region-wide process of democratisation, Cairo had made token gestures,[†] but by late 2005 it had had enough. It was time to bring home to the White House and Foggy Bottom that opening up the political field would serve only to empower the Islamists and destabilise the state. The Algerians had similar if more complicated reasons for legalising and manipulating the FIS, and the results of the first round of the 1991 elections were instrumentalised in the same way in the regime's endless dialogue with Paris. But the Egyptian regime, or rather Gamal Mubarak's team in the NDP leadership, miscalculated. They thought the Brothers would win thirty or forty seats at most and panicked when they did far better than that, which is why the Mubaraks

---

[*] During the 2005 election I witnessed the Brothers in action in the Fayoum, for years the fiefdom of former NDP secretary-general, Yousef Wali; the Brothers' very well-organised campaign covered the district with marches and meetings and deservedly took the seat.

[†] Notably the decision to license Ayman Nour's new party, El-Ghad, in October 2004, and then slightly liberalising the rules regarding presidential elections in the constitutional revision of May 2005.

had to compensate by ordering a massive crackdown, while Washington looked the other way.[*]

There are many other points of contact between the Egyptian and Algerian experiences. In Algeria since 1962, as in Egypt since 1952, the military has been the source of power, rather than the party, which has been no more than a state apparatus, subject to close control by the president and the intelligence services – an empty shell, as Boumediène once admitted. But the Algerians discreetly deviated from the Egyptian model early on in one important respect that we can fully appreciate only now, thanks to Hazem Kandil's important book.[†]

Kandil effectively rewrites the inner history of the Free Officers' state and his book deserves to spark sustained debate. It provides an exceptionally detailed account of the endless power struggle in both Nasser's and Sadat's regimes and offers startling new accounts of the major crises that occurred in each of them. Disputing conventional histories that portray Nasser from 1954 onwards as wholly dominating the state, Kandil argues that, when he took over the government, Nasser effectively lost control of the army. Having delegated command to Abdel-Hakim Amer, he found his supposed long-time friend acting increasingly against him, turning the army into his fiefdom by promoting friends and cronies, however incompetent, and thereby replicating eventually the army's corrupt and demoralised condition under King Farouq, which is what had prompted the Free Officers' conspiracy in the first place. The increasingly antagonistic relationship between the two men gave rise to a kind of trench warfare conducted by the intelligence services they respectively controlled, and eventually played a major part in Nasser's three great failures: the short-lived union

---

[*] Seeing the Brothers' first-round tally far exceed their expectations, the authorities in the second and third rounds resorted to fraud but also to brazen interference in the polls, shutting voting stations on polling day and preventing voters from entering them, in addition to arresting the Brothers' campaign staff (ICG, 'Egypt's Muslim Brothers', 2).

[†] Hazem Kandil, *Soldiers, Spies and Statesmen: Egypt's Road to Revolt* (London and New York: Verso, 2012).

with Syria in 1958–61, the abortive intervention in the Yemen, and, above all, the catastrophic defeat by Israel in June 1967. It was in part to get Amer out of his hair that Nasser agreed to the union with Syria in the first place, appointing him as Cairo's proconsul in Damascus, a move that helped doom the union but failed to solve Nasser's problem, since he couldn't stop Amer resuming command of the army on his return. Amer's reluctance to promote competent officers who might have helped equip the army for serious fighting, Kandil suggests, was a major factor in the Yemen fiasco. Above all, we learn that it was not Nasser but Amer who was responsible for the fatal game of brinkmanship – the deployment of troops into the Sinai, the closing of the Straits of Tiran – that gave Israel its pretext and opportunity to crush Egypt in the Six-Day War, while Nasser struggled in vain to head off the consequences of Amer's folly.

Whatever such revelations – which other historians may challenge – mean for specialists working on Israel, Jordan, Syria and US policy, they also shed light on Algeria. On taking power in 1965, Boumediène made sure to keep the defence portfolio and, following Nasser's success in at last ridding himself of Amer in August 1967, he succeeded in provoking his turbulent chief of staff, Tahar Zbiri, into mounting an abortive coup four months later, the crushing of which consolidated Boumediène's control. More evidence that the Algerians kept on watching and learning from Egypt is provided by Kandil's fascinating account of the Sadat era. Perhaps its most controversial element is his suggestion that part of the army leadership was behind Sadat's assassination in October 1981. Kandil is unable to nail this claim all the way down but makes a good case in view of the fact that the assassins were junior army officers and that the military commander of Tanzim al-Jihad, the group that pulled it off, was a defector from military intelligence who was spared execution and finally released from prison in March 2011. Is it just a coincidence that shortly before Sadat was killed, President Chadli replaced the head of Algerian military intelligence with a regular army officer and then transferred the service from its home in the defence ministry to the presidency? It may be; coincidences happen. But the Chadli regime had already taken a big leaf out of Sadat's book, closely imitating his purge of Nasserists and the left in the early 1970s in its own purge of Boumediènists and leftists beginning in 1980.

That the Egyptian army commanders had reason to resent Sadat is clear from Kandil's account of the 1973 October war, when the generals were beside themselves at Sadat's failure to press the advantage they had gained by crossing the Suez Canal. His refusal to seize the main passes in Sinai enabled the Israelis to turn the tables. This resentment was aggravated by the terms to which Sadat agreed at Camp David, another tortuous episode Kandil explores in depth. In effect, Amer lost Sinai and Sadat made no serious attempt to regain it; together they created Egypt's Sinai problem, which Mubarak was content to manage rather than resolve and which is now exploding.

It is in this episode, in the way Sadat prostrated himself and his country before the Americans, that we can discern both the origins of the army's eventual refusal to rescue Mubarak, Sadat's faithful successor, and the origins of the convergence Owen describes between Arab 'republics' and monarchies. While the syndrome of presidents for life was not pioneered by Egypt – it was Bourguiba who started it and who also pioneered the *infitāḥ* that was to become central to Sadat's economic policy – it was Sadat who pioneered the distinctively monarchical presidency, modelling himself on the shah of Iran and aping his flamboyance. As Kandil describes it, Sadat's strategy for retaining power was essentially to make himself dependent on and indispensable to Washington, in his eyes the only foreign power that mattered, reducing Egypt to a client state – or even a servant state – while making the US the external guarantor of his rule.

Algeria under Chadli went some way along a similar path, except that it spread the risk between Washington and Paris and always kept some room for manœuvre. On taking over, Mubarak moderated Sadat's strategy, while maintaining its fundamental elements, dropping the irritating flamboyance and regal manner, at least at first, and renegotiating some aspects of the relationship with the US. He also continued Sadat's determined effort to control and sideline army commanders, prudently following the course Sadat had set while reducing the zigzags. As a result, it might be said that Mubarak, succeeding where Sadat came to grief, managed to secure for the presidency a degree of autonomy from the military that amounted to the virtual negation of the Free Officers' state.

VII

The return with a vengeance of the Egyptian army to the centre of government does not, as some have suggested, mean the advent of Mubarakism without Mubarak, since the extreme autonomy of the presidency is no more, even if Sisi takes the job. Moreover, an important element of Mubarak's prolonged balancing act was his tacit reliance on the Muslim Brothers to provide needed services and to keep order in those parts of society the state could or would no longer bother itself with. That compact is now broken. Whether there will be a substantive as opposed to purely rhetorical reversion to Nasserism in domestic policy remains to be seen but it's unlikely. Reliance on Saudi money and Israeli co-operation would seem to rule it out in foreign affairs, unless the full recovery of Egyptian sovereignty in the Sinai becomes a genuine objective of the army. So the startling influence of the Tamarrud movement over the political reflexes of the young 'revolutionaries' may prove short-lived. If definitive disillusion sets in, the latter may at last begin to realise how profoundly they have ended up repeating the tragic error of the Algerian secularists and the Algerian left after 1989, in their failure to develop a positive vision of the way to achieve freedom, justice and dignity that they could confidently oppose to the Islamists' one.

3

The Hijackers

Syria is the terminus of the Arab Spring, of the wave of contestation radiating from Tunisia that, combining profoundly justified popular anger and the Arab elites' endlessly recurring investment in imitation, has dashed against the rocks of other Arab states with such calamitous consequences.

The trajectory of the wave has formally resembled that of the Tunisian uprising itself, which began on the periphery of the Tunisian state but quickly exhibited a centripetal dynamic, gaining in organisation, purposefulness, support and sophistication as it approached the core, and so acquiring the power not only to capture the capital but also, crucially, to begin reordering Tunisian political life on the basis of representative government and the rule of law. Tunisia itself is on the periphery of the Arab world, with Algeria and Morocco to its west enjoying the advantages and disadvantages of even more peripheral locations. The shock wave the Tunisian revolution triggered barely ruffled Algiers and Rabat and headed east, cresting in spectacular fashion in Cairo, then engulfing Libya in the backwash from Mubarak's fall before resuming its centripetal thrust and attaining Syria, the 'beating heart of Arabism'.

Syria is where the Banū Umayya clan of the Prophet's tribe, the Quraysh, established the Umayyad dynasty to rule the first Islamic empire from Damascus. It is where the venture of absorbing the Arab world into the Ottoman Empire got started with the Ottomans' victory in the battle of Marj Dabiq (1516 CE); where the Arab *nahda*, the cultural renaissance of the Arab world, blossomed in the course of the nineteenth century; where the unified Arab kingdom that the British promised the Hashemites (descendants of the Prophet's own clan, the Banu Hashem), who led the 1916–18 Arab revolt against Ottoman rule, was to have its capital in Damascus. It is also where, in the aftermath of the Second World War, the most modernist, politically developed and socially radical version of the dream of Arab unity was conceived by the founders of the Arab Socialist Ba'th (Resurrection) Party.

The country today is in ruins: there are more than 200,000 dead, many thousands of them children; about 4 million refugees in Iraq, Jordan, Lebanon and Turkey, some 7 million people internally displaced and many towns largely destroyed. The movement sparked by the Tunisian revolution has ended up consigning Egypt to a new phase of military dictatorship bleaker than any before and precipitating the descent into mayhem of Libya, Yemen and Syria. The most substantial beneficiary in the region of this turn of events practises the most zealously intolerant, retrograde, vindictively sectarian and brutal form of Islamist politics seen in our lifetimes. Islamic State – with its capital and organising centre in Raqqa in northern Syria – now exerts control over much of Syria and Iraq and is spreading its tentacles south to the Gulf states and west to North Africa. How is this dreadful turn of events to be understood?

Jean-Pierre Filiu, who teaches at Sciences Po in Paris after a career in France's diplomatic corps which included tours of duty in Jordan, Syria and Tunisia, argues in his new book that the Arab revolutions (as he calls them) have been foiled – except (as of 2015) Tunisia – by successful counter-revolutions organised by the 'deep state'.* In Syria – as in Egypt and Yemen – the deep state is the hard core of a regime that strongly resembles those of the Mamluks in Egypt and the Levant long ago.[1] He holds the Syrian 'Mamluks' responsible not only for the devastation of their own country but also for the rise of Islamic State, with

* Jean-Pierre Filiu, *From Deep State to Islamic State: The Arab Counter-Revolution and Its Jihadi Legacy* (London: Hurst, 2015), x, xii, 1–19.

which, he suggests, they have been in cahoots.[2] The 'Mamluks' are the main – indeed the only – villains in his story. His solution is to keep the revolutions going at all costs and get rid of the 'Mamluks' whatever it takes.[3]

The notion of the deep state became fashionable in media coverage of Egypt in 2011. Filiu notes that the term originated in Turkey, where it connoted not merely the secretive apparatuses of the state such as the police and intelligence services but above all the shady nexus between them, certain politicians and organised crime.[4] Part of his argument is that the deep state is beyond the law: its members see themselves as custodians of the higher interests of the nation and believe this authorises them to get up to all sorts of unavowable things, not only working with criminal elements but even engaging in what would otherwise be regarded as criminal acts. The sense that they have an unqualified right to do whatever they choose, he argues, is premised on a patrimonial view of the state and a paternalistic view of the people, both views determined by the collective self-interest of the deep state actors themselves.[5]

There is of course truth in all this. But all states – at any rate, all states that endure – have their hidden depths and, for very cogent reasons, make a point of veiling what they get up to by means of what the French call *le secret d'État*. In the Ben Barka affair of 1965–6, the leader of the Moroccan left was abducted and murdered during a visit to France as the result of a conspiracy involving a large cast of characters including French police and intelligence agents, Moroccan agents, the Moroccan interior minister and French gangsters. A few of those involved – mainly the gangsters – eventually stood trial and went to jail. Paris's prefect of police, Maurice Papon, was obliged to resign and others, including the head of the SDECE (France's equivalent of MI6 at the time), took early retirement.[6]

The state and the deep state are not two things but all of a piece, in what we call democracies as well as in dictatorships. Talk of the deep state in Egypt suggested that its discovery was an unpleasant surprise, which indicated a good deal of naivety on the part of the Egyptian revolutionaries. Would-be revolutionaries who set out to transform a state – let alone overthrow it – need to know what they're up against before they start. Why, then, does Filiu make so much of this? The answer is that he links his thesis about the counter-revolutionary behaviour of the deep state to his thesis that the states in question are ruled by 'Mamluks'.

The original Mamluks were the slave soldiers employed by the Abbasid dynasty from the late-ninth century onwards. Dynasties established on the basis of descent from the Prophet's family, clan or tribe often faced equally plausible rival claims; troops recruited from the dynasts' own clan or tribe could never be wholly loyal, since they would also owe obligation to other ambitious individuals or families. The answer was to form armies of slaves imported from far afield, non-Arabs and non-Muslims: Kipchak Turks, Circassians and Georgians and, in a later period, Albanians and Greeks. Eventually the strategy backfired. Because the military profession was reserved to Mamluks, some of them rose to positions of great power and transcended their original slave status, and a Mamluk elite eventually emerged. In 1250 it seized power in Egypt and Syria and established the Mamluk Sultanate, with its capital in Cairo. Later the Ottomans would recycle and refine this recruitment strategy with the *devshirme*, the 'harvest' of young boys from Christian families in the Balkans and southern Russia, who would be taken to Istanbul, converted to Islam and trained for careers in the army (as janissaries), the palace or the bureaucracy. The key principle was that the army should not be recruited from the free-born Muslim population.[7]

Filiu is not the first to posit a parallel between the historic Mamluks and contemporary regimes in the Middle East and North Africa. As he acknowledges, the Egyptian scholar Amira El-Azhary Sonbol wrote a book on this theme.[*] But the idea is older than that. In *The Arab Predicament*, the late Fouad Ajami included a discussion of two writers who hit on this notion at the same time.[8] In 1969 Sami al-Jundi published *Al-Ba'th*, his critique

---

[*]   Amira El-Azhary Sonbol, *The New Mamluks: Egyptian Society and Modern Feudalism*, with a foreword by Robert Fernea (Syracuse, NY: Syracuse University Press, 2000).

of the movement he once served with enthusiasm, arguing that, under the rule of the 'Military Committee' of the Ba'th, Syria was regressing to the Mamluk era.[9] The following year, Muhammad Jalal Kishk, an Egyptian Islamist, published *Al Qawmiyah wa 'l-Ghazw al-Fikri* (Nationalism and the Cultural Invasion), in which he referred to the leftwing Ba'thists then running Syria (Salah Jadid and his associates) as 'socialist Mamluks'.[10] Kishk's thesis was that the creation of a state sector of the economy with the nationalisations decreed by the regime in the name of social-ism had not entailed progress beyond the capitalist forms of property and production relations that had begun to develop following the 1858 Ottoman land reform, but a regression to earlier, pre-capitalist, forms of both, an argument that prefigured Sonbol's talk of a 'new feudalism' in the Egyptian case. Four years later, in 1974, the British scholar Ernest Gellner canvassed a different version of the idea in an essay on the role of Salafi Islamism in the Algerian national revolution, in which he spoke of the new Algerian elite as largely composed of 'the mamluks of the modern world', not in virtue of its socialist policies but rather because of the way this elite (the civilian technocrats as well as the military) was constituted through 'atomic, one-by-one recruit-ment' to minimise its ties to the governed and insulate it from them as the original Mamluks had been insulated.[11]

Filiu largely ignores these authors and distinguishes his idea from Sonbol's by insisting that he is not positing 'new Mamluks', but highlighting a parallel with the original Mamluks in their heyday, the era of the Mamluk Sultanate (1250–1517 CE).[12] Just as the Mamluks in power pretended to be serving the Caliph – reduced to a mere figurehead – and secured legitimation for their rule by this ploy, so today's 'Mamluks' pretend to be serv-ing the People, securing a dubious legitimation via rigged elec-tions and plebiscites.[13] This line of argument enables Filiu to reach, by a different route, a similar conclusion to Gellner's, making the key issue the 'Mamluk' regimes' legitimacy deficit. This is a more serious matter today than it used to be.

Since the international military intervention in Libya, an alleged legitimacy deficit can be a pretext for externally engi-neered regime change. Gellner's case, developed in a less hysterical world, stated dispassionately and thoughtfully argued, was that the elite's nationalist legitimacy would wear out in time, and its 'socialism' would not compensate for this because it cut little ice with the Algerian public – both reasonable suppositions – and that they would accordingly not only need the endorsement of the religious leaders, the *'ulama*, but also become politically beholden to them, a *non sequitur* that subsequent events have not confirmed. Filiu offers – in a polemical book that betrays deep hostility to the nationalist cause in France's former possessions in the region – a more radical view: that the 'Mamluks' were entirely illegitimate from the outset as crude usurpers of the original national revolution, which they had hijacked at independence, and he insists that this was the case in Algeria before broadening the charge to apply it to Egypt, Syria and Yemen.[14] In effect, Filiu imports Turkey's deep state into his analysis of Arab states, takes the 'Mamluks' from Cairo to Algiers, misrepresents Algerian history in these exotic terms and concludes that this 'Algerian matrix' is the key to understanding Syria and Yemen.

The claim that Algeria's independence was hijacked by the army – the French term is *confisquée*, which has different connotations – and that Algeria's rulers have been illegitimate from 1962 onwards recycles the propaganda of the French army during the Algerian war: the National Liberation Front (Front de Libération Nationale, FLN) and its National Liberation Army (Armée de Libération Nationale, ALN) were not revolutionaries, but *fellaga* (bandits), utterly illegitimate. Filiu's argument thus deploys a hardy perennial of *revanchard* French discourse on Algeria and reflects the extent to which this discourse has moved from the extreme right to invest the centre ground of French public life. The hijacking or confiscation thesis is tendentious. Almost without exception the key people in the Algerian regime when I first visited the country in 1972 had impressive records of service in the national revolution. That certain once prominent personalities had lost out in the FLN's internal politics did not seriously detract from the government's legitimacy in the Algerian public's estimation or in mine.

Revolutionary politics are by definition unbound by law and rough in the extreme. Disputes among the revolutionaries are resolved by force and manœuvre. Some leaders come out on top, others have their moment then get the chop. Oliver Cromwell led the parliamentary cause to victory by defeating the royalist forces with his New Model Army, then purged the radical elements, suppressed Parliament itself and thereafter ruled as Lord Protector. The Jacobins took charge of France in the summer of 1793, after other revolutionary factions had made a mess of everything, and sent many of them to the guillotine while bringing a new order out of chaos. Did Cromwell hijack the English revolution? Did Robespierre and Saint-Just hijack the French one? Did the Bolsheviks hijack the Russian revolution? You can always make a case for such views, taking the side of the Levellers or the Girondins or the Mensheviks or Kerensky or the Left Social Revolutionaries. The people who storm the Bastille are rarely if ever the people who construct a new political order on the ruin of the old regime; the latter can always be accused of having hijacked the revolution. Revolutions are like that. If you don't like this sort of thing, what are you doing enthusing about putative revolutions in the Arab world?

II

Before we can clarify what is to be done about Syria, there are two questions that need to be answered. The first is why the nationalist movements in these countries, and Syria in particular, were militarised. Without an answer to this question, demilitarisation – the indispensable task of a serious democratic opposition – cannot be undertaken with any prospect of success. The second question is: who have been the real hijackers of the Arab uprisings from 2011 onwards, and how have they gone about it?

Algerian nationalist politics were militarised in 1954. Until then political parties led by civilians had peacefully put forward variants of the nationalist ideal. But successive governments in France refused to make any serious concessions. The founders of the FLN came out of the most vigorous nationalist party, the Parti du Peuple Algérien (PPA), having decided that, once all legal options proved fruitless, there was nothing for it but to fight their way out of the French embrace.[15] The pre-eminence of the army in Algeria dates from 1954, not 1962. The militarisation of Algerian nationalism had its tragic side, but there was nothing gratuitous about it and it secured Algeria's independence. The political primacy of the military was not seriously questioned in independent Algeria until the 1980s but, because the explicit challenge to it from 1989 onwards came from the Islamists, the Westernised and secularist wing of the middle class looked to the army for protection, giving it fresh, if temporary, endorsement. The demilitarisation of Algerian politics became a matter of public debate with the winding down of the violence after 2001. But achieving it requires a reinvigoration of civilian politics, and that will take time as well as new thinking. The serial wars of intervention in the Middle East and North Africa since 1990 and the 'global war on terror' since 2001 have provided the most unfavourable context for such a change that one could imagine.

The notion that the military are 'Mamluks' and hijackers is most persuasive in the Egyptian case. For all its shortcomings, the political life of Egypt after the end of the British protectorate in 1922 was an improvement. Egyptian sovereignty was massively qualified by the 'four reserved points', according to which the British retained control over 'security of imperial communications' (primarily the Suez Canal), defence, protection of foreign interests and minorities, and the Sudan. But Egypt had a measure of freedom and, however unsatisfactory, a political life to call its own. And then, between 1952 and 1954, the army took over. Those Free Officers who argued that, after some house-cleaning, they should return to barracks and reform the army while allowing civilian party politics to resume were defeated by Nasser and his followers, with the Americans, fixated on the Cold War and wanting an anti-communist strong man rather than democracy, arbitrating in Nasser's favour.[16] Under Nasser, the new regime turned Egypt into a political desert but made headway in achieving full independence by securing the British evacuation of the Canal Zone in 1954 and nationalising the canal and seeing off the tripartite aggression in 1956, Nasser himself gaining immense popularity and legitimacy in the process. But he lost the Sinai to Israel in 1967 and

Egypt has never fully recovered it. In order to get it back, Nasser's successor, Anwar Sadat, prostrated himself before the United States and Egypt has remained a depressed client state to this day. In the process, Sadat increased his own freedom of action by encouraging the army to develop its economic interests as a surrogate for an active political role, a strategy continued by Mubarak. The army commanders became at least partially independent of Egypt's economy and society, insulated from the populace to a considerable degree (in that sense resembling Mamluks), while maintaining close relations with their American counterparts. The recent emphatic remilitarisation of Egyptian political life, after just two and a half years of inevitably turbulent civilian politics, owes a great deal to this history, but Filiu does not mention the American connection.

The Syrian case is very different. The militarisation of Syria's political life occurred in fits and starts. It began with Husni al-Zaim's coup in March 1949, the first military coup in the Arab world, launched with American encouragement if not prompting.[17] Four and a half months later Zaim was killed during a second coup, carried out by Colonel Sami al-Hinnawi. Hinnawi soon lost out to Colonel Adib al-Shishakli, who took command of the army in December 1949. Shishakli did not at first take over the government but used the army's capacity for persuasion to shepherd civilian politicians before assuming overall political control – though still operating behind civilian front-men – in November 1951. To consolidate his authority, he did what Nasser was soon to do in Egypt: he banned all political parties and set up the Arab Liberation Movement as a regime-controlled surrogate. But by this point the army itself had been politicised. In February 1954, a number of senior officers (including some linked to the Ba'th Party and others to the Communists) rebelled; to his credit, Shishakli went into exile rather than allow a civil war to erupt, and civilian party politics resumed. But, four years later, the army commanders, supported in varying degrees by civilian politicians, gave up on Syria as a viable political entity and begged Nasser to take them into a political union. The terms he imposed were the abolition (again) of all political parties in Syria, to bring it into line with Egypt, and the subordination of Syria to Egyptian stewardship. That Syria's elite, which didn't lack political sophistication or principle, should have allowed this to happen was an index of its despair at ever resolving the geopolitical – and therefore existential – problems the Syrian state faced.

III

The carving out of the mandate territory of Palestine and the British protectorate of Transjordan amputated historic Syria's southern regions, about two-fifths of its overall territory and coastline, while state frontiers were erected between Damascus, Beirut and Jerusalem. As the mandatory power in Syria and Lebanon, the French sliced off further districts – Tripoli, the Biqā', Ṣāida (Sidon) and Ṣūr (Tyre) – and added them to Lebanon, creating a Greater Lebanon that was more than twice the size of the old Ottoman *mutasarrifiyya* (governorate) of Lebanon, and reducing Syria's coastline to the districts of Alexandretta, Latakia and Tartus in the far north-west.[18] As if that wasn't enough, France then ceded to the British the whole of the Mosul region, which it had been awarded in the 1916 Sykes–Picot agreement. In 1918, advised that the region probably contained huge oil reserves and that the Royal Navy would require oil, Lloyd George told his French opposite number, Clemenceau, that he wanted Mosul, and Clemenceau provisionally agreed.[19] The deal finally went through in 1926 and Syria lost this territory too, as well as the prospect of significant oil wealth, while Mosul and its population became 'Iraqi'. Finally, in 1939, the French ceded the Alexandretta (Iskenderun) district – comprising about 40 per cent of what was left of Syria's coastline – to Turkey, which renamed it the province of Hatay. Independent Syria has never accepted this, arguing that France violated the terms of her mandate; a map I bought in Damascus includes the Iskenderun region in Syria. But Syria's case has received no international support. France's last act in her nonchalant serial *charcutage* of the country reduced its coastline to the provinces of Latakia and Tartus.

That the infant democratic republic of Syria was not a viable state on its own was common ground among its politicians during the first decade of independence. But they could not agree on what to do about it. Some sought to recover the territory lost in the imperial carve-up. This idea had support in Lebanon too, where many people still thought of themselves as Syrian. In Beirut in 1932, a Greek Orthodox Christian called Antun Saada founded the Parti Populaire Syrien with an explicitly irredentist purpose; subsequently renamed the Syrian Social Nationalist Party, it had support in Syria in the late 1940s in both civilian and military circles. In 1948, politicians from Aleppo founded the People's Party: Aleppo's prosperity had historically depended on its strong trading links with Mosul, and the loss of Mosul in 1926 had caused an immense prejudice to the city and its merchant elite. The People's Party accordingly favoured developing political ties with Iraq and even envisaged some kind of federal arrangement. But Iraq is more than twice the size of Syria and far richer, and would have dominated any political union. Above all, under the Hashemite monarchy it was seen as a British client and Syrian nationalism in all its varieties had developed strong anti-imperialist reflexes; free at last of the destructive ministrations of France, few Syrians wanted to come even indirectly under the British sway. This geopolitical predicament was sharpened by the foundation of the state of Israel, seen as a menacing development in itself but also signifying that recovering lost territory appeared equally impossible in the former mandate of Palestine as in the British-backed kingdom of Jordan. But it was the efforts of the Americans and British to exploit the Cold War in order to subordinate Arab states, beginning with the Baghdad Pact of 1955, that brought the crisis to a head. Nasser's refusal to bow to this pressure, followed by his successful defiance of the British–French–Israeli attack in 1956, and, more generally, his championing of the principle of non-alignment, made him seem an indispensable ally, if not Syria's saviour.[20]

Three and a half years after the formation of the United Arab Republic of Egypt and Syria in 1958, few Syrians still supported it. In September 1961 a military coup led by an anti-Nasserist officer backed by Jordan and Saudi Arabia succeeded and the UAR disintegrated.[21] The bewildering series of coups and counter-coups that followed the Egyptian overlords' departure was finally ended by the Ba'th Party, which was able to take power in 1963 and perform the Jacobin function of bringing, as in France in 1793–4, a new order out of chaos because it had by then acquired decisive influence in the army. For this was not the Ba'th Party of its founders, Michel Aflaq, Salah al-Din al-Bitar and Akram al-Hawrani, who had gone along with the UAR idea with varying degrees of enthusiasm. It was a new or Neo-Ba'th that took power in 1963, under the secret leadership of something called the Military Committee, formed by army officers serving in the higher reaches of the UAR's military structures in Cairo.[22] Its most dynamic figure was Salah Jadid, a leftist whose views determined Syrian government policy from 1966 onwards.[23] Committed to pan-Arabism, Jadid was also committed to the Palestinian cause. Influenced by advisers who had just returned from Algeria in raptures over the success of the guerrilla struggle there, Jadid and his supporters bought into this simplistic understanding of the Algerian story and encouraged the Palestinians to wage guerrilla war on Israel from their bases in Syria, disregarding the Israeli practice of massive retaliation.[24]

Ever since the Syrians had decided that the UAR was a false solution, reducing their country to the unbearable condition of an Egyptian colony, the pressure to find another solution had been immense. Jadid's adventurist policy had simply compounded the problem, contributing as it did to Israel's devastating pre-emptive war in June 1967 and the aggravation of Syria's vulnerability by the loss of the Golan Heights. The Syrian minister of defence at that point was Hafez al-Asad, one of Jadid's colleagues on the Military Committee, and long a close ally. But Asad decided Jadid's policy was folly and they became rivals. In November 1970, Asad seized power with a programme of making Syria a viable and defendable country, whatever it took. A central element of his strategy was building strong alliances with distant powerful states that had no ambitions to take Syria over, among them the Soviet Union and, from 1979, Iran. The other key element was the search for national unity at home in an effort to secure consent to the by now long-established authoritarian aspect of Syria's government.

Asad's 'corrective revolution' was popular at first. He moved to the centre ground in domestic as well as foreign policy, abandoning Jadid's doctrinaire leftism, allowing an appreciable measure of liberalisation in economic matters, courting Sunni business circles and consulting widely with Syria's notables. He rebuilt the armed forces and other state institutions, and even allowed four other political parties of the Syrian left to operate, on condition that they did so as members of a National Progressive Front in which the Ba'th retained primacy.[25] In short, Asad performed the function in the Syrian national revolution that Cromwell had performed in the English revolution: he stabilised it so that the country could be governed and defended. In the process, he induced the Syrian Ba'th to concentrate on making Syria itself, at last, a viable state. The retreat from the romantic pan-Arabism that had encouraged the Ba'th to seek the Egyptian embrace did not signify a repudiation of pan-Arabist principles but a new political realism. Asad's Syria saw itself as the champion of the Arab cause, but from 1970 onwards its policy was pan-Arabism in one country.

In what sense, then, can Asad and his wing of the Ba'th be accused of hijacking Syrian independence? They were not responsible for the militarisation of Syrian political life, a process which began years before they took power. And it was they who sought more coherently and more effectually than any of their predecessors to make independence a reality. The tragedy for Syria is that Asad lived so long.

Under Asad, Syria was a republic ruled by an autocrat. A republican autocrat is a contradiction in terms. Cromwell ruled Britain as a republican autocrat and engaged British political life in an impasse. When he died the army commanders tried to maintain the status quo by getting his son to succeed him. The prototype of what the Arabs call *tawrith al-sulta*, the inheritance of power that occurred with Bashar al-Asad's succession in 2000, occurred in seventeenth-century England. But Richard Cromwell seriously tried to liberalise the Protectorate; the army felt threatened and deposed him after nine months.[26] Asad fell ill in 1983 and it seemed for a moment that his younger brother Rifat would take over, in what would have been an anticipation of the Cuban scenario. But Asad recovered, sent Rifat into exile and carried on for another sixteen and a half years, grooming his eldest son, Bassel, to succeed him. When Bassel died in a car crash, he summoned Bashar to be groomed in his place. So in Syria, unfortunately, the Cromwellian succession worked; in England it had, fortunately, been a fiasco.

IV

With Asad's death, autocracy gave way to an oligarchy in which Bashar was the public face of a regime he could not dominate as his father had done.[27] Allowed to make minor reforms and to bring on younger men of his own choosing, he was undoubtedly made aware of red lines that could not be crossed. In this respect Syria resembles Algeria and Yemen, and for that matter Mubarak's Egypt. All of them have been national security states whose rulers have calculated that liberalising in earnest would compound their already serious national security problems, enabling hostile powers to manipulate the new political parties that liberalisation would bring.

It does not follow that such regimes are entirely unreformable. But qualitative political reform can only come about if they are put under sustained pressure by effective movements from below articulating demands which can be defended as strengthening the state by enhancing its legitimacy. This is the lesson that much of the opposition in Algeria has drawn from the bitter experience of the 1990s: positive change can only come from non-violent activism that seeks to establish a national consensus on a project of reform.* The theoretical

---

* This assessment of the growing sophistication of the Algerian opposition seemed to have been vindicated by the initial behaviour of the mass movement known as the *Hirāk* which succeeded in February–April 2019 in compelling the army commanders to drop their plan to

possibility of such a thing happening in Syria in 2011 was destroyed almost at once.

The brutal repression with which the regime responded to demonstrations in Deraa in the far south of the country back-fired; it ensured that the revolt would spread across Syria, initially in the form of increasingly angry demonstrations but soon as an armed insurrection, much as the celebrated 1925 revolt against the French spread across the country from its starting point in the south, as Charles Glass points out in a powerful essay.[28] But the militarisation of the revolt was to prove disastrous. A lot then depended on the leaders of Syria's opposition. A major meeting was convened in Antalya in southern Turkey. One of the most respected Syrian exiles, Burhan Ghalioun, a Sunni Muslim from Homs who taught political sociology at the Sorbonne, explained his refusal to attend:

> It is a collection of many of those who want to benefit from and exploit the revolution to serve private agendas, including, unfortunately, foreign agendas. Unfortunately, very few of those participating are really interested in serving the revolution or sacrificing for it.[29]

The organisers of the meeting were the Syrian Muslim Brothers. Formally the conference was convened by the human rights activist Ammar al-Qurabi and the public intellectual Abderrazaq Eid, but its proceedings turned out to be under the pre-eminent influence of the Muslim Brothers, who were looking to Turkey for patronage – Erdoğan was happy to oblige – and it was the Brothers who were responsible for its decision to rule out negotiations with the regime and commit the opposition to ousting Asad.[30] A key part of their strategy was the co-option and manipulation, as front-men, of Syrian democrats like Ghalioun.

---

give the incapacitated President Bouteflika a fifth term in violation of the Constitution. Intelligently constitutionalist, immaculately peaceful and immensely effective at first, the Hirāk was subsequently suborned into adopting an anti-constitutional stance and went down to inevitable defeat; see my article 'The Hirāk and the Ides of December', *Jadaliyya*, 19 November 2019.

On 23 August a body called the Syrian National Council (SNC) was formed to 'represent the concerns and demands of the Syrian people' and established its headquarters in Istanbul.[31] A few weeks later Ghalioun was named as its chairman.[32] He seems to have negotiated an understanding that enabled him at first to exercise some influence in favour of non-violence; on 28 October the SNC's spokesperson, Bassma Kodmani, referred to the 'frightening possibility' that the Libya scenario would be replayed in Syria, and added:

> This is not what we want to have happen in Syria . . . In Syria, the majority is concerned that the price of violent opposition is very high; the majority know that there are long-term consequences. Nobody wants a war; nobody in the opposition wants to see a bombed Damascus.[33]

Unfortunately, on the last point, she was mistaken. Plenty of people wanted a war.

The regime seems to have believed it had to suppress the revolt quickly and at whatever cost before it addressed the grievances that had led to the unrest. But, if this was what it had in mind, it was a miscalculation, as officers unable to stomach the repression began to desert. On 29 July five such officers announced the creation of the Free Syrian Army (FSA).[34] In September the FSA absorbed another grouping, the Free Officers Movement.[35] By October the FSA had gained Ankara's support and was allowed to site its headquarters in Turkey's Hatay province.[36] By December it was liaising with the SNC, and the SNC's hopes of leading a non-violent movement were evaporating. Ghalioun had continued to chair the SNC but was kept on a short leash, being re-elected only for three-month terms and driven by degrees to go along with the militarisation of the anti-Asad movement. In May 2012 he abruptly decided that his position had become untenable and resigned.[37]

On 11 November 2012, a new body to speak for the Syrian opposition abroad was established, the National Coalition for Syrian Revolutionary and Opposition Forces, or Syrian National Coalition for short, and the Syrian National Council folded itself into this organisation, securing twenty-two of the sixty seats on its ruling body.[38] The National Coalition was sponsored by Qatar and its founding meeting was held in Doha. It elected as its president Moaz al-Khatib, a Sunni from a distinguished Damascus family who had served as imam of the Umayyad mosque. But he did not last long either, resigning on 21 April 2013. As he explained, in an interview with Al Jazeera the following month,

> the people inside have lost the ability to decide their own fate . . .
> I have become only a means to sign some papers while there are
> hands from different parties involved who want to decide on
> behalf of the Syrians.[39]

Anonymous sources told Al Jazeera that al-Khatib was not a 'team player'. In January, without consultation, he had publicly offered to negotiate with the Syrian government. Presumably he believed his colleagues would dissuade him and so presented them with a *fait accompli*; in any event, the ploy failed. The possibility of a negotiated political solution had resurfaced, only to be nipped in the bud a second time.

Some reports suggest that, in sponsoring the National Coalition, Qatar was doing Hillary Clinton's bidding. Qatar's move irritated the Saudis and incited them to closer involvement. Riyadh was flatly opposed to any negotiations with the government and advocated arming the rebels; Washington, London and Paris were soon publicly considering the idea. By this time, however, the armed rebellion was no longer dominated by the supposedly moderate FSA. Explicitly jihadi movements, notably the al-Qaida affiliate Jabhat al-Nusra, were gaining ground. This development signed the revolution's death warrant.

That this was the case emerges clearly from Jonathan Littell's account of the condition and outlook of the armed rebellion in early 2012.* Littell got himself smuggled into Syria from Lebanon by a rebel network and witnessed what was going on in Qusayr

---

* Jonathan Littell, *Syrian Notebooks: Inside the Homs Uprising* (London and New York: Verso, 2015).

and the rebel-held neighbourhoods of Homs. His book, a diary of eighteen intense days, consists of his raw and confusing daily jottings, reflecting the confusion through which everyone was living. He writes from a frankly partisan viewpoint, but his testimony is nonetheless moving, showing in accounts of numerous incidents the endearing humanity of the people he is with, the courage of adults and children alike, the dedication in particular of doctors and nurses working in the makeshift clinics, the hospitality and generosity of all and sundry, and even their sense of humour, manifested at moments when everyone bursts into laughter for some reason despite the ever-present terror in a city where regime snipers cover the main thoroughfares and people never know whether they can cross a street in safety or whether their next attempt will be their last. But Littell also bears witness to the fact that the 'revolution' is winging it on a hope and a prayer. The local FSA officers are brave and businesslike, but there is no sense that the FSA is operating like a real army with a plan of campaign. It is reacting rather than acting; its local commanders have no strategy. Several of Littell's interlocutors make clear that they have been counting on a Libya-style Western intervention – NATO coming to the rescue – which indicates that they have a realistic assessment of the revolution's unaided prospects but cannot calculate the international realpolitik.[40] And several of them repeatedly express apprehension about their revolt being rebranded a jihad.[41] They did not explain why, and Littell seems not to have asked them. But they probably realised, even if they could not articulate this clearly, that once jihad was proclaimed the initiative would pass to others – including foreign jihadis – and that this would be the point of no return for that reason, but also for another reason.

The rebels Littell writes about were mostly Sunnis. They were pious Muslims, or at least believers, even those who liked a drink and a smoke, but in the main they were not sectarian. A few of them were; one FSA officer confessed to Littell that Zarqawi was his idol.[*] But the majority seem to have hated the

---

[*] Littell, *Syrian Notebooks*, 48; Abu Musab al-Zarqawi was the ferociously sectarian and sanguinary leader of al-Qaida in Iraq until his death in 2006.

regime for political reasons and could distinguish between Alawites in high positions and Alawites in general. They exemplified, perhaps in its dying moments, Syria's tradition of religious tolerance. This outlook represented a continuation of the original spirit of the uprising in Tunisia, the demand for the dignity that only the end of arbitrary rule can bring. Littell says that 'they dream less of democracy, a concept that no doubt is very vague to them, than of the rule of law'.[42] It is not at all certain that they wouldn't have understood democracy, given that between 1945 and 1958 Syria had experience of it, however disappointing. But the moment the armed revolt became a jihad, it became an explicitly Sunni affair and, in justifying their fight against the regime, the Sunni jihadis were bound to engage in *takfir*, that is, condemn the regime as infidel, and damn the Alawites as infidels into the bargain. And so a rebellion against arbitrary rule became a sectarian war of religion, virtually from one day to the next.

It is often suggested that the Asad regime contributed to this transformation. This is certainly true in part. It was bound to rally the Alawite community behind itself; it also enlisted the support of the Lebanese Shia Hizbullah movement. And as long as its main military antagonist was the FSA, that is, a rebel army led by deserters, it naturally refused to give this recognition by broaching a negotiation, if only because of the dangerous effect this might have on its remaining troops' morale. But there is another reason why the regime should have concentrated its fire on the non-jihadi rebels and so allowed the jihadis to make headway. This is almost exactly what the Algerian generals did in the 1990s in order to turn public opinion against the Islamists by tarring them with the extremist jihadis' atrocities. It should not surprise anyone familiar with the Algerian story that the Asad regime may have resorted to a comparable strategy. But, if the regime decided to take advantage of the jihadis in this way, this does not for a moment absolve of responsibility those external actors backing and bankrolling the jihadis and supplying them with arms.

I see no point in moralising about the behavior of Saudi Arabia, Qatar and Kuwait. Turkey as a NATO member is a different matter. The Gulf states are Sunni sectarian monarchies sitting on disadvantaged Shiite minorities, with Iran, a Shiite power that was the chief gainer from the overthrow of the Ba'thist regime in Iraq in 2003, just across the water. They were bound to want to topple the Asad regime – the central link in the Iran–Damascus–Hizbullah alliance – if the opportunity presented itself. The problem that most urgently needs to be faced is the policy of the Western powers.

V

It was clear early on that the NATO intervention that had taken place in Libya would not be repeated in Syria. Russia had gone along with UN Security Council Resolution 1973, which authorised NATO's war on Qadhafi's peculiar state, but Russia's ties to Syria were far stronger, and, with Putin stiffening Russian sinews following his return to the presidency in May 2012, any attempt by Washington, London and Paris to secure a mandate for a second regime-change war under UN auspices was bound to be vetoed. Instead of seeing how different the Syrian case was, the Western powers recycled as much of their Libya strategy as possible. They repeatedly insisted that 'Asad must go' as the key element of their position. They repeatedly cast the Asad regime as the sole villain of the story and forced Russia and China to put themselves in bad odour when they vetoed Security Council resolutions pushing this line.[43] They set up a Friends of Syria organisation on the earlier Friends of Libya model to whip UN member states into line and deprive the Damascus–Moscow–Tehran alliance of possible allies or useful neutrals.[44] They undermined the Syrian government's claim to international legitimacy by persuading the Arab League to suspend Syria's membership on 12 November 2011 and later to admit the Syrian National Coalition instead as Syria's legitimate representative in March 2013.[45] And they sabotaged the efforts of the UN special envoys, first Kofi Annan, then Lakhdar Brahimi, to broker a political compromise that would have ended the fighting.

On 30 June 2012, a meeting of what was described as an 'action group' on Syria, comprising US secretary of state Hillary Clinton, Russian foreign minister Sergei Lavrov, British foreign secretary William Hague, French foreign minister Laurent Fabius, the foreign ministers of China, Iraq, Kuwait, Qatar, Turkey, the secretaries-general of the United Nations and the League of Arab States and the European Union's high representative for foreign and security policy took place, at Kofi Annan's invitation, in Geneva. During the meeting (known as 'Geneva I'), Annan issued a communiqué announcing that the action group had agreed on the need for a 'transitional government body with full executive powers' which could include members of the present Syrian government and of the opposition.[46] Following the communiqué, Clinton declared that Asad could not himself remain in power and was promptly contradicted by Lavrov.[47] Matters were patched up sufficiently for the final communiqué to declare that the meeting had agreed on:

1. the establishment of a transitional governing body with full executive powers that could include members of the government and opposition, and should be formed on the basis of mutual consent;
2. the participation of all groups and segments of society in Syria in a meaningful process of national dialogue;
3. a review of the constitutional order and the legal system;
4. free and fair multi-party elections for the new institutions and offices that would be established;
5. full representation of women in all aspects of the transition.[48]

The devil was in the detail of the first point, since it could be read as meaning that opposition forces could veto the nominations of any of the proposed Syrian government members of the transitional body – such as Asad – just as the government could veto nominations of opposition figures. It was clearly Asad's position that was in dispute.

Six weeks earlier, I had attended a seminar held under the Chatham House Rule somewhere in the United States and addressed by a senior official involved in devising and executing Western policy on the Syrian crisis. It was made clear to the audience that the policy was to secure regime change – that is, the eviction of Asad as the precondition of everything else – and that the authors of this policy were intent on negating Annan's efforts to secure a negotiated settlement. Annan abandoned the job as mission impossible in August 2012.

What was surprising was that the immensely experienced Brahimi then agreed to take it on. One of the dynamic young FLN diplomats who made his country's case during the Algerian war, Brahimi had later been, successively, ambassador to Cairo and to London, under-secretary general of the Arab League, Arab League special envoy for Lebanon, Algeria's foreign minister, and UN special representative in turn to South Africa, Haiti, Afghanistan (twice) and Iraq. When I heard he was tackling the Syrian problem I assumed that he believed he had a chance of resolving it. In the event, he was unable to and, having given it his best shot, eventually resigned in his turn. Why did he fail?

After immense labours, Brahimi succeeded in convening a major international conference ('Geneva II') in January 2014. On the very first day, the US secretary of state, John Kerry, declared: 'There is no way, no way possible, that a man who has led a brutal response to his own people can regain legitimacy to govern.'[49] So the US position was unchanged: Asad had to go, which meant that the Syrian government would not engage in talks on the formation of the transitional authority. The Geneva II talks got nowhere.

Brahimi resigned on 13 May 2014. In an interview with *Der Spiegel* the following month, he was asked to what extent the dispute was about Asad:

BRAHIMI: The issue of President Assad was a huge hurdle. The Syrian regime only came to Geneva to please the Russians, thinking that they were winning militarily. I told them 'I'm sure that your instructions were: "Go to Geneva. But not only don't make any concessions, don't discuss anything seriously."'

SPIEGEL: What about on the other side?

BRAHIMI: The majority among the opposition were against coming to Geneva. They preferred a military solution and they came completely unprepared. But at least they were willing to start talking with President Assad still there as long as it was clear that, somewhere along the line, he would go.[50]

The point here is not that one side was slightly more or slightly less intransigent, but that, by making the future of Asad the central question and insisting on his departure, the Western powers, in conjunction with Saudi Arabia, Qatar, Kuwait, the United Arab Emirates and Jordan – not one of which is a democracy – as well as Turkey, which under Erdoğan has slid a long way towards authoritarian rule, made it impossible for a political solution to be found that would at least end the violence. It is in ways like this that the Arab uprisings were really hijacked.

The Tunisian revolution was a real revolution not because it toppled Ben Ali, but because it went on to establish a new form of government with real political representation and the rule of law. The hijacking of the Arab uprisings by the Western powers has been effected by their success in substituting for profound change a purely superficial regime change that merely means the ejection of a ruler they have never liked (Saddam, Qadhafi, Asad) or have no further use for (Mubarak), and his replacement by someone they approve of. In seeking this change in their own interests, they have repeatedly shown a reckless disregard for the consequences of their policies, from Iraq to Egypt to Libya to Syria.

Three days after Brahimi's interview, on 10 June 2014, Islamic State fighters heading east from northern Syria captured Mosul.

VI

The Islamic State came out of Iraq, as Patrick Cockburn explained in his pioneering account, *The Jihadis Return* (2014), now republished in an updated edition with a new title.[*] The

---

[*] Patrick Cockburn, *The Rise of Islamic State: ISIS and the new Sunni revolution* (London and New York: Verso, 2015).

movement initially called the Islamic State in Iraq (ISI), then the Islamic State in Iraq and Syria (ISIS) or in Iraq and the Levant (ISIL), had roots in al-Qaida in Iraq, which, under Abu Musab al-Zarqawi, waged sectarian war on the US-sponsored regime in Baghdad and the Shia in general until Zarqawi's death in 2006. Al-Qaida in Iraq were jihadis; Jabhat al-Nusra in Syria are jihadis; the Armed Islamic Group in Algeria were jihadis. But Islamic State is something else.

Cockburn provides an invaluable outline history of IS while anchoring this in a powerful critique of Western policy in Iraq and Syria and an unsparing analysis of Shia politics in Baghdad. In their book, Michael Weiss and Hassan Hassan lean much further towards Filiu's thesis – that the rise of IS can be blamed in large part on the Asad regime – and they devote a chapter to the dealings between the Syrian intelligence services and Sunni jihadi groups in Iraq.* There can be little doubt that such dealings occurred. Syria opposed the Anglo-American war on Iraq in 2003, and the destruction of the Iraqi state created a zone of insecurity the length of Syria's eastern border. Syria was bound to make it its business to get a handle on what was going on in western and northern Iraq by establishing contacts with and infiltrating whatever armed movements emerged there. But I think Cockburn is right when he dismisses as a conspiracy theory the idea that Asad helped create IS, not because I refuse to consider conspiracy theories (conspiracies occur), but because the theory ignores the fact that IS and the Asad regime are fighting each other. Besides, Asad has had sound military reasons to concentrate on other fronts and leave IS in the north-east for later. As Lakhdar Brahimi told *Der Spiegel*, if there has been more to the regime's calculus than that, 'It is probably the government's way of saying: "This is the future you will have if we are not there anymore."'

Hassan and Weiss refer indiscriminately to IS and other jihadis groups as 'takfiris'. But not all jihadi groups are *takfiri*. Bin Laden's al-Qaida was originally waging a classic jihad

---

* Michael Weiss and Hassan Hassan, *ISIS: Inside the Army of Terror* (New York: Regan Arts, 2015), 99.

against 'Crusaders and Jews' – that is, the West and (at least notionally) Israel. The question of *takfir* arose where would-be jihadis took on their own, nominally Islamic, governments, as in Egypt and Algeria.* Sunni doctrine endorses jihad against infidel powers but condemns rebellion against a Muslim ruler as *fitna* – division of the community of believers, the supreme evil – so rebels have to legitimise their revolt by denying their rulers' Islamic credentials. This is what Zarqawi's group did in confronting the new Shia regime in Baghdad, and it is what Jabhat al-Nusra and others have been doing in Syria. Such *takfiri* jihadis rarely if ever have a state-building project of their own with which to replace the state they are fighting. The leaders of IS have such a project. While their movement has been fighting states whose Islamic credentials they deny, they have been constructing a new state in remote regions where the former central power has, at least temporarily, lost all purchase. As such, the movement they most resemble is the Taliban.

In his *Der Spiegel* interview, Lakhdar Brahimi was asked what he thought the future holds. He replied that Syria would become 'another Somalia ... a failed state with warlords all over the place'. But we already have this, in Libya. What is taking at least partial shape in Syria – unless the country is partitioned, which is also in the cards – is another Afghanistan.

When the Afghan jihadis – backed, like their Syrian successors today, by the Gulf states and Anglo-America – finally overthrew the secular-modernist Najibullah regime, they immediately fell out among themselves and Afghanistan collapsed into violent warlordism. But, unlike Somalia, Afghanistan was rescued by a dynamic movement that suddenly appeared on its southern marches and swept all before it, crushing the warlords and finally establishing a new state. Western audiences were invited to be horrified by the nature of this state. But, in the aftermath

* *Takfir* means the passing of judgment on something or someone, especially an institution or a ruler that claims to be Islamic, as in fact un-Islamic, infidel.

of the jihad our governments had sponsored and our media had enthusiastically reported, secular modernism was no longer on offer: militantly retrograde Islamism was the only political discourse around, and it was inevitably the most fundamentalist brand that won. The victors called their state an emirate, the realm of an *amir* (commander, prince). IS calls its state a caliphate – *khilāfa* – and this matters.

No doubt strictly local factors have facilitated IS's project. Their capital, Raqqa, a large town in a strategic location on the Euphrates in the centre of northern Syria, has long had ties with Iraq. When Hafez al-Asad, during his conflict with Saddam Hussein, ordered purges of pro-Iraqis in the Syrian Ba'th party in the 1980s, the second purge, in 1985, targeted the party branch in Raqqa, which pro-Iraqis by then controlled. A few miles west of Raqqa is the site of the battle of Siffin, where the Umayyad pretender Mu'awiya confronted the fourth caliph, Ali, in 657 CE as the Sunni-Shi'i schism took shape. Much further to the west, to the north of Aleppo, near the Turkish frontier, is the town of Dabiq. In 1516 it was the Ottomans' victory over the Mamluk Sultanate in the battle of Marj Dabiq that opened the way for their conquest of the Arab lands. But the name of Dabiq resonates for another reason; in Islamic eschatology, Dabiq is one of the two possible locations of a battle in which it is believed Muslims will defend themselves and their lands against an invading Christian army and which will result in a Muslim victory and mark the beginning of the end of the world. *Dabiq* is the title of the Islamic State's official online magazine.

Since the abolition of the Ottoman caliphate in 1924, its restoration has been proposed by various Sunni Islamists: it has long been a declared aim of Hizb ut-Tahrir (the Islamic Liberation Party), and in 1994 the Armed Islamic Group in Algeria named the members of a restored caliphate's new government. These rhetorical gestures led nowhere. But IS has done what others talked of. It has an army comprising highly equipped regular forces as well as guerrilla forces; it controls a large territory, it has an oil industry, it has a tax system; it has a system of local government and a system of justice. It fights like a state, sees like a state and punishes like a state. It carries conviction and meets with belief. It does not care that it horrifies us; it knows that millions of Muslims have been horrified by what our governments have been doing to them.

The Taliban did not call their state a caliphate because they had no wider ambitions; their emirate was simply a new and better form of the Afghan state. IS, on the other hand, is reconnecting northern Iraq and northern Syria – reverting to what the Sykes–Picot agreement envisaged before Lloyd George amended it – and it is not a simple emanation of jihadi Islamism. The former members of Zarqawi's al-Qaida in Iraq, whom IS's leader, Abu Bakr al-Baghdadi, took with him into the new project, haven't been building IS by themselves.

When the Taliban began their drive across Afghanistan, they had the backing of a neighbouring state. The movement had matured in the madrasas of north-west Pakistan, and the Pakistani intelligence services were discreetly supporting it. Pakistan had every reason to be weary of the vacuum to the north, and what better way to fill it? Remarkably, IS appears to have grown and spread without the backing of any other state. Except that isn't quite right: it has had the backing of an ex-state – the Ba'thist state overthrown in 2003.

As Hassan and Weiss explain, after the 1990–1 war, Saddam acted to shore up his regime by enhancing its religious legitimacy, broaching an ideological merger of the 'pan-Arabism in one country' that he, like Asad next door, had long pursued with the themes of resurgent Islamism. Iraqi Ba'thists developed ties with Sunni religious figures and the gulf between formerly divergent outlooks was bridged. The leader of IS, Al-Baghdadi, born in 1971, comes from a tribe with claim to a noble ancestry that goes back to the Prophet's tribe, the Quraysh. But his birthplace, Samarra, was a Ba'thist stronghold and his family undoubtedly had Ba'thist connections. So he is likely to have been open to the idea of working with former Ba'thists if the terms were right.

The 'Islamic faith campaign' that Saddam set in motion was orchestrated by his loyal lieutenant Izzat Ibrahim al-Douri, who belonged to an important Sufi order, the Naqshbandiyya. When Baghdad fell to US troops, al-Douri went on the run and was never tracked down. Reported at intervals to have died, he was busy building an insurgent network of his own, Jaish Rijāl al-Tarīqa al-Naqshbandiyya (the Army of the Men of the Naqshbandi Order), which is rumoured to have played a considerable part in the Sunni insurgency between 2003 and 2006. The relationship between al-Douri's organisation and IS is unclear; it may be an alliance rather than a merger. But there is no doubt that numerous senior figures in the IS are former Ba'thists, including some former officers of the Iraqi army who had nowhere else to go after Paul Bremer's fateful decision in May 2003 to dissolve the army and dismiss all members of the Ba'th Party from the state administration. The presence in its upper ranks of ex-Ba'thist officers largely explains the military prowess that IS has demonstrated. But there may be more to the Ba'thist connection than that.

In a lecture at Harvard's Kennedy School last March (2015), the Palestinian scholar Yezid Sayigh argued that the Iraqi Ba'th supplied the organisational template for Islamic State and that this has shaped its geopolitical perspectives and strategy. Unlike the Syrian Ba'th, which limited its strategic ambitions to its 'near-abroad', the Iraqi Ba'th in its heyday had ambitions far afield. No doubt Baghdad's eternal rivalry with Cairo had a lot to do with this. The Iraqi Ba'th recruited members and established branches across the Arab world, in Jordan and Lebanon but also in Libya and Mauritania; Sayigh suggested that the reason IS has been following the same script is that Ba'thist *savoir-faire* has been available to it. And this in part explains the logic of the decision to call the state a caliphate. Pan-Arabism is a concept that has had its day but pan-Islamism has become contemporary again, and the architects of a caliphate, if they continue to succeed, have a chance of outflanking all their rivals within Sunni Islamism and attracting allegiance across the Middle East and North Africa, and even beyond (IS may already be making headway in the Caucasus). So we may be seeing the resurrection of a form of Arab nationalism in the medium of fundamentalist pan-Islamism.

VII

Cockburn argues that 'for America, Britain and the Western powers, the rise of Isis and the caliphate is the ultimate disaster'.[51] There are certainly grounds for thinking he is right. But there are also grounds for wondering. His book went to press before he could take account of the extraordinary revelation that US intelligence had anticipated the rise of Islamic State nearly two years before it happened.

On 18 May, a document from the US Defense Intelligence Agency (DIA) dated 12 August 2012 was published by a conservative watchdog organisation called Judicial Watch, which had managed to obtain this and other formerly classified documents (notably about the Libyan mess) through a federal lawsuit. The document not only anticipated the rise of IS but seemed to suggest it would be a desirable development from the point of view of the international 'coalition' seeking regime change in Damascus. Here are the key passages:

> 7b. Development of the current events into proxy war ...
> Opposition forces are trying to control the eastern areas (Hasaka and Der Zor), adjacent to the western Iraqi provinces (Mosul and Anbar), in addition to neighbouring Turkish borders. Western countries, the Gulf states and Turkey are supporting these efforts. This hypothesis is most likely in accordance with the data from recent events, which will help prepare safe havens under international sheltering, similar to what transpired in Libya when Benghazi was chosen as the command centre of the temporary government ...
>
> ...
>
> 8c. If the situation unravels there is the possibility of establishing a declared or undeclared Salafist principality in eastern Syria (Hasaka and Der Zor), and this is exactly what the supporting powers to the opposition want, in order to isolate the Syrian regime.

So American intelligence saw IS coming nearly two years before it took Mosul, and was not only relaxed about the prospect but, it appears, positively interested in it. The precise formula used in paragraph 8c is intriguing. It doesn't talk of 'the possibility that ISIS might establish a Salafist principality' but of 'the possibility of establishing' a Salafist principality. So who was to be the prime mover in this process? Did IS have a state backing it after all?

A second piece of evidence is a map prepared by Lieutenant-Colonel Ralph Peters of the US War Academy and published in the *Armed Forces Journal* in June 2006. It shows a 'New Middle East' that, as imagined by Colonel Peters, would annoy most of the region's current governments. What is striking is that, in place of Iraq and Syria, it suggests there could be three states: an 'Arab Shia' state extending up to Baghdad, a 'Sunni Iraq' and then 'Syria', with the last two shorn of their Kurdish districts, now included in a new state of 'Free Kurdistan'. On its own the map proves nothing beyond one man's imagination and the fact that a journal found it interesting enough to print. But it suggests that the partition of Iraq has been envisaged in senior US circles as a possibility for the last nine years. With the advances IS has made over the last year, talk of partition, both of Iraq and of Syria, has been increasing.[52]

What we can make of this is, of course, unclear. At one extreme, conspiracy theorists will argue that it supports their claim that the Western powers have been deliberately creating chaos for unavowable reasons of their own. At the other end of the spectrum, one could hypothesise that the DIA document may have been read by four unimportant people in Washington and ignored by everyone else. In the middle, showing more respect for the DIA, we could imagine something else: the possibility that, in 2012, American and other Western intelligence services saw ISIS much as they saw Jabhat al-Nusra and other jihadi groups – as useful auxiliaries in the anti-Asad drive – and could envisage its takeover of north-eastern Syria as a helpful development with no worrying implications. If Islamic State escaped whatever influence Western intelligence services may initially have sought to have on it and went its own way, this means that people have been playing with fire.

I don't pretend to know what the truth is. But there is no need to prove malign intent on the part of the Western powers. The most charitable theory available, 'the eternally recurring colossal cock-up' theory of history, will do well enough to discredit the policy that has been followed with such dreadful consequences. If, as I would argue, a more sophisticated theory is indeed required, I suggest we start by recalling the assessment of C. Wright Mills when he spoke of US policy being made by 'crackpot realists', people who were entirely realistic about how to promote their careers inside the Beltway, and incorrigible – and dangerous – crackpots when it came to formulating foreign policy. Since it is not only American but also British folly and incompetence that are in the dock, I would also recall the assessment of Ernest Bevin, who remarked that 'superiority is claimed by the middle class in the realms of government, when as a matter of fact their work is a monument of incompetence'.

Western policy has been a disgrace, and Britain's contribution to it should be a matter of national shame. Whatever has motivated it, it has been a disaster for Iraq, Libya and now Syria, and the fallout is killing Americans, French people – and now British tourists in Tunisia – in addition to its uncounted victims in the Middle East.[53] The case for changing this policy, at least where Syria is concerned, is overwhelming. Can Washington, London and Paris be persuaded of this? Cockburn quotes a former Syrian minister's pessimistic assessment that 'they climbed too far up the tree claiming Assad has to be replaced to reverse their policy now'.[54] But at least one significant American voice has been arguing for the last five months that this is indeed what they should do.

No one was a more zealous advocate of the 'support the revolution/regime-change' policy than the US ambassador to Syria from 2010 to 2014, Robert Ford. He believed in the policy of backing the 'moderate' elements fighting the regime and unhesitatingly called for them to be armed. But he drew the line at the more extreme jihadis, and notably at Jabhat al-Nusra, unable to accept that the US could support an affiliate of al-Qaida. This wasn't a problem for Paris, apparently. In early May, on a visit to Qatar, to which France had just sold twenty-four Rafale jets, François Hollande declared that it was French policy to aim for a transition in Syria 'that excludes President Bashar al-Assad, but comprises all opposition groups as well as some individual components of the regime'.[55] *All* opposition groups, *pardi*. And this was not a departure from the established French line: in December 2012, his foreign minister, Laurent Fabius, declared, with reference to Jabhat al-Nusra, that 'sur le terrain, ils font du bon boulot' (on the ground, they are doing a good job).* Ford couldn't stomach this and had the courage to accept that the policy he had championed had failed.

What can be done about Islamic State? As things stand, very little. As Cockburn was among the first to point out, air power will not stop it, and nor will the corruption-ridden and demoralised Iraqi army; meanwhile, the much more combative but ferociously sectarian Shi'ite militias are driving Sunni Iraqis into Islamic State's arms. Sending in Western troops would be folly, a gift to the enemy. Training a few hundred Iraqis here or a few hundred Syrians there is obviously not a serious policy but a fatuous surrogate for one. What does this leave? The answer is that, unless the Syrian army takes on Islamic State, IS will stay in business indefinitely.

On 10 June the *Telegraph*'s defence correspondent reported that Western officials were working to persuade Moscow and Tehran to abandon Asad. The argument they apparently put forward was that, since he is losing the war, the strategic priority for Russia and Iran must be to prevent IS capturing Damascus. Even if you accept the first part of the premise, there are gaping

---

* Isabelle Mandraud, 'Pression militaire et succès diplomatique pour les rebelles syriens', *Le Monde*, 13 December 2012. A subsequent *Le Monde* article claimed that the quotation of Fabius's remarks had been 'corrupted', and that he had never said that the Al-Nusra Front 'is doing a good job'; see Adrien Sénécat, 'Laurent Fabius et le "bon boulot" du Front Al-Nosra [*sic*] en Syrie, histoire d'une citation dévoyée', *Le Monde*, 21 March 2017. In fact, what Fabius said can be interpreted as his own positive judgment on Jabhat al-Nusra or as reporting *sympathetically* the positive judgment of the Syrian opposition in contesting the American authorities' decision to place Jabhat al-Nusra on the list of terrorist organisations.

holes in the idea as reported by the *Telegraph*. If Asad is dropped, what next? If the regime holds together and carries on regardless, the jihadi movements and IS will continue to fight it. Why should the Syrian army do better in those circumstances than it is doing now? If the regime implodes, as it could well do, its army can hardly be expected to keep fighting and hold the IS at bay. And if it implodes but 'moderate' Sunnis are somehow eased with magical promptness into the saddle, the state will not maintain its strong relationship to Iran; it will reverse course in deference to its Gulf sponsors, and Tehran will have suffered a strategic defeat that will greatly weaken its alliance with Hizbullah. Why should the ayatollahs agree to this? And in such circumstances Moscow would be bound to lose most of its purchase on Damascus as well. The notion that getting rid of Asad will facilitate the defeat of Islamic State is wishful thinking, a crackpot's daydream. If the Western powers genuinely want an end to Islamic State, they must will the necessary means to this end.

Think-tankers shrink from proposing policies they know governments will not want to consider. But I'm not a think-tanker. And, apart from wanting an end to the war in Syria for its own sake, I want and believe that every real democrat would want Tunisia, the sole democracy in the Arab world, to be defended from the depredations of all forms of terrorism. Western governments must be induced by public opinion in their own countries to drop the veto on a negotiated end to the war in Syria that the demand that Asad must go has amounted to. This stance, pre-empting the right of the Syrian people to decide the matter, has always been wrong in principle and catastrophic in practice. This does not mean that they have to declare that Asad can stay. That too would be wrong in principle. But they could moderate their position: they could say that they believe Asad should step down before long, but that they recognise it is for the Syrian people to decide. They could encourage those elements of the opposition that originally wanted to negotiate with the regime to do so. They could suggest that the formation of a national unity government, to include respected figures representing the non-violent opposition, would be a positive development. And they could give an undertaking to the Syrian regime that, as soon as a negotiated agreement between Syrians has been reached on the way forward, they will support the regime's efforts to re-establish government control of the national territory. They have much to atone for, but that would be a start.

4

What Was the Arab Spring?

On 28 August 2011, the flag of Qatar was raised over Tripoli, the capital of Libya in the days when Libya was a state, which it had just ceased to be. On 5 June 2017, the Kingdom of Saudi Arabia, the United Arab Emirates, Bahrain, Egypt and Kuwait all severed diplomatic ties with Qatar and cut all sea and air communications with it. Further client-states or client-statelets of the Gulf monarchies – the Maldives, Mauritania, Yemen, not to mention the Tobruk-based 'government' of Libya – quickly followed suit, while the Saudis closed their land border with Qatar, the only land border it has.

Between these two dates a striking transformation had occurred, the supersession of the 'Arab Spring' by what Marc Lynch calls, with some reason, the 'new Arab Wars'.* This mutation in the content and dynamics of international politics in the Middle East and North Africa is nominally the principal subject of Lynch's book but not its only subject. As important to it is Lynch's concern to face up to the disappointing – if not calamitous – outcome of the 'Arab Spring', which he, like so many others, had welcomed and approved, and try to salvage as much of his original analysis as possible from the wreckage of the unjustified hopes it authorised. As such, it stands as a very useful, if far from comprehensive, antidote to the 'revolutionary'

---

* Marc Lynch, *The New Arab Wars: Uprisings and Anarchy in the Middle East* (New York: Public Affairs, 2016).

cheerleading of Gilbert Achcar's earlier study.* A third element is Lynch's preoccupation with evaluating US policy and President Obama's particular responsibility for this over the period in question and, as far as possible, exonerating them both, rather than criticising, let alone condemning, either of them.

Lynch's concerns are partly shared by Robert Worth, who also has had to come to terms with grim outcomes so at odds with his original expectations. A key difference is that Worth is interested above all in the micro-history, the human stories of what happened on the ground in one country after another, stories he has shown great enterprise in getting hold of and tells with engaging sympathy and skill.† Lynch, a Washington-based political scientist, wants to give and persuade us of his view of the big picture and knows very well that for good or ill the US has been a central player. Worth disarmingly declares, 'I have little to say about the role of the United States and other Western powers, because I believe it was mostly secondary.'[1] Achcar tends to a similarly dismissive view of the role of the powers,[2] a position consistent with his exaggerated celebration of the revolutionary potential of 'the people'. Lynch knows better, at any rate where the salience of the US role is concerned. But he too authorises himself to say little or nothing about the British and French roles, a symptomatic oversight and a serious one.

The term 'Arab Spring' gained currency only with the fall of Egypt's president, Hosni Mubarak, on 11 February 2011. It subsequently embraced the whole chain of sensational events that developed in the wake of the Tunisian revolution, which began on 17 December 2010 and culminated four weeks later with the overthrow of President Zine el-Abidine Ben Ali on 14 January, that is, in the depths of winter. The events in Tunisia helped to prompt the rash of nationwide rioting that occurred in Algeria between 4 and 10 January, but these disturbances were politically aimless, and many well-informed Algerians

* Gilbert Achcar, *The People Want: a Radical Exploration of the Arab Uprising* (London: Saqi, 2013).

† Robert F. Worth, *A Rage for Order: the Middle East in Turmoil, from Tahrir Square to ISIS* (London: Picador, 2016).

believed, quite plausibly, that they were instigated by the regime's intelligence services to let the air out of the balloon in good time before it went up in accordance with someone else's flight plan, a piece of statecraft that had to be undertaken before the revolution in Tunisia climaxed and set a dangerous example for others to follow. So the shock wave from Tunis did not spread west, only east.[3]

The first big demonstrations in the Middle East took place less than a fortnight after Ben Ali's eviction, in Cairo on 25 January and in Yemen two days later. Then Mubarak's fall on 11 February gave a further, decisive, boost to the movement. Street protests started in Bahrain on 14 February and the rebellion against Mu'ammar Qadhafi got under way in eastern Libya on the 15th. It was only in the wake of this entire chain of events – and not as a simple effect of the Tunisian revolution in itself – that serious unrest occurred in Morocco in the form of the 20 February Movement, whose leaders made it clear that, while seeking reforms, they were targeting neither the monarchical character of the Moroccan state nor King Mohammed VI personally, who accordingly felt able to make concessions enough to restore calm and take Morocco out of the Arab Spring frame before it had become trapped in it.[4]

By this time the Libyan rising seemed to be carrying all before it, but by early March the government's forces were counter-attacking effectively and by mid-March threatening to crush it completely. In Bahrain, too, the protest movement was unable to capitalise on its initial momentum, and on 14 March Saudi and Emirati forces crossed onto the island to suppress it. But, the very next day, the shock wave resumed its initial forward movement, with the onset of demonstrations in Syria; two days later the UN Security Council authorised Western military intervention in support of the Libyan rebellion and French jets began bombing Qadhafi's forces on 19 March.

With very few exceptions, Western commentators on these events approved of all these developments at the time, expressed strong support for the protestors and rebels everywhere except Bahrain, and confidently suggested that the movement was heading in the right direction: the overthrow of autocracy by popular forces that carried with them the promise of democratic or at least representative and law-bound government. This suggestion was utterly mistaken.

II

Western discussion of events in the Arab world since 25 January 2011 has been characterised by a degree of confusion, to which media and academic fashions have contributed, about what is being discussed. The confusion is illustrated by the existence of three different names – the 'Arab Spring', the 'Arab Uprising (or *intifāda*)', and, using the plural, the 'Arab Uprisings (or *intifādāt*)' – for the series of events in question. The first is the name the Western media gave this series; the second the name preferred by some journalists and many academics, especially those concerned to emphasise the role of the Arab insurgents in order to credit this with revolutionary significance; as Lynch formulates this thesis, 'The Arab uprising was a singular event, uniting the entire Arab world within a single, incredibly potent narrative of the possibility of change.'[5] The third names these events in sober and factually accurate terms – uprisings did, after all, occur – but does not emphasise the linkages between them. In the light of the eventual calamitous outcome, 'the Arab Spring', viewed from one angle, can be seen to be the name of a hallucination, shot through with wishful thinking, which precluded a lucid appreciation of the events in question. The 'Arab Uprising/ *intifāda*' does not necessarily encumber itself with wishful thinking (although some of those who use it contrive to do this) but, by employing the singular, attributes an essential – rather than contingent and contrived – unicity to the series of events it names, and so proposes its own way of mystifying them.

The only thing that had, from the outset, an intrinsic unity in the wake of the Tunisian revolution was the shock wave that spread out from it. What would happen once that wave made landfall in different parts of the highly variegated political topography of the Middle East and North Africa was bound to be a plurality of distinct situations with sharply differentiated implications, by no means necessarily promising ones. What gave a subsequent unity to these situations was the overarching construction placed upon them. In so far as talk of the 'Arab Uprising' tended to credit them with a uniform revolutionary potential, it was, if anything, even more of an hallucination than the talk of 'the Arab Spring', which is why I have come, reluctantly, to regard the latter as the appropriate term to use, on one condition. This is that the Tunisian case is understood not to belong to the series to which the term refers, because the Tunisian revolution was not only prior to the shock wave that founded this series but also determined by quite other logics.

'The Arab Spring' names not only the edifice of wishful thinking with which the Western media and many academics misinterpreted these events as they unfolded but also the construction of *policy* that was erected, to great effect, on these several risings, depending on them the way a bridge depends on the foundations built into the river bed on which the pillars which support the bridge themselves rest. This bridge was constructed not by any of the insurgents but by external powers in every case, and what its arches, so glittering when viewed from afar, actually spanned was the distance between the condition of the Middle East as it was in late 2010 and the landscape of desolation it has since become. What the rebellions came to have in common, over and above the shock wave that generated them, was the way they were subsequently inflected by external actors and the way the dynamics of co-optation and confiscation interfered with and overlaid the original dynamics of the conflict between the domestic forces in contention, whereas the latter alone determined the onset of the revolutionary situation in Tunisian and its provisional outcome.

In saying this now, I am not speaking with the benefit of hindsight; I am repeating what I said at public events in Paris and London in the spring and summer of 2011, by which time I was already convinced that the Egyptian and Libyan actors of the Arab Spring were riding for a fall.[6] And that is why I think it is a mistake to counterpose an 'Arab Winter' to the 'Arab Spring'.

The Arab Spring, properly understood, was not a failure but at least a partial success. It achieved its primary purpose, the purpose initially orienting the political actors who actually attained and thereafter exercised practical hegemony within the dramatic flow of events. If you want to know what that purpose was, look around you and consider what you see. The extremes of desolation to which the Arab Middle East has been reduced, from Tripolitania to Mosul and from Aleppo to Aden, are not of course the intended consequences of that purpose, but they are the consequences of what was intended and achieved, the immediate neutralisation and eventual defeat of revolutionary aspirations everywhere east of Tunisia.

At the critical level of ideas, this outcome was achieved through the substitution of a secondary objective for the primary one. The revolt in Tunisia was sparked by the gesture of Mohamed Bouazizi in committing suicide rather than live with the shame he had experienced at the hands of local officials in Sidi Bouzid. It expressed the widespread popular refusal of the injustice borne of contempt – al-hagra (al-haqara in standard Arabic) – that ordinary people so often suffer in the form of abuse of power by governments, local power-holders and state agents of all kinds. This refusal, a willed negation, had a clear, positive implication – the demand for dignity. For this to be met, it had to be developed into the more focused, explicit, political demand for real as opposed to merely nominal citizenship, the demand that governments treat the governed with respect and do so because they are obliged to do so, a state of affairs that could arise only once the form of government had been changed to allow for effective political representation. Whether this change required the fall of the head of state as the precondition of everything else was a secondary consideration, depending on circumstances. But whether or not this was required, it was not the ultimate objective. In Tunisia, the overthrow of President Ben Ali was followed very swiftly by a series of other developments, because the initial popular revolt was promptly harnessed, generalised and developed by an experienced and well-organised force, the national trade union (Union Générale Tunisienne du Travail, UGTT), which had far-reaching democratic ends in view – and, incidentally, no counterparts elsewhere.

III

One of the first commentators to employ 'the Arab Uprising' to name his object of analysis was Gilbert Achcar, a Lebanese Marxist and professor at the School of Oriental and African Studies (SOAS) in London, whose book, first published in French, garnered the high praise of the no longer remotely left-ish *Le Monde* before appearing in an English translation that wears *Le Monde*'s endorsement with pride. Achcar's initial view of the Arab Uprising was not a merely hopeful one, it was virtually apocalyptic. While studded with quotations from Karl Marx, not to mention Trotsky, it appeared not to be mindful of Gramsci's recommendation of 'pessimism of the intellect' since, in addition to proffering a Marxian political economy of the Uprising, it also entertained and encouraged grand expectations of where this was headed.

That Achcar should have published his book when he did is curious. It is not that Marxism has nothing to offer when it comes to analysing the events in question; it has, and Achcar's account of the political-economic background and context of the events he discusses has merit. Nor can it be said that Marxists had no part of the uprisings. Leftists of several – including Marxist – varieties played active parts in the overthrow of Ben Ali in Tunisia, and a grouping called the Revolutionary Socialists – recognised by the Socialist Workers' Party (SWP) in Britain as its Egyptian counterpart – played a role in the initial Tahrir Square demonstrations and at several junctures thereafter. The problem is that the commodity Achcar had to purvey was simply a kind of Marxist Olympianism. What he did is provide a Marxist analysis of what was wrong with the regimes the uprisings were challenging, and what their weaknesses as well as their ugly aspects were. He thus clearly put himself on the side of the uprisings and validated them from a revolutionary social-ist point of view, while claiming to go one better than liberal analysis in explaining their genesis. The remarkable thing is that he should have thought it appropriate to produce his political economy of the uprisings when he did. As the late Tony Cliff, the founder of the International Socialism group that became the

SWP, was fond of reminding his adepts, 'Minerva's owl flies out at dusk', when the day is done. The time for a considered scholarly exploration, radical or not, of the political economy of the uprisings was in the evening, after the event, not high noon. What onlookers with the ambition to influence events needed to publish at high noon was a concise set of intelligible thoughts that might guide the actors in the desired direction, a critical commentary on the action, not Olympian explanations of why the villain was so villainous or why there was a play at all, both of which could be taken for granted by that stage. And because Achcar got high noon and dusk muddled up, he allowed himself some extreme reflections that tempted fate, and to which history has not been kind at all.

In his provisional balance sheet of the uprising in Libya, Achcar made no mention whatever of Qadhafi's repeated offers to negotiate and insisted:

> The man could only be overthrown by force of arms; the ineluctable precondition for his downfall was his military defeat. The only real choice was between civil war and allowing the uprising to be crushed, without fighting back.[7]

This was, of course, exactly the position of the Western powers, which stonily rejected all Qadhafi's offers of ceasefires and talks and the urgings of the African Union and the International Crisis Group that these should be taken seriously, and whose military intervention Achcar approved without qualification. In assessing the position as of October 2012 (when his original French text went to press), Achcar suggested that Libya had experienced by far the most complete of all the Arab revolutions thus far:

> The dynamics of the Libyan uprising ... make it the only one of the Arab uprisings that, at the time of writing, had completely "broken" the state of the old regime ... Libya has, so far, undergone a radical political revolution, but not a radical social revolution. The state superstructure and the ideological superstructure have been shattered.[8]

While noting the chaotic aspect of the resulting situation, Achcar was clearly pleased with the success of 'the politically radical nature of the uprising' in shattering the Libyan state. While requiring more – a radical *social* revolution – to satisfy him completely, the destruction of the Libyan state was enough for him to assure us that a radical political revolution had been achieved. He did not waste a single word on assessing the capacity of the victorious rebels to constitute a new state or on how this might be done, or whether, indeed, there was any prospect of it at all. Apparently, in his opinion, a radical political revolution did not need to constitute a new and better state; it was enough for it to shatter the previous state.

In defending this position, Achcar took issue with the International Crisis Group and me personally in a long footnote, in which he suggested that I had 'grounded [my] position on mistaken premises', and expressed the hope that I would repent and confess my errors.[9] While he omitted to inform his readers what that position was or what its premises had been, he was not wrong to suppose that his viewpoint and mine were diametrically opposed. The ICG's position, as explained in its press releases of 10 March and 13 May 2011, in its Open Letter to the United Nations Security Council of 16 March 2011, and in its full-length report of 6 June 2011, was that, while the Jamahiriyya was finished and Qadhafi's time was up, it was vital to preserve the necessary minimum of state continuity and avoid a collapse into anarchy and that, to that end, the UN Security Council should secure a ceasefire and the onset of negotiations between the regime and the rebellion on the modalities of a transition to a post-Qadhafi, post-Jamahiriyya form of government.[10] As its media release of 10 March 2011 pointed out,

Determined Western intervention could help topple the regime but at considerable political as well as human cost and would risk precipitating a political vacuum in which various forces engage in a potentially prolonged and violent struggle for supremacy before anything resembling a state and stable government are re-established. Such a vortex could draw in Libya's neighbours and gravely compromise prospects for democratic development in Tunisia and Egypt as well as create a humanitarian catastrophe on Europe's doorsteps.[11]

I can no longer speak for ICG, but I do not think that it has the slightest reason to regret its position of thirteen years ago, and I know I don't. I have always taken the view that a complete political revolution is one that constitutes a new state in place of the state it has overthrown, and that the destruction of a state where forces capable of constructing a new one are absent is liable to be experienced as a catastrophe by the people of the country in question. And I have seen no reason to revise the judgment I made at high noon in February–March 2011, that what passed for the leadership of the Libyan rebels would be unable to constitute a new state.

On Syria, Achcar told his readers that 'the rebellion had to choose between three options': they could either 'admit defeat and give up' or 'demand international protection' – both of which he dismissed as non-starters – or 'recognise that the regime could only be overthrown by force of arms'.[12] His premise for this was 'a concrete analysis' that 'could only lead to the conclusion that nothing but a civil war would topple the Syrian regime'.[13] In effect, he recommended the last of these, and a civil war was fought and the democratic aspirations of the original protestors were rapidly engulfed and lost sight of; much if not most of Syria as a country and a society was destroyed, and the regime was not toppled. The question is: what to make of Achcar's past positions now that Minerva's owl has taken flight? No doubt some of his readers at SOAS and elsewhere who like explorations to be radical found his preaching of civil war eleven years ago impressive and convincing. *How about now?*

In fact, he himself has been obliged to abandon the position he adopted in 2012–13. In his latest book, *Morbid Symptoms: Relapse in the Arab Uprising*, he finally recognises that his prescription of civil war to topple Asad was not, in fact, a very good idea and he suggests a different one:

In order for any progressive potential to materialise in an organised political form among the Syrian people at large, the precondition at this stage is for the war to stop. In that regard and given the abysmal situation that has arisen in Syria after four years of war, the appalling level of killing and destruction, and the immense human tragedy represented by the refugees and displaced persons (about one half of Syria's population), one can only wish for the success of the international efforts presently being deployed to reach a compromise between the Syrian regime and the mainstream opposition.[14]

I broadly agree with this (while wondering what he meant by 'the mainstream opposition') and regret only that Achcar did not say this sooner. *Morbid Symptoms* was published in May 2016. I stated my own position along these lines at some length in *LRB*, ten months earlier, in July 2015. But in fact I first stated it at a public event held at the Harvard Kennedy School on 6 May 2013 (and recorded in a podcast available for download online).[15] In this talk, I argued that no good could possibly come of the violence in Syria and that the US should enlist Russia's co-operation in undertaking the complex diplomacy and horse-trading that it would take to persuade the protagonists – not only the regime and the rebels but also, crucially, Saudi Arabia, the other Gulf states, Iran and Turkey – to stop the war. I said this fifteen months before ISIS captured Mosul and twenty-seven months before Russia began deploying active forces in support of the Syrian government. As of 6 May 2013, most of Syria's towns and cities were largely intact and the estimated death toll stood at some 90,000, an already appalling figure which may, however, have been an overestimate. By May 2016 it had at least tripled if not quadrupled – the UN Special Envoy Staffan de Mistura gave his own figure (for what that was worth) of 400,000 in late April 2016 – and it may well exceed 500,000 today.[16] And the world knows what has happened to so many of Syria's towns and cities and to the numbers of refugees and internally displaced persons over the last ten years.

IV

Contemplating failure and disappointment, whether in love or war or politics, almost always includes revolving in one's head a triad of thorny questions. When did things go wrong? Whose fault was it? And what lessons are to be learned from the fiasco? Whether the right lessons are drawn depends heavily on how the first two questions are addressed and answered. And the business of identifying the right answer to the first is liable to be gravely prejudiced by the impulse to rush to judgment in addressing the second.

Achcar has no doubt where the blame belongs. The Arab Uprising was defeated by the combined assaults of two distinct reactionary forces: the deep states of the countries in question and reactionary Islamism. His position is thus similar, although not identical, to Jean-Pierre Filiu's thesis (reviewed in Chapter 3), that the 'new Mamluks' of the deep state were the villains of the story, with the difference that, whereas Filiu placed less emphasis on the role of the Islamists (except in Libya, where he allocates particular blame to the Muslim Brothers), Achcar has the Islamists and deep states equally in his sights.

Lynch may appear likewise to regard the deep states as the villains of the piece; he certainly condemns Arab autocrats and 'the determined refusal by entrenched elites to allow for progressive change'.[17] But his argument is more interesting than that for two reasons. First, he places unprecedented emphasis upon the role played by the Gulf Arab states – as distinct from the 'deep state'/'Mamluks' in Egypt or Syria – in influencing the course of events. He insists early on that 'autocratic regimes, in their single-minded pursuit of survival, are the root cause of the instability . . . The region's autocrats . . . are the problem and not the solution', and further that 'the Arab uprising failed because the regimes they challenged killed it', an outcome he denounces as 'a crime'.[18] But what is important about this is that he includes Arab monarchies on the charge sheet and goes on to explain in detail their behaviour and influence in particular cases – not only Bahrain, Yemen and Syria but also Libya and even Egypt. Second, he does not regard the 'revolutionaries' as above criticism at all and identifies several of their limitations. Thus, while regionwide factors or 'drivers' and the influence of the Gulf monarchies – Qatar, Saudi Arabia and the United Arab Emirates in particular – are central to his analysis, he insists that 'this is not to downplay . . . the responsibility of domestic political actors for their own failures'.[19] He notes early on that 'the uprisings have proven to be far more successful at breaking the status quo than at building better alternatives', and goes on to observe more particularly that 'revolutionaries failed to translate their mobilizational capacity into enduring political parties' – important observations that warrant further development.[20]

In placing the Gulf Arab states at or at least near the centre of the story, and allocating to them a substantial portion of the responsibility for what went wrong, Lynch has not only innovated in the Western narrative of the Arab Spring/Uprising but has also deviated from the mainstream Western discourse on the Arab world. The condemnation of Arab 'authoritarianism' purveyed by this discourse has long targeted the regimes of the so-called republics alone – Algeria, Egypt, Iraq, (Libya), Sudan, Syria, Tunisia and Yemen – and the monarchies have been largely spared Western opprobrium. Morocco and Jordan have generally had a favourable or at least sympathetic press; Oman, to some extent Kuwait and (until 2011) Bahrain have been overlooked, the UAE also largely overlooked except in respect of the vast commercial opportunities it offers, Qatar praised for its lead in freeing up the Arab media with Al Jazeera; and Saudi Arabia treated (until the Khashoqji scandal) with the respect that power and wealth usually elicit, except by those exercised over its promotion of Islamic fundamentalism and its treatment of women.

Lynch's thesis about the central role of the Gulf monarchies performs three functions in his overall argument: a unifying function, a transitional function and an apologetic function. Since, as he shows, these monarchies were players in every situation – Bahrain, Egypt, Libya, Syria and Yemen – their role in itself was a major factor giving unity to the Arab Uprising, if only or at least primarily in the sense of its negation, and justifying analysts' use of the singular. Second, their central role in the real politics of the Uprising was of course the main stepping stone to what superseded this Uprising: the 'Arab Wars'. Third, to hold the Gulf monarchies responsible to a substantial degree for the disastrous outcome of the Uprising is of course not only to relativise the responsibility of this or that deep state – which is not what Lynch intends – but also, and crucially, to minimise the blame accruing to the United States and to President Obama in particular.

The answer that Lynch provides to the question of when it all went wrong is that 'the period between the fall of 2012 and first half of 2013 was a tipping point. This is when the Arab uprisings decisively shifted on to the track to damnation.'[21] His opinion on this point is broadly consistent with his comparatively sophisticated and reasonable view of who the culprits were. But there is a problem in situating the turn in 2012–13 and thereby suggesting that all had been well before that point. Lynch needs this version of the chronology in order to sustain his view of the Libyan uprising as initially a good thing, and of the Egyptian uprising as initially a good thing: the Arab Uprising(s) as a whole was (were) a good thing but then got perverted and derailed, and Washington is not to blame, all sorts of Arabs are: this is Lynch's thesis in a nutshell. But it does not work as well as he would wish. Lynch tries hard to make it work in respect of the Libyan story in particular but, given his own understanding of the role of the Gulf monarchies, he is unable to devise a coherent version of this story that is consistent with his non-negotiable postulate that the military intervention that secured Qadhafi's overthrow was justified, while his account includes evidence that undermines other key parts of the Western powers' propagandist narrative.

5

The Reconstruction of Statelessness in Libya

The story the Western powers fed to the world about Libya was that they were intervening to support a popular uprising against a cruel and hated despot, and thereby acting to further the Arab Uprising in general by saving it from defeat (and its supporters from massacre) in Libya, and that the intervention was not remotely imperialist in character since it had been invited by the Libyan leadership of the revolt, the National Transitional Council (NTC), and was approved by the rest of the Arab world as represented by the Arab League. A corollary of this story is that things went wrong only after the overthrow of Qadhafi; up till then, all had gone well.

This is the line that President Obama took in his conversation with Jeffrey Goldberg, in which he claimed that 'we averted large-scale civilian casualties, we prevented what almost surely would have been a prolonged and bloody civil conflict', before acknowledging that 'despite all that, Libya is a mess'.

'When I go back and I ask myself what went wrong,' Obama said, 'there's room for criticism, because I had more faith in the Europeans, given Libya's proximity, being invested in the follow-up' ... He noted that Nicolas Sarkozy, the French president, lost his job the following year. And he said that British prime minister David Cameron soon stopped paying attention, becoming 'distracted by a range of other things'.

Obama also blamed internal Libyan dynamics. 'The degree of tribal division in Libya was greater than our analysts had expected. And our ability to have any kind of structure there that we could interact with and start training and start providing resources broke down very quickly.'[1]

'The degree of tribal division' is a red herring. If the analysts in Washington discounted it, they were not in error; the problem lay elsewhere. As for the absence of 'any kind of structure', Obama's use of the phrase 'our ability' where 'the Libyans' ability' would make better sense is symptomatic of Washington's difficulty in deciding who really 'owned' post-Qadhafi Libya. But what registers most clearly is that the French and the British were to blame for failing to be 'invested in the follow-up'. This is after-the-event buck-passing, if not scapegoating; there was no British or French prior commitment to engage in the kind of follow-up that would have enabled Libya to avoid the 'mess' it became. The report of the House of Commons Foreign Affairs Committee, published five months after the article in the *Atlantic*, offers a less casual discussion of what went wrong but echoes a key part of Obama's self-serving argument in its claim that 'former Prime Minister David Cameron was ultimately responsible for the failure to develop a coherent Libya strategy'.[2] Former prime ministers are easy targets, as Tony Blair knows well; however much to blame they may truly be, they can also be used to take away the sins of everyone else.

While concerned to defend Obama's handling of the Libyan crisis, Lynch does not reproduce Obama's line of argument, but develops a different argument that undermines the warmongers' original story in fundamental respects. A key element of this story was the insistence that *the leadership of the revolt was Libyan*, that the NTC represented a broad groundswell of Libyan opinion and had legitimacy in virtue of that fact, and that Libyans accordingly 'owned' and never ceased to 'own' their rebellion and the 'revolution' it became. This key element of the story in turn presupposed another, namely that the role of other Arabs was primarily that of a chorus providing supportive 'noises off', a source of legitimating rhetoric and some practical support, above all money and arms, but not much more than that. In particular, there was at first no explicit, public, suggestion that troops from other Arab countries were going to be involved in the fighting. The military intervention was, from 23 March onwards, a NATO affair, operating on a UN mandate that was, supposedly, strictly interpreted and involving the combined French, British and American air forces, with modest contributions from other NATO members (Canada, Italy, Norway et al.), plus a very modest presence of British and French special forces on the ground, with the bulk of the ground fighting being handled by the Libyan troops at the disposal of the NTC.*

We now know better. That Qatari forces were involved on the ground finally emerged into full view in August 2011, when their role in orchestrating the capture of Tripoli by fighters from Zintan and Misrata could no longer be obscured. Lynch now tells us that from 'quite early on' both Qatari and Emirati special operations forces, in addition to NATO's, 'became actively involved, embedding in rebel units to provide training and to call in air strikes'.[3] According to a report by the Royal United Services Institute in September 2011, Emirati special forces had established themselves from April onwards in the Zawiya district on the coast near the Tunisian border, from where they were able to supply rebel units with equipment and provisions, and Qatar had established training facilities in Benghazi and in the Nafusa mountains in May, while acting also from June onwards to convey 'French weapons and ammunition supplies to the rebels including by establishing an air strip at Zintan'.[4] But it was not only Qatari and Emirati special forces that were in action; some 100 Egyptian special forces were deployed in eastern Libya as early as February and March to train rebel units, while an unspecified number of Jordanian special forces were also deployed for the same purpose.[5] Meanwhile there were thirty to forty British special forces, the same number of French special forces, plus some ten Italian special forces

---

* The transition to NATO command began on 23 March and was complete on 4 April; see Anthony Bell and David Witter, 'The Libyan Revolution', 4 parts, Institute for the Study of War, Washington DC, September 2011, Part 2: 'Escalation and Intervention', 9.

engaged on the ground – from Tobruk and Benghazi in the east to Misrata, Zawiya and Zintan in the west – and even twelve Bulgarian special forces and a Bulgarian frigate deployed offshore to interdict or at least limit the Qadhafi regime's control of the coast, so that arms for the rebels might be landed and the amphibious aspect of the eventual assault on Tripoli prepared.[6]

In the Annual Chief of Defence Staff Lecture at the Royal United Services Institute (RUSI) on 14 December 2011, General Sir David Richards commented as follows on the way the military intervention made use of Arab special forces:

> Integrating the Qataris, Emiratis and Jordanians into the operation was key. Without them and their defence chiefs' leadership, especially the huge understanding they brought to the campaign, it is unlikely that the NTC's militias could have successfully acted as the land element without which the campaign would have been impossible.[7]

This crucially relativises the role of the Libyan rebel forces – already relativised by the strategic primacy of NATO's air campaign – but it also understates the amount of 'integrating' that actually went on. For the British and French military chiefs and the officers commanding their special forces on the ground, 'integrating the Qataris, Emiratis and Jordanians into the operation' was only part of the exercise, and was in fact the easy part, since these forces were disciplined professionals but also largely if not entirely the product of prior British or French training. The second part of the exercise was the way in which these various special forces then worked to integrate the plethora of Libyan *katā'ib* (brigades; sing.: *katība*) only nominally, if at all, obedient to the NTC into a coordinated military campaign.[8]

The NTC could be said to have a functional army for as long as non-Libyan military expertise was directing and coordinating its troops. The factor integrating the *katā'ib* into this army was an external one. It was predictable that the moment this external factor, its mission deemed accomplished, was withdrawn, the NTC's 'army' would disintegrate and the *katā'ib* would become laws unto themselves.

Was this not foreseen? How could it be that experienced British and French generals did not foresee this? And if, as may well be the case, they did indeed foresee it, why was this allowed to happen?

II

With the end of the war against Qadhafi in late October, the men with guns on the rebel side underwent an abrupt transition of their own. From revolutionaries – *thuwwār* – receiving the plaudits of the West as artisans of the revolution and living proof that the revolution was 'Libyan-owned', they became something far less positive, indeed negative if not sinister – *militias* – and were soon identified as the key problem of the post-Qadhafi 'state'.[9] They had served their purpose, were no longer needed and had become a nuisance. This 180-degree turn in onlookers' evaluation of the Libyans who had done any fighting took no interest in the fighters' actual outlook, which in many cases had remained constant. This emerges clearly from Worth's fascinating account, in which he introduces us to Jalal Ragai and Nasser Salhoba, the leaders of a *katība* in Tripoli, and presents an engaging portrait of them.[10] Suddenly some militiamen at least have names and faces and interesting stories to tell; they come across as resourceful, apparently inclined to treat their prisoners – elements of Qadhafi's security forces, including former torturers and killers – humanely (at any rate in the presence of foreign journalists), and displaying an extraordinary, if understandably macabre, sense of humour.[11] If these vignettes cannot be relied on as furnishing a generally valid picture, they can certainly be read as an antidote to the wholly abstract and negative depiction of the 'militias' that has been the common coin of Western commentary since late 2011. But what does this signify? Worth remarks:

> Rebels like Jalal and his men started out in 2011 as liberators who hoped to restore law and order, but soon became a law unto themselves. It was up to them to decide whether their country became something more than an archipelago of feuding warlords.[12]

Except that it wasn't.

There was no way the leaders of the many hundreds of independent brigades scattered across the country could take such a decision. The national anarchy in which they had their being from September 2011 onwards was not of their making and could not be transcended by them. For as long as it lasted the most they could do was to try to behave with restraint. But no other force existed that could transcend this anarchy either. That this was the truth of the matter took a long time to sink in, because it had to make headway against the resistance of determined prejudices. The day after Qadhafi was lynched, Chatham House published on its website a piece by the head of its Libya Working Group which assured us that

> the outlook for security is good: Gaddafism is done for without Gaddafi . . . There will be a general instinct to cooperate with the new government, the police and the victorious armed forces. Libyan towns and the Libyan desert are likely to be as safe as or safer than equivalents in other North African countries . . . The promised interim government will be announced shortly . . . The transition will start formally. That is not a problem.[13]

As an expression of the extraordinary delusions to which British official optimism is nowadays prone, this would be hard to beat. For there was a problem and it was that there was no government or police or armed forces – other than the *katā'ib* – for the good people of Libya to cooperate with.

It would take the killing of the United States ambassador Chris Stevens and three other US personnel on 11 September 2012 for the West to begin to wake up to Libya's bleak reality. From that point on, numerous Western think tanks and other voices would vie with one another in insisting that the imperative for the new Libyan republic was to establish security as the precondition of everything else, and that this meant dealing with the *katā'ib*.[14] The problem was that nobody had a clue how to do this. The air was filled with cries that these cats must be belled if not neutered or at least herded, but not a single mouse or dog could put forward a realistic proposal as to how these things might be done.

As Worth mentions, the tactic of the interim governments of Abderrahim El-Keib (November 2011 to November 2012) and Ali Zeidan (November 2012 to March 2014) was to buy them off, both selectively and *en bloc*, co-opting certain brigades to provide security for government personnel and institutions on the one hand, and paying them all a wage for not doing anything in particular on the other.[15] This inevitably made matters worse, sharpening rivalries between the co-opted and the non-coopted while encouraging new brigades to form in order to get on the payroll. Moreover, quite apart from mercenary considerations, the widespread insecurity prompted the formation of new *katā'ib* in many places simply to provide a makeshift security at the local level. It is generally agreed that there were some 17,000 fighters during the war against Qadhafi, and about 140,000 registered militiamen by 2014.[16] (This second figure may be an underestimate; by early 2012 estimates of registered militia members ranged from 120,000 to 200,000; seven months later the total was estimated at 'up to 250,000 members on the government payroll'.[17]) But it is not at all clear that any other option was available to either of these hapless prime ministers by the time they took office, because in both cases office conferred little or no power. El-Keib was elected by the NTC with the support of only twenty-six out of the fifty-one NTC members present and voting, and the fact that the NTC did not fully support him was made repeatedly evident during his year in office.[18] Zeidan held his mandate from the General National Congress (GNC) elected in July 2012, but he in turn had as many problems with the GNC as El-Keib had had with the NTC. He had been elected with ninety-three votes in favour and eighty-five against; this support of less than half of the Congress's 200 members did not provide an effective mandate to govern and was wholly insufficient to give him or his 'government' any authority over the *katā'ib*.[19]

III

The election of the General National Congress was celebrated in Western commentary as a great success. It had been free and pluralist, and reasonably well organised and conducted. This commentary took additional satisfaction from the fact that the Justice and Construction Party that had been set up by the Muslim Brothers won only seventeen seats and was outdistanced by Mahmoud Jibril's National Forces Alliance (NFA), which won thirty-nine.[20] One wire service even went so far as to call the NFA's performance 'a landslide'.[21] What nobody pointed out was that the Congress thus elected made effective government utterly impossible.

The law that governed the election stipulated that the Congress should have 200 members, but that 120 of these should be elected as individuals standing (notionally) as independents, and that only 80 members might be elected as explicitly representing political parties.[22] These rules made it impossible for any party to win a majority. But it was worse than that in at least three respects. First, the law provided for two different types of individual candidacies: those in single-member constituencies, where election was on the first-past-the-post rule, and those in multi-member constituencies, where election was on the basis of share of total single non-transferable votes. Second, the remaining eighty seats were to be decided on the basis of proportional representation in multi-member seats contested by rival party lists.[23] Thus the Congress would consist of three distinct categories of members elected on quite different principles, with very different relationships to their electors. Third, it was widely rumoured that a significant proportion of the 120 notionally independent individual members did in fact have partisan allegiances but were coy about them, so that the arrangement had the character of a confidence trick played on the electorate. Libyans were unwittingly voting for candidates whose party affiliations were being concealed; how could this possibly be reconciled with democratic principles? Finally, it not only made it impossible for any party – even Jibril's NFA (in reality not a party at all but an alliance of some forty-four political groupings) – to form a government on its own, but also made it impossible for any party to act as the decisive architect and leading element of a stable governing coalition. It condemned whatever governing team eventually obtained an initial mandate of sorts to base itself on shifting sands, the entirely unreliable support of numerous Congress members whose allegiances were uncontrolled by definite party affiliations and so liable to be erratic. It guaranteed that such a 'government' would be congenitally weak and unable to govern in the proper sense of the word, and would accordingly carry no authority with the *katā'ib*. But the NTC's role in guaranteeing this outcome went far beyond the perverse rules it laid down for the election of the Congress.

The NTC committed itself to dissolving itself once the Congress had been elected, and it did indeed dissolve itself, in August 2012.[24] This did not mean that henceforth the Congress was the NTC's full successor and locus of national sovereignty – 'the supreme power in the State of Libya', as the NTC had described itself – for the NTC's actions precluded that. The NTC's description of itself in the phrase just quoted was contained in Article 17 of the 'Constitutional Declaration' it published on 3 August 2011. This Declaration presented itself as binding on the Congress that would be elected in July 2012, and was widely regarded as such. It committed the Congress:

- to appoint a new interim government within thirty days;
- to establish a body to draft a constitution and see to it that this body completed its task within sixty days;
- to submit this draft within thirty days of approving it to a referendum, which, in order to ratify the draft constitution, required a two-thirds majority of those Libyans voting, failing which the entire procedure would have to be repeated until this demanding majority was secured;
- to hold, within 180 days of the enactment of an electoral law in accordance with the new Constitution, fresh elections to a new body, the Legislative Power, and to dissolve itself immediately when the new body assembled.[25]

It even dictated to the Congress which member it should choose to preside its very first meeting, and which it should choose to act as its secretary and how exactly this meeting should then elect the Congress's president and vice-president.[26]

All these manic instructions were contained in the August 2011 Declaration, but the NTC *still* could not leave bad enough alone. In March 2012, in response to militant federalists demanding autonomy for Cyrenaica, the NTC further pre-empted the future Congress by stipulating that the body to draft the Constitution should be composed of sixty persons drawn from the three historic regions – twenty each from Tripolitiania, Cyrenaica and the Fezzan – regardless of their vastly unequal populations.[27] And, as if saddling the Congress-to-be with all this was not enough, on 3 July 2012, just two days before the elections to the Congress, the NTC announced that the body the Congress was required to establish to draft the Constitution would not, in fact, be established by the Congress but by a popular election which the Congress was required to organise.[28] Thus the NTC dictated that the Congress should arrange for its own legitimacy and authority to be qualified and rivalled if not nullified by another popularly elected body, and made not the slightest attempt to define what the relationship between these two popularly elected bodies should be.

In this way the NTC arranged for itself to have a kind of vampirish life after death. Although it would officially cease to exist as soon as the Congress met in August 2012, its vision, its detailed road-map, would survive it and determine developments. It had never been an elected body itself, but its stated views were to pre-empt the deliberations of the elected Congress. Although secularist critics of the NTC might complain about the way its chairman, Mustafa Abdul Jalil, pre-empted any elected assembly when he proclaimed in August 2011 that the Sharī'a would be the main source of law in the future Libyan state, this proclamation was able to presuppose a national consensus on the question and provoked no major controversy. But the subsequent behaviour of the NTC required everyone in Libya to treat *The Constitutional Declaration* as holy writ no less binding than the Qur'ân and the Sharī'a, without the NTC having any genuine, let alone divine, authority to warrant this whatever.

A political revolution is a moment, brief or protracted as the case may be, of radical change from one kind of state and form of government to another. It is a moment that is governed by no laws, when the various social forces in contention struggle with one another to shape the future and those possessing the most weight, political coherence and aptitude for resourceful statecraft win out. Such a process cannot be predicted, let alone scripted, stage-managed and scheduled in advance, *ever*. That the NTC tried to lay down precisely how events had to unfold and the exact timing of every one of them is evidence that its members had no idea of what a revolution is. And one other arrangement that the NTC made as an irremediable *fait accompli* furnished proof that, in addition to not understanding revolutions, the NTC had no idea of government.

In early September 2012, the newly elected Congress voted to prohibit its members from holding the position of minister or prime minister.[29] In line with this, Ali Zeidan had to resign his seat in Congress as the representative of the electors of Jufra in order to be nominated for the premiership.[30] This rule was not Congress's invention; it recycled the much earlier decision of the NTC, embodied in the Constitutional Declaration (Article 21), that prohibited members of the NTC from holding any executive public office, which meant that none of the members of the 'interim government' it finally appointed in November 2011 could be members of the NTC.

The rule that no member of the government could be a member of the legislature ensured that the government would be at the mercy of a notionally sovereign assembly in which neither it nor individual ministers had any voice at all. This would conceivably have been all right if there had been a powerful presidency and the council of ministers was appointed by the president and enjoyed powers that he delegated to them, and if there had existed a substantial party connection between the president and his cabinet on the one hand and a significant number of the members of the legislative branch on the other. But, in the absence of that arrangement, the Libyan 'governments' have simply existed in mid-air, with no footing in the Parliament and no bodies of armed men to rely on, a self-evidently hopeless position.

This rule was imposed in a partial – but wholly unreflecting – imitation of the American constitutional principle of the separation of powers. As such, it expressed the influence of the expatriate Libyans who had studied in American universities or lived in America for long periods and who took the American Constitution – as they understood (or misunderstood) it – as the gold standard of democracy, to which they had to pay fealty in order to win Western support.

But it also expressed something else.

IV

The formation of the National Transitional Council or, as it was initially known, in a more exact translation of the Arabic [*al-majlis al-waṭanī al-intiqālī*], the Transitional National Council (TNC) was announced on 27 February 2011, a mere ten days after the Day of Rage which, two days after the initial unrest of 15 February, had really launched the uprising.[31] Qadhafi's former justice minister, Mustafa Abdul Jalil, was named as its chairman, and the former head of the National Development Corporation, Mahmoud Jibril, who had returned to Libya from a sojourn in Abu Dhabi on 28 February, was one of the most prominent figures listed as members of the NTC on 27 February and was subsequently named as the head of its executive board when this was finally formed on 23 March.[32] Worth remarks of Abdul Jalil that he was 'the kind of man who made you believe in the Libyan cause'.[33] It was Jibril who, thanks to the good offices of Bernard Henri-Lévy, was invited to Paris to meet President Sarkozy on 10 March and went on to meet Hillary Clinton on 14 March, a meeting she later claimed had been decisive for her.[34]

Lynch explains the formation of the NTC as follows: 'The Libyan rebels urgently needed a political body to represent them abroad. Qatar again took the lead, sponsoring the creation of the National Transition Council.'[35] The suggestion that the NTC owed its foundation entirely to Qatari sponsorship is questionable, but there is no doubt about Qatar's early prominence in supporting it, nor about the way this galvanised other Gulf states into taking a piece of the action for themselves, nor about where this led. 'Getting rid of Qaddafi wasn't enough,' Lynch tells us; 'each wanted to dominate the new Libya"',[36] an observation he elaborates later on:

> Qatar, the UAE and Saudi Arabia were initially on the same side, mobilizing their distinctive resources against Qaddafi and in support of the rebels. This unity did not last. As in Yemen, Egypt and Tunisia, they were competing with each other from the start for influence with power brokers in the anticipated new Libya. The competition for rebel proxies in Libya helped to ensure that its transition would fail, and it set the stage for even worse to come in Syria . . .
>
> . . . As the NTC began to evolve from a coordinating body for the international community into a proto-government in waiting, the struggle for representation and its relationship with the armed militias took on an ever greater significance. The external powers jockeyed to get their people into leadership positions, leading to debilitating internal politicking at a time of urgent military threat.[37]

This sinister line of development was facilitated by the uncertainty that the NTC's own members evinced about their collective purpose and role. Press reports of the meetings held in Al-Bayda in Cyrenaica on 24 and 25 February 2011 initially suggested that these had the object of forming an interim administration or alternative government but, in officially announcing the formation of the NTC on 27 February 2011, its spokesman, Abdelhafiz Gougha, emphasised that the Council was *not* a provisional government.[38] This uncertainty may have seemed to have been resolved on 5 March, when the NTC published a statement declaring itself to be the 'sole representative of all Libya', but it was not obvious what this meant for practical purposes, and it was subsequently qualified by the announcement on 23 March that the NTC had established an executive board, which was understood to mean a body performing at least some governmental functions.[39] However, beyond some basic administration, undertaken by local committees in Benghazi and other towns controlled by the rebellion, and the payment of salaries, it is unclear that any serious governing was going on. When Britain's international development minister, Andrew Mitchell, visited Benghazi on 4 June, he was so impressed that he allowed himself to enthuse that

> The NTC are much better than anyone thought they would be. The thing I noticed was how quickly, when they had driven out the Gaddafi forces ... they stabilised Misrata, which was in a bad way. I saw it for myself in Benghazi – there was traffic control. Although the rubbish wasn't being collected, the fact was that the police were evident and they were able to provide order.[40]

Providing a degree of routine order – on traffic if not rubbish – in towns enthusiastically loyal to the rebellion was not a major feat and was never the issue. And it says something about the British government's grasp of the Libyan end of the project to overthrow Qadhafi that he supposed the NTC controlled Misrata. The NTC never ran Misrata at all; order there was secured by the newly formed seventeen-member Misrata City Council, which operated independently of the NTC, as did the local councils established elsewhere in Tripolitania.[41]

Lynch arrived in his book at a very negative conclusion: 'The NTC's members ... commanded little local constituencies or support on the ground. More liberal-minded Libyans wondered about the democratic legitimacy of a self-appointed and Western-backed council.'[42] This is in line with the assessment furnished by Anthony Bell and David Witter in the first part of their four-part study, 'The Libyan Rebellion':

> Libya's new government, the rebel National Transition Council, is far from a capable government-in-waiting. Despite receiving international recognition and support, the NTC is only a

transitional body that has not yet articulated a clear roadmap for Libya's political future. The NTC itself is fraught with internal divisions and possesses an unclear decision-making structure. It has little institutional capacity to carry out policies and has not exercised control over the numerous armed rebel factions. Lastly, the NTC's leaders are self-selected and it is dominated by officials from eastern Libya, giving it tenuous political legitimacy over the western half of the country.[43]

These are pertinent observations, but the key point is not so much the NTC's supposedly insufficient legitimacy as its meagre 'institutional capacity'. It was vital to develop this if the NTC was to be able eventually to fill the vacuum that would inevitably arise with the end of the Jamahiriyya and Qadhafi's departure. It could be developed only if the NTC began actively to govern the regions of Libya that were in rebel hands. The fact that much of Cyrenaica was in rebel hands from late February onwards gave the leaders of the rebellion the opportunity to establish a rival centre of state formation in eastern Libya, with its capital in Benghazi. The remarkable thing is that they did not take it. They tried to proceed directly to the overthrow of Qadhafi instead, when they were yet to possess anything remotely resembling a disciplined and competent army that they could call their own and so had to rely on external powers – France, the UK, the US, Qatar, the UAE et al. – to compensate for their crying deficit in the military sphere. They made no effort between February and August 2011 to establish new bodies under their authority to maintain order and security in the 'liberated' areas of eastern Libya. And the extent of their failure in this was made clear in the wake of the NTC's migration from Benghazi to Tripoli in August 2011, when it turned out that what they had left behind in Benghazi – and Cyrenaica as a whole – was a vacuum, promptly filled by militant federalists on the one hand and the welter of armed Islamist groups on the other, and the conditions for the murder of Ambassador Stevens and his associates were established.

Institutional capacity is not easily acquired. That a new political movement possesses substantial institutional capacity presupposes that its leaders possess something else: political ability. In lobbying President Sarkozy on the NTC's behalf in March 2011, Bernard-Henri Lévy talked up the political qualities of the NTC very vigorously. When it came to composing the narrative of his adventure six months later, Lévy could not resist recounting all the ways in which he had taken the lead in order to get his Libyan interlocutors to make elementary political moves.

Lévy's role did not end with his notorious phone call to the Élysée from Benghazi on 5 March; it began with it. He rendez-voused with Jibril in Paris, where they were joined by Ali Zeidan and Ali Essaoui, and himself attended their meeting with Sarkozy on 10 March.[44] On 14 March, the day Jibril met Hillary Clinton, Lévy drafted 'L'Appel de la dernière chance' addressed to 'Amis du monde entier' on behalf of the NTC, and secured its publication on 16 March in *La Règle du Jeu*, the literary review that Lévy had founded in 1990.[45] On 25 March, prompted by Sarkozy's mildly exasperated complaint that 'our friends in Benghazi' needed to be 'a little more apparent', he drafted, on Jibril's behalf, a letter from the NTC to President Sarkozy in which the NTC 'recognises France's pre-eminent role' (to which Jibril added a paragraph recognising Lévy's role).[46] Meanwhile, from 10 to 31 March Lévy spent his spare time in Paris lobbying left and right on the NTC's behalf, doing battle with the sceptics, swearing his geese were swans, before flying to New York to spend a week doing the same over there.[47] Back in Benghazi on 8 April, he attended a dinner offered by the chiefs of Libya's tribes at a farm near Benghazi and proposed to the gathering that they draw up a *Manifesto for a United Libya*. Having obtained his hosts' agreement to this, he then proceeded, aided by his sidekick Gilles Hertzog, to draft the text in question himself, as the numerous spelling mistakes of Arabic words confirm, and subsequently arranged for its eventual publication on 27 April under the title 'Toutes les Tribus de Libye ne font qu'une', accompanied by Lévy's 'décryptage', in *La Règle du Jeu* once more.[48] The next day he persuaded Abdul Jalil to deliver his first ever speech as chairman of the NTC and then drafted it for him.[49] Three days later, on 12 April, he himself addressed the populace of Benghazi in a speech delivered in the open air to the crowds on the Corniche.[50] The next day it was back to Paris to greet the rebellion's military commander, Qadhafi's former interior minister Abdelfattah Younis, and to shepherd him around his programme of meetings. A week later Lévy was busy helping to arrange for Mustafa Abdul Jalil himself at last to visit Paris in his turn.[51] On 20 April he was at Le Bourget to welcome Abdul Jalil and proceeded to give him detailed advice as to how to make the most of his talks with the French authorities, insisting notably that he should:

- remind Sarkozy of his invitation to Benghazi;
- remind Sarkozy of the French promise to Younis to 'arm the Berbers of the mountains';
- demand 300 special forces troops, to 'guide the airstrikes'; and
- demand the training, shared with the UK, of a unit of elite Libyan commandos with which, at the right moment, to capture Kufra.

In his lobbying for a military intervention, Lévy had exaggerated the extent of the NTC's authority and capacities wherever he went. But in his relations with its leading members and in his own behaviour, which, in the euphoria of late 2011, he felt he could safely recount in detail, he betrayed a very different assessment of his protégés' possibilities. If we assume that Lévy has not simply invented all this, was what he gave Abdul Jalil on 20 April advice, *or instructions*? By this stage Lévy had graduated from the cheerleader for the NTC he initially seemed to be to a role that went far beyond that of self-appointed *consigliere* and appoximated to that of minder if not road manager.

There is, I believe, a mystery here that remains to be elucidated. Whatever the truth regarding the precise nature of Lévy's personal engagement, it is clear that, in acute contrast to his sales talk about the NTC, he was well aware of its deficiencies where the political art was concerned and was working hard to compensate for these.

These deficiencies were inherent in the NTC's real nature. The NTC was what it said it was, a council.[52] It functioned as a secretive legislature that refused to undertake governing responsibilities. Although it eventually set up an 'Executive Board', it retained a supervisory authority in relation to this that hampered it, while failing to establish either an effective army or an effective police. In fact, the NTC failed so completely to do these things that it is difficult to suppress the thought that it actually did not want to do them.

To establish an effective army or police would have been to create or midwife bodies that would have quickly eclipsed the Council in terms of real power. But there is reason to think that to do this would also have offended a key feature of what we might well call the Libyan ideology – what the British anthropologist John Davis called 'the notion' (or 'image') 'of statelessness'. As he explained, this was both widespread in Libyan society and linked to 'the tribal rejection of government'.[53] And it was given a new lease of life following the discovery of huge deposits of high-quality oil, since this meant that the popular rejection of government from below would be reinforced from above by the state's ability to dispense with taxation and its corresponding freedom from social pressure to concede political representation.[54]

Chatham House's expectation that 'Gaddafism is done for without Gaddafi' took it for granted that the form of government in Libya owed everything to Qadhafi's wayward ideological outlook, and nothing to local realities or Libya's own traditions. This was a misapprehension founded on a failure to understand Libyan history. Qadhafi's Jamahiriyya was certainly peculiar but, far from being the gratuitous concoction of a madman, amounted to an idiosyncratic solution to a real problem: how to reconcile a nationalist ambition to establish a unitary nation-state with Libyan society's longstanding and profound antipathy to any state at all. His solution – encouraging the society to suppose that it was governing itself through People's Congresses and Revolutionary Committees while he and his associates were managing the distributive state and otherwise exercising power informally through personal networks mobilising kinship links and hinged on his own charisma – was objectionable from a Western liberal point of view but not at all absurd as is widely supposed. That this is the truth of the matter is borne out by the NTC's behaviour: its insistence, in deference to popular attitudes, that it was not a provisional government; its willingness to let the population manage its own affairs at the local level through local councils, whoever these consisted of and whether they were elected or not; and the fact that not only did it not integrate the *katā'ib* into a new model army or establish a new national police force but seems never to have seriously tried to do so.

The outcome was a new dispensation that, in addition to the weakness of its institutions, shared other features with its predecessor. The city or town councils which proliferated across the country, if unevenly, from February 2011 onwards, dominated by local notables, provided a kind of government acceptable to local populations which the Jamahiriyya's People's Congresses had ceased to offer. The military councils that headed up the *katā'ib*, the principal repositaries of revolutionary virtue, at city or district level, replaced Qadhafi's Revolutionary Committees.[55] Thus the old tandem of Popular Congresses and Revolutionary Committees had been replaced by a new tandem that was structurally similar to it, no matter how much the two tandems differed in their subjective content. But the neo-Jamahiriyya differed in structural terms from the original in one major respect: it had no Guide or 'Brother Leader', no head of state and no commander in chief. Qadhafism was dead in this respect, at least for the time being, but what this meant is that the neo-Jamahiriyya lacked the factor that made the Jamahiriyya functional and enabled the Libya it governed to conform to Weber's definition of a state and accordingly secure. The so-called revolution did not transcend Qadhafi's Jamahiriyya, it merely decapitated it, loosing anarchy upon the country in doing so.

The TNC never really led the rebellion against Qadhafi. The Libyan case is not an exception to the general rule that the Arab Spring uprisings were leaderless, but an instance of this, with unusually dreadful consequences – unusually dreadful, that is, until the Syrian uprising got going. By the time the TNC (subsequently NTC) was formed on 27 February 2011, this rebellion was in full swing, with no overall leadership but plenty of leaders at the local level making things happen: agitators organising demonstrations, local notables forming councils, veterans of the Libyan Islamic Fighting Group organising attacks on state institutions, defectors from Qadhafi's army taking their own initiatives. The NTC did not instigate these activities, it merely surfed on them. It made a point of including within itself representatives of as many local councils as it could as the foundation of its claim – directed to the outside world from the start – to be representative of the Libyan people. Inclusiveness did not imply coherence, but the opposite; nothing beyond the shared detestation of Qadhafi's regime – no agreed programme or strategy – united its membership and public audience. But *inclusiveness*, a key term in the lexicon of neo-liberalism's post-democratic discourse, worked where attracting Western support was concerned: the more inclusive it was, the more representative it could claim to be, the more legitimate it could be made to appear under Western eyes and the more legitimate Western (and Middle Eastern Arab) partisanship and interference could pretend to be. The trend of development embodied in the NTC disposed it to seek and depend upon external support as the core if not the whole of its strategy, since it was incapable of devising any other strategy for itself, while exposing its own shallow procedures to outside investment and manipulation. Lynch suggests that the NTC should be seen as the victim of the way Gulf Arab influence insinuated itself into its counsels.[56] But the truth is that it invited this, as it invited the insinuation of Western influence as well.

In Cairo, in the early hours of 22 February 2011, I drafted a memorandum in which I told my ICG colleagues that

> The great danger in immediate, not to say gung-ho, intervention by the 'international community' is that it could precipitate the fall of the Qadhafi regime and the disintegration of the entire power structure before any politically viable alternative to it has had time to cohere. If Libya becomes a power vacuum, it will also become a vortex which sucks other forces in.[57]

With the capture of Tripoli and the killing of Qadhafi, Libya became that vortex. After presiding fecklessly over the vortex for a year and systematically queering the pitch for its successors, the NTC dissolved itself, which is to say it abdicated. Abdication had been in its DNA from the beginning. But the replacement of a peculiar and exasperating state by a peculiar and exasperating vortex was the achievement of the international military intervention that got under way on 19 March 2011, notionally for humanitarian reasons but in reality to salvage the NTC, its reception committee, within which the vortex had existed in germ from the day it was set up.

V

The role of the Western powers was an integral feature of the Arab Spring. This role was comparatively discreet in Egypt in January–February 2011 and an oblique, irresolute and dissembling – although persistently mischievous – affair in Syria. But it was a self-righteous, mostly public and spectacular affair in the case of Libya, so it is the Libyan case which offers the opportunity to appreciate the Western role in depth and detail. Three controversial issues are at the centre of this story: the question of 'mission creep'; the question of whether an end to the war could have been negotiated with Qadhafi; and the question of whether the stated rationale of the intervention – to head off the massacre that was supposed to be in prospect in Benghazi – was ever more than a cynical pretext.

Lynch recognises that 'the military intervention in Libya opened the door to the proxy wars which would shape the fate of the Arab uprisings'.[58] But he tries to sustain his original positive view of this intervention, and of President Obama's decision to back it, claiming that

> The intervention succeeded in its short-term goal of protecting Libyan civilians by preventing a near-certain massacre ... Had Obama not acted, America would certainly have been blamed for allowing the uprising to end in bloodshed.[59]

The military intervention that Obama's action made possible did not prevent the uprising from ending in bloodshed. It determined the political content of the outcome, not the presence or absence of bloodshed at the finish, and it is entirely possible that it ensured that the blood of far more Libyans was shed than would have happened had Qadhafi managed to end the uprising in March. The bloodshed in which the uprising ended was accepted as an integral aspect of the intervention's success. Lynch is confusing the issue here; whether or not the uprising would end in bloodshed was never the question. What was at issue is whether a massacre was 'near-certain'.

This claim was the principal justification for the intervention. The House of Commons Foreign Affairs Committee discounted this claim in its September 2016 report, noting that 'the proposition that Muammar Gaddafi would have ordered the massacre of civilians in Benghazi was not supported by the available evidence'.[60] This judgment quickly provoked the ire of Bernard-Henri Lévy:

> Sarkozy and Cameron are criticised in the committee's report for overstating the threat Gaddafi posed to civilians and acting without first taking the time to 'verify the real threat that the Gaddafi regime posed to civilians'. Like the other arguments, this is just not serious. How do you verify 'a real threat'? Should we have waited (as happened in Syria) until 100,000 people had died . . .?[61]

I yield to no one in my disinclination to agree with anything M. Lévy may say, but he has a point here. The Committee's judgment was made five and a half years after the event. The question is what judgement could and should have been made in the heat and dust of the action, at high noon. Lévy's counter-claim that the only sound judgment that could and should have been made at high noon was the judgment he himself made – that a military intervention was indispensable to prevent the massacre that would otherwise have occurred – is entirely false. But it is scarcely to the credit of the House of Commons that its Foreign Affairs Committee finally got it right five and half years after the event. The question that should have been addressed is why the House of Commons got it wrong in March 2011 and allowed Cameron to wage his gratuitous and indefensible war. For the truth of the matter is that *all the available evidence at the time indicated clearly that a massacre of civilians was neither imminent nor likely.*

Citing Qadhafi's speeches, Lynch argues that

to an international community primed by memories of Rwanda and Srebrenica, and guided by a highly partisan Arab media, his words signified impending doom . . . The Obama administration blanched at the prospect of what one senior official vividly warned could quickly become 'Srebrenica on steroids'.[62]

Whatever 'the international community' – which exists only as a figure of speech in the rhetoric of Western warmongers – may be primed by is not my problem, but it should not be necessary to spend long on the comparisons with Rwanda and Srebrenica.

That these were false analogies was self-evident to me at the time, as I explained to my ICG colleagues. The slaughter in Rwanda and Bosnia arose out of conflicts between distinct populations defined by their respective ethnic identities: Hutu and Tutsi, Bosnian Muslims and Serbs. The conflict in Libya pitted Qadhafi, his regime and its supporters against their opponents; the issue was an entirely political one, not an ethnic one. (The one element of ethnic cleansing that occurred, as a sideshow of the main drama, was the work of rebel elements targeting and often lynching 'Africans' on the pretext that they were 'mercenaries' in Qadhafi's pay; the Qadhafi regime committed no acts of this kind.) The social conditions for 'another Srebrenica' – let alone 'another Rwanda' – were conspicuous for their absence. It is an index of the degree of hysteria that had been whipped up by mid-March 2011 that such rubbish should have been taken seriously by anyone. It is, or should be, a sobering thought that this rubbish was entertained and recycled by senior figures in the Obama administration and the British government.

That this was the truth of the matter is tacitly acknowledged by Achcar. Although he approved of the intervention, he does not pretend that the situation of Benghazi resembled Rwanda or Bosnia. He opts instead for the superficially more plausible analogy with what happened in Syria in 1982, when security forces of Hafez al-Asad's regime, under the command of his brother Rif'at, slaughtered thousands in quelling a revolt in the city of Hama.[63] Achcar fully endorses the Western powers' pretext for intervening but he argues that what they really feared was another Hama and that they were right to do so (although none of them spoke of another Hama).[64]

No one knows for sure how many died in Hama. The lowest credible estimate is 5,000. Many higher estimates – 10,000, 20,000, 30,000, even 40,000 – exist, and have to be taken seriously.[65] There is no doubt the carnage was dreadful. The massacre came after several years of a Muslim Brothers' terrorist campaign against the regime, including numerous assassinations of regime officials. The regime's siege of Hama was a reaction to an uprising in the city, instigated by the Brothers, which began with the proclamation of jihad from the minarets of the city's mosques and was swiftly followed by the murders of seventy regime officials and party members in twenty-four hours. The regime's response clearly reflected the decision to end the three-and-a-half-year-long insurgency once and for all. This was the final settling of accounts with the Muslim Brothers, after years of violence which the Brothers had initiated.[66]

But Achcar's analogy with Hama will not work. Hama was encircled by Rif'at al-Asad's security forces. It was completely sealed off and then the districts held by the insurgents were pulverised.[67] Benghazi was not encircled or sealed off. Qadhafi's troops were encamped on the southern edge of the city – that is, the vanguard units were; according to the *Telegraph*, citing Al Jazeera, Qadhafi's troops were still advancing towards Benghazi along the road from Ajdabiya at 20.16 hours on the evening of 18 March – and the northern and eastern sides of the city were open and free of egress.[68] I asked the Libya specialist I had commissioned to research and write the ICG report on Libya what she thought the rebels were likely to do. Her answer was that they would withdraw from the city and take to the countryside and the mountains. The highlands known as

Al-Jabal al-Akhdar (the Green Mountain), are not far to the east and would have provided a refuge and new base for the rebels, or at least a secure staging post on their escape route to Egypt. She saw no reason to expect them to stay in the city to be rounded up or wiped out and neither did I. So the analogy with Hama joins the analogies with Rwanda and Srebrenica in the waste-paper basket.

This leaves the apologists of the intervention with one final argument, the argument from Qadhafi's rhetoric. Lynch rests much of his case on this.

> On February 22, Qaddafi warned that he would mow down protestors with tanks if need be. Such extremely hard-line rhetoric, aimed at domestic audiences, badly undermined his prospects abroad. Qaddafi's tone may have been intended to restore the fear and perceived inevitability upon which his regime had for decades depended. But such public commitments created their own reality ... His apocalyptic language thus played into the hands of the Libyan opposition and their Arab backers. The exterminationist language helped them enormously in their campaign to win American and ultimately United Nations and NATO military backing.[69]

Lynch here gives a misleading paraphrase of Qadhafi's speech of 22 February 2011; nowhere in this did Qadhafi warn that he would 'mow down protestors with tanks'. He referred to the use of tanks to repress protests in China (Tiananmen Square in June 1989) and Russia (the bombardment of the Duma ordered by Boris Yeltsin in October 1993) but repeatedly spoke of mobilising not tanks but a march of his supporters to deal with the situation in Libya. Moreover, not only did he distinguish between the rebels and the civilian population in general, but he further distinguished, within the rebellion, between the instigators and leaders of this on the one hand and, on the other hand, the young people involved, who, he suggested, were being manipulated, and made it clear that it was not these but the ringleaders that he was after.[70] As for his speech on 17 March, which was the speech that really mattered as far as his intentions towards the people of Benghazi were concerned, this repeatedly made clear that he was coming after the diehard rebels and nobody else.

> Those who would surrender their weapons, who come in without their arms, we will forgive them and will have an amnesty for those who put down their weapons . . . Throw away your weapons and we will collect these and you are safe . . . Those infidels and traitors, we'll have to deal with, we promise to deal with, but the peaceful individuals of our people should remain, whether they want to stay at home or go out to the squares. But they should put down their weapons, throw away their weapons. There is no danger. They should not feel unsafe . . . Those who have been forced to follow the infidels . . . those also will be forgiven, will be granted amnesty . . . The world has to see . . . that Benghazi is a free city. It is not a city of traitors.[71]

The fact that Qadhafi offered an amnesty in this speech was reported at the time in the daily paper *USA Today*, in addition to the *New York Times* and news agencies,[72] and must have been known to the US government and other governments, but they ignored it. Moreover, in offering an amnesty on this occasion, Qadhafi was repeating what he had said a fortnight earlier, prior to his forces' counter-offensive, on 2 March.[73]

The propaganda of the warmongers cherrypicked Qadhafi's speeches, latching onto a few fierce phrases here and there and ignoring everything else. This propaganda has had staying power. In his oral evidence to the House of Commons Foreign Affairs Committee (FAC) on 19 January 2016, Lord Hague, who was foreign secretary in 2011, claimed 'we had to make a decision about what to do in the face of the threat to Benghazi, and the possibility – indeed, the stated intention – that the Gaddafi Government would kill large numbers of people'.[74] That claim was a lie. And it speaks volumes about the seriousness of the FAC's 'examination' that Lord Hague was allowed to get away with it. What one pundit has called 'Gaddafi's fixation on making a bloody example of Benghazi' was a myth from start to finish.[75] There never was any such 'stated intention', as the former foreign secretary, who was served while in office by MI6, must have known.

When read in their entirety Qadhafi's speeches provide no indication that he intended to perpetrate a general massacre in Benghazi, but clear evidence of exactly the opposite intention.

Ironically it is Lévy, the French mountebank, who gives the game away. At yet another unguarded moment in his self-celebrating narrative, he compares the Qadhafis to the Ceauşescus, betraying what one suspects he knew perfectly well all along: Benghazi was never the Libyan Srebrenica or the Libyan Hama; it was the Libyan Timişoara.[76]

VI

The Libyan war of 2011 indisputably turned out to be a regime-change war. The thesis that this was the result of 'mission creep' presupposes that the war began as something else. This is the view to which the House of Commons Foreign Affairs Committee clings, when it asserts that 'a limited intervention to protect civilians drifted into a policy of regime change by military means'.[77] Thus the burden of the committee's critique of David Cameron's handling of this matter is that decisions were made in regrettable haste, in disregard of 'the available evidence', but there is no suggestion that they were not made in good faith. The intention was good, the fear of a massacre was genuine and the mission was indeed meant to protect civilians, but things then 'drifted' and went awry. If anyone was to blame for this drift, it was, we are assured, Sarkozy and the French; for, as Lord Richards told the Committee, the problem was that the French military had not built into its game plan the possibility of a pause after Qadhafi had been forced to withdraw from Benghazi, and so the 'limited intervention' just went on and on, and 'morphed' of its own accord into a war to the finish.[*] [78] In

---

[*] Sir David Richards was created a life peer with the title Baron Richards of Herstmonceux in February 2014.

fact, Lord Richards's view was a mild version of the thesis that the 'mission creep' was Paris's fault. The Committee's collective finding went much further, stating that 'France led the international community in advancing the case for military action in February and March 2011. UK policy followed decisions taken in France.'[79] This version of events is not reliable at all.

It is possible to take seriously the view that the war began as 'a limited intervention to protect civilians' only if we confine ourselves to the Committee's remarkably narrow consideration of the events of mid-March 2011. The moment we widen our gaze, an entirely different view of the logic of these events becomes possible, if not mandatory. The decision to treat the approach of Qadhafi's troops to Benghazi as the preliminary to a crime against humanity, and thus as a *casus belli*, can be properly appraised only if we look at what preceded it.

The drive to war began on 21 February in the form of the widely canvassed demand for a no-fly zone, prompted by the sensational but entirely mendacious reports that Qadhafi's air force was slaughtering peaceful demonstrators. This propaganda lie was given global reach by Al Jazeera, as previously noted, but, as I subsequently discovered, it did not originate there. The first instance of it that I have seen was on CNN on 19 February, but it was not given emphasis, appearing only in paragraph fourteen, in the words, 'hovering helicopters fired into the crowds'.[80] It was then picked up by the British press the next day, in a story on Libya in the *Daily Telegraph*, the first paragraph of which began: 'Snipers shot protesters, artillery and helicopter gunships were used against crowds of demonstrators.'[81] Thus as a big story the aerial slaughter lie was *made in London*, with Al Jazeera simply amplifying it, and it was London, not Paris, which took up the demand for a no-fly zone. President Sarkozy had joined the chorus of condemnation of the regime's repression but in less vehement terms than David Cameron, and had initially called for a political solution, not military intervention. On 25 February he went with the flow in declaring that 'Mr Gaddafi must leave' but also warned that 'regarding a military intervention ... France would consider any initiative of this type with extreme caution and reserve'.[82]

This position reflected the concern of an important element – possibly the majority – of French senior officials that the destruction of the Libyan state could have major destabilising effects in the Sahel, notably in Mali and Niger, as well as severely impacting Tunisia, and in some degree Algeria as well, a concern shared by at least some senior officials in Whitehall.[83]

The international condemnation of the repression was strong enough to get a resolution through the United Nations Security Council on 26 February; UNSC 1970 imposed sanctions and an arms embargo, and referred Qadhafi to the International Criminal Court, but said nothing about a military intervention or a no-fly zone.[84] The Pentagon and President Obama were no more keen to get the US into another war than was the French government.[85] As for the British government, it could not publicly champion a military intervention until several hundred British nationals, in addition to most of the embassy staff, had been brought home from various points in Libya on 25–26 February but, once these matters were resolved, Cameron started pressing for a no-fly zone, as he told the House of Commons on 28 February.[86] In the meantime, on 26 February, President Obama had declared that Qadhafi 'had lost the legitimacy to rule and needs to do what is right for his country by leaving now'.[87] On 27 February the NTC had announced its existence to the world and Hillary Clinton had declared that the US would assist the opposition.[88]

These developments occurred against the backdrop of the rapid spread of the rebellion across much of the country and, crucially, to the west, notably Misrata, Zawiya and Zuwara on the coast and Nalut and Zintan inland, south-west of Tripoli in the Nafusa mountains, home of Libya's Berbers.[89] 'Muammar Gaddafi isolated in Tripoli bolthole,' reported the *Guardian* on 23 February; the influential blog Informed Comment reported, '90% of Libya in rebel hands' the next day, and the apparently unstoppable progress of the revolt continued over the following days.[90] This was the context in which the British government let it be known that it was heading moves to plan a military intervention.[91]

In its rhetoric at this juncture, the British government surfed uninhibitedly on the *Telegraph*'s and Al Jazeera's fake news story. The UK's ambassador to the UN, Peter Gooderham, had already given credence to this on 25 February, in the run-up to the Security Council debate the next day.[92] Cameron followed suit on 1 March when he declared that it was not 'acceptable to have a situation where Colonel Gaddafi can be murdering his own people using airplanes and helicopter gunships', although he had made no mention of this mendacious claim in addressing the House of Commons the previous day.[93] The same day, 1 March, Foreign Secretary William Hague even claimed that a no-fly zone would be 'legal' without a UN Security Council mandate.[94] This was immediately rejected by his French opposite number Alain Juppé, who insisted that there would be no military intervention without a UN mandate, a position promptly reiterated by French prime minister François Fillon.[95] In Washington the next day, moreover, the chairman of the Joint Chiefs of Staff, Admiral Mike Mullen, told the House Appropriations Sub-Committee on Defense that he and his colleagues 'have not been able to confirm that any of the Libyan aircraft have fired on their own people'.[96] This fact was given no media coverage at all, but it would have been noted by all Western governments. Continued deployment of this fake news story by representatives of these governments accordingly assumed the character of lies.

In the meantime, the original, non-violent, peaceful democracy protestors of the Western media's collective imagination had morphed into armed *thuwwār* (revolutionaries) who appeared to be carrying all before them, so the original, purportedly humanitarian, considerations underlying the initial denunciation of Qadhafi's behaviour no longer seemed so cogent. But then the tide turned in the military situation as Qadhafi's forces began to retake the towns that had been initially overrun by the rebellion: Bin Jawad on 6 March, Zawiya on 10 March, Ras Lanuf the next day.[97] It was at this point that Western discourse underwent a key development.

Cameron and Hague were wedded to their proposal of a no-fly zone. The problem was that not only the US government and Obama in particular (not to mention Russia) but also NATO and the European Union remained reluctant to endorse let alone actively support a military intervention, and the prospect of securing the UN mandate that Paris had insisted was indispensable was accordingly uncertain to say the least.[98] Hague defined the terms of a solution to this problem on 8 March when he declared that a no-fly zone would have to have 'a clear legal basis, a demonstrable need and strong international support and broad support in the region and a readiness to participate in it'.[99] This approach was adopted by NATO at a meeting of defence ministers in Brussels on 11 March; the meeting agreed to continue planning for all military options but withheld endorsement of the no-fly zone demand, with Secretary-General Anders Fogh Rasmussen echoing Hague's three main criteria, if in a slimmed down version, in his own statement that 'demonstrable need ... a clear legal basis ... and ... firm regional support' were all required.[100]

'Broad' (or 'firm') 'regional support' was initially understood to mean the support not only of the Arab League but also of the African Union.[101] What remained at issue was the meaning of 'demonstrable need'.* Hague gave his interpretation of this on 8 March:

> Clearly it is unacceptable that Colonel Gaddafi unleashes so much violence on his own people and we are all gravely concerned about what would happen if he were to try to do that *on an even greater basis* [emphasis added].[102]

This line was amplified by Cameron later that day when he spoke of the need to

> prepare for what we might have to do if he goes on brutalising his own people. I had a phone call with president Obama this afternoon to talk about the planning we have to do in case this continues and *in case he does terrible things* to his own people [emphasis added].[103]

---

* NATO's own communiqué speaks of 'demonstrable need, a clear legal mandate and solid support from the region': 'NATO ready to support international efforts on Libya', 10 March 2011.

It was by this time tacitly accepted that a civil war was in progress and that the regime could not be expected not to try to win this. It followed that its efforts to defeat the armed rebellion did not in themselves justify international military intervention. As the *Guardian* reported on 9 March, Hague's 'on an even greater basis' criterion and Cameron's 'terrible things' criterion would apply 'if aerial bombing by pro-Gaddafi forces causes mass civilian casualties'.[104] NATO's 'demonstrable need' criterion meant 'a major atrocity by Gaddafi against civilians' but it was recognised that there was as yet no sign of this; as a NATO source told the *Guardian* that same day, 'Gaddafi ... had not done enough to trigger intervention under international law.'[105] So the *Guardian* concluded on 10 March that 'unless there is an atrocity in Libya, the chances of military intervention are increasingly slim'.[106]

Qadhafi's forces recaptured Brega on 13 March, Zuwara (in the west) on 14 March and Ajdabiya on 17 March, which left them poised to recapture Benghazi.[107] They did all this without committing any atrocity; in most of these engagements the death toll was barely in three figures. It was consequently necessary to invent the 'major atrocity' that had not yet happened, in the shape of the 'mass civilian casualties' that it was claimed were certain to happen in Benghazi unless a military intervention forestalled them. In this way the Western powers and their Gulf Arab allies abandoned the preconditions for their intervention that they had themselves established, ignoring all three of their own criteria of justification: no atrocity had occurred, the African Union had refused its support,[108] and, to cap it all, the Security Council Resolution 1973 that supposedly authorised the intervention was immediately complied with by Qadhafi when he announced his agreement to the Resolution's first demand of a ceasefire, an exasperating detail which Cameron and Obama and the NTC promptly dismissed as neither here nor there.[109]

The point is that London was playing hunt-the-trigger before Qadhafi got anywhere near Benghazi. Cameron and Hague were looking for a pretext for military intervention, to turn NATO and Obama round, before the alleged prospect of a

massacre offered itself. And the criterion of what would constitute a trigger had to be drastically watered down to make the
alleged prospect of a massacre meet the bill.

There was no 'mission creep', no 'drift' to a regime change
war because the intervention was never about protecting civilians but always about regime change, as the director of the CIA,
Leon Panetta, acknowledged some weeks later.[110] If it had been
about protecting civilians, it would not have taken place because
there was no demonstrable need for it. But Barack Obama was
incapable of thinking for himself about this faraway country of
which he knew nothing, and once he had been panicked by the
hysteria-inducing talk of Rwanda and Srebrenica into changing
his stance on 17 March, all the Western ducks were in a row and
regime change could proceed. No massacre was imminent, but
the fantasy of the prospect of one had been conjured into existence. The logic was not that a military intervention was needed
to prevent a massacre but that the deliberately fabricated and
wholly false prospect of a massacre was needed to justify the
military intervention which had been resolved upon for quite
other reasons.

VII

Lord Richards was not alone in being concerned at the refusal
to mark a pause that would have allowed for negotiations with
Qadhafi once the operation around Benghazi had ended. Several
senior generals and Pentagon officials were so dismayed that
negotiations were being ruled out, for which they blamed Hillary
Clinton, that they took the extraordinary step of opening their
own line of communication with the Qadhafis and exchanged
several messages with them before being emphatically ordered
to stop it.[111]

Sarkozy, not Clinton, was the source of the problem. The veto
on negotiation with Qadhafi at any point at all after 17 March
was the condition of French participation in the military effort.
Sarkozy also tried to secure an independent role for France but
was obliged to accept the NATO framework and the American

hegemony this implied. To compensate for and mask the reality of this subordinate role, France and its client, Lebanon, were allowed to do the honours in proposing UNSC 1973 (in reality mainly drafted by Susan Rice, with British assistance), and Sarkozy then indulged himself and France in a theatrical display of purely symbolic independence and 'leadership' on 19 March, sending French jets to open the aerial assault on Qadhafi's troops ahead of the agreed timetable. In this way, Sarkozy's France appeared to leapfrog over its British and American allies, transforming itself from reluctant recruit to eager frontrunner. But this was just for show; the important point was Sarkozy's insistence that there should be no negotiations. London and Washington evidently agreed to this condition and Clinton simply stuck to that agreement thereafter. What motivated it?

The French government's longstanding concern for stability in North and West Africa only partially explains Sarkozy's initial reluctance; he had his own, very personal, reason for this too. And it was his personal predicament that explained his veto on negotiations with Qadhafi once he had finally committed himself to participating in the military intervention.

Neither Cameron nor Obama had a personal political invest-ment in Qadhafi that could inhibit them from going to war, but Sarkozy had. As interior minister in 2002–4 and 2005–7, he had naturally had dealings with Qadhafi concerning security and immigration issues, and had visited Tripoli on several occasions; once elected president, he hosted Qadhafi's state visit to France in December 2007 and concluded important trade deals. Hugely embarrassed by the outcome of the events in Tunisia, where his foreign minister, Michèle Alliot-Marie, had imprudently supported President Ben Ali to the extent of publicly offering him French *savoir-faire* in suppressing unrest, Sarkozy clearly decided he had no option but to join the international chorus calling on Qadhafi to go, but dragged his feet when invited to support military action. Under pressure from London, he seems to have decided that he had to show willing, while quietly counting on Robert Gates and Hillary Clinton, not to mention NATO and the EU, to ensure that Obama would not back Cameron's drive to war. His strategy of running with both the hare and the hounds nearly worked.

This is why Bernard Henri-Lévy was necessary to the warmongers. The initial *casus belli*, Qadhafi's alleged recourse to aerial slaughter of peaceful demonstrators, had been demolished by the testimony of Gates and Admiral Mike Mullen on 2 March and a new reason to oppose Qadhafi was needed. Lévy supplied this once he got to Benghazi on 5 March. 'I have just met the Libyan Massouds,' he told an initially bemused Sarkozy as soon as he got through to the Élysée on his cell phone.[112] The reference here was to Ahmed Shah Massoud (1953–2001), 'the Lion of the Panjshir', the iconic commander of the Tajik forces in north-eastern Afghanistan who led opposition to the Soviet-backed regime in Kabul and later kept the Taliban at bay for years. In short, the new case for intervening was that the NTC were heroes, authentic resistance fighters and, ideologically speaking, fully deserving of France's support in the civil war that was now under way, irrespective of whatever Qadhafi could or could not be accused of. At this point, when the rebels seemed to be carrying all before them, Lévy's suggestion was tempting enough for Sarkozy to embrace it to the extent of publicly 'saluting' the NTC in the name of France. But then Qadhafi's forces started regaining ground, and the Libyan Massouds no longer looked like winners, so Lévy reverted to a variant of the original pseudo-humanitarian case: if France allowed the rebellion to be crushed, the Tricolore would be spattered with the blood of the Libyan rebels.[113] Why did this pseudo-patriotic *chantage* work on Sarkozy?

On 16 March 2011, Euronews published an interview with Saif al-Islam Qadhafi in which he accused Sarkozy of accepting Libyan money to finance his election campaign in 2007 and demanded that the money be returned, adding 'we are ready to reveal everything'.[114] An interview which his father gave to *Le Figaro* around this time, in which Qadhafi accused Sarkozy of betraying him, was suppressed; it was broadcast by France 3 in 2014.[115] In March 2012, the French online investigative journal Mediapart began publishing stories and supporting documents alleging that Sarkozy's 2007 presidential election campaign had been illegally financed to the tune of €50 million (£42 million) by the Libyan government, and that the deal had been negotiated in Tripoli by close colleagues of Sarkozy.[116] That such a deal was agreed in principle has been established; doubt remains as to whether the money was ever actually received by Sarkozy, and this aspect of the story is currently *sub judice*.

February–March 2011 was not the best time for this story to break from Sarkozy's point of view, and his only hope of preventing it was to succeed in his tightrope act and hold out to the end against the military intervention he never favoured, since without his full support Cameron could not expect to swing Obama. This was the ace in his hand, and it was Lévy's mission to trump it, which he managed to do, cornering Sarkozy by supplying arguments for French participation in a military intervention that he could not easily dismiss; moreover, it is entirely possible that Lévy had advance knowledge of the story that Euronews broke on 16 March, and that Sarkozy knew this. It seems that the Qadhafis understood Sarkozy's situation and held their version of the story back until it became clear, between 10 and 14 March, that he had finally crumpled under the pressure and joined the war party in earnest.

The Euronews interview was ignored by the rest of the Western media. Its influence on events was that of a lesson and a warning to the Western leaders; it showed what could happen in the event of a negotiation, when Qadhafi finally had the opportunity to be listened to and heard. Sarkozy simply could not risk this. Cameron, Clinton and Obama went along with him and Qadhafi was a dead man walking from that point on, his declarations ignored or distorted, his role in Western eyes solely that of target, as his end made clear. 'We came, we saw, he died,' chortled Hillary Clinton, acknowledging Washington's share of responsibility for the lynching as well as for the policy that had required Qadhafi dead whatever the cost.[117]

Given the political weakness of the NTC, a serious negotiation with the regime to secure agreement on the modalities of the transition to a post-Jamahiriyya Libya was an indispensable condition of preserving a minimum of state continuity and public order, let alone the possibility of an eventual evolution towards any measure of democracy. The refusal of the intervening powers to countenance a negotiation at any point doomed Libya to the anarchy that has ravaged it ever since.

6

The Playing of Tahrir Square

In Libya, an armed rebellion against Qadhafi was co-opted by the Western powers and Gulf monarchies and turned into a war for regime change in a manner which ensured the disintegration of Libya into prolonged anarchy and consecrated Qatar, Saudi Arabia and the United Arab Emirates into independent actors in the military sphere. In the process, the Arab spring pivoted in a way that anticipated and prepared the ground for the destruction of Syria. It would not have pivoted in this way had it not been for the massive determining influence of London and Paris at this precise juncture, which it takes a truly exceptional American myopia to overlook. But this was not the first time the Arab Spring pivoted in a new direction under Western influence. The first instance of such pivoting occurred in Egypt and established the conditions which precluded a democratic outcome of the Egyptian uprising and made possible the resurgence of the Free Officers' state in its most brutal ever version at the expense of the actors of the uprising and the aspirations which had motivated them.

The fall of Mubarak did not occur as the achievement of a revolution; it was the achievement of a military coup that was carried out on the back of a mass protest movement that, having for the most part no sense of direction, no precise idea of where to go from Tahrir Square, demanded the departure of Mubarak as an end in itself – that is, as a fetish. In this way, the Arab

Spring crystallised, with Western blessing, as a movement that sought merely to evict the reigning autocrat in one country after another, with no wider ends in view, and so in a manner consistent with Western interests, in a series of episodes that vainly imitated formal aspects of the Tunisian revolution without emulating it. In the immediate Egyptian context, the significance of the way Mubarak fell is that it took Egyptian politics out of the existing constitutional framework when the forces capable of giving Egypt a new democratic constitution did not exist. The extreme gravity of the implications of this development was obscured by the mindless enthusiasm with which not only the protesters but above all the Western media greeted and celebrated this event.

The ins and outs of what happened during the eighteen critical days from 25 January to 11 February 2011 are almost entirely ignored by most authors who have discoursed upon the Arab Spring. Achcar offers a brisk political economy of the outcome of the uprising which has the merit of recognising that this was a coup rather than a revolution while leaving open the possibility that the revolution was ongoing, with the army's coup a discrete moment in a more profound process, but he does not attempt to provide a political history of the uprising. Worth and Kirkpatrick both provide accounts of 'Police Day' (25 January) and the 'Day of Anger' (28 January) that convey the drama and exhilaration of the first stages of the uprising, but largely ignore what was happening on the regime's end of events and the concessions Mubarak offered in his speech on the night of 31 January–1 February. The drama continues in their accounts with the 'Battle of the Camel' (2–3 February) and the violence this involved, but then they fast-forward to the intoxicating dénouement of Mubarak's fall on 11 February, saying precisely nothing about the intervening nine days. It is as if the logic of events could be taken for granted, as if the fall of Mubarak was a matter of course and could be celebrated unconditionally, whatever had really brought it about and irrespective of its consequences. Except that we – and now they – know better.

Worth remarks of those first heady days of the Arab Spring that 'in that moment, to be cold and reasonable felt almost like treason' and, of the insurgents, 'you could not help rooting for them'.[1] This is a plausible explanation of the character of Western media coverage of the Egyptian uprising, not to mention its successors. The inability of Western journalists to think about the implications of the events they were witnessing because of the intensity of their identification with the protesters and rebels they were observing was not the least striking feature of the story they were covering. While it was natural and inevitable that the courageous Egyptians in Tahrir Square and elsewhere should have experienced Mubarak's fall as a resounding victory, the world's media offered no counterpoint to their wishful thinking when a counterpoint was badly needed.

To appraise Mubarak's fall as an unqualified victory for the people was to assume that the uprising was indeed a revolution and that the revolution was a success and on course for further successes. It accordingly displaced the question that eventually arose – when did it all go wrong? – to a later stage.

II

Achcar's answer to this question can be inferred from his answer to the related question: Who was to blame? In addition to the 'deep state', the other villain of the story, as he tells it, was the Society of the Muslim Brothers. The 'deep state' owed no loyalty to the revolution and its counter-revolutionary impulses could be taken for granted and should have been anticipated. But, in Achcar's view, the revolution was not merely defeated, it was betrayed – and it was the Muslim Brothers who betrayed it. Moreover, they betrayed it repeatedly: when they agreed to meet Mubarak's newly appointed vice president, Omar Suleiman, on 6 February 2011;[2] when they supported the SCAF's interim constitutional revision on 19 March 2011, despite the opposition of liberals and leftists to this;[3] when they took part in the legislative elections in November 2011–January 2012, dissociating themselves from the liberals' and leftists' protests against the SCAF at that juncture; and when, following Mohamed Morsi's election to the presidency in June 2012, they made further concessions to the

SCAF, pursued a neo-liberal economic policy and then tried to drive through a controversial new constitution.

The 'revolution betrayed' thesis is distinct from the claim that the success of the demonstrations in Tahrir Square and elsewhere was the achievement of liberals and leftists but then hijacked by the Islamists. This claim, supported by Hazem Kandil among others, was given wide credence in Western media coverage.[4] As David Kirkpatrick ruefully comments,

> We set ourselves up for disappointment. 'Where did it go?' I was often asked later, in New York or London. What happened to the non-violent, secular-minded, Western-friendly, Silicon Valley uprising that we cheered in Tahrir Square? Who stole that revolution? That image of the revolution was as much about Western narcissism as it was about Egypt.[5]

This narcissism prevented the Western media from seeing clearly. As both he and Robert Worth show, the uprising was by no means purely 'secular-minded'; the Muslim Brothers were involved in the protests from the outset. Worth provides an especially poignant account of the political itinerary of Mohamed Beltagy, an impressively energetic and courageous activist who was a leading light of the MB members who were in Tahrir Square on 25 January and throughout the next seventeen days. Beltagy and his followers got to Tahrir Square at about midnight, but other young Brothers and Sisters had been there for hours. As Worth and Kirkpatrick both report, a committee formed in mid-January to organise the first protest included members of the MB's youth wing.[6] Kirkpatrick further reports: 'A female Brotherhood lawmaker led a contingent of Islamist women who pushed through police lines all the way to Tahrir Square. Islamist women may have been the first to make it.'[7] Moreover, Kirkpatrick rightly records the Brothers' role in helping to provide organisational coherence to the Tahrir Square occupation thereafter, in organising field hospitals and other logistical requirements and especially in defending the occupation against the violent assault of the *baltagīya* (thugs) during the Battle of the Camel (on 2–3 February). Worth sums things up with the comment that the Islamists 'were the ones who'd made the uprising succeed, with their numbers, their discipline, their bravery under attack'.[8]

The sole basis for the claim that the Brothers hijacked a revolution made by others is the fact that the MB leadership officially supported the protest only on 27 January, not before then, while allowing MB members to take part as individuals. This delay is easily explained. There was no certainty whatever on 25 January that the protest planned for that day would be a success and for the MB to endorse it from the start would have been foolhardy in the extreme in view of the huge assets it had to protect, its organisation and membership, and the extensive network of charities and businesses that it had built up since the early 1970s. The 'revolutionaries', such as Ahmed Maher's 6 April Youth Movement, and liberals, such as Mohamed ElBaradei's supporters, had only very modest organisational assets to put at risk or none at all. Moreover, the reticence of the Muslim Brothers' leaders also served the cause of the protest; had they endorsed it on day one, they would have been making a gift to the regime, enabling it to denounce the seizure of Tahrir Square as an Islamist insurrection. And whether or not this ploy had worked, they could have been accused by the secular activists of claiming ownership of the movement – that is, precisely, of hijacking it.

The hijacking thesis is groundless. The 'revolution betrayed' thesis differs from it in acknowledging that the Brothers played a part in the Egyptian 'revolution', as Stalin and his supporters played a part in the Russian revolution before incurring Trotsky's charge of subsequently betraying it. But for Achcar to put forward this thesis is problematic, given that he had already insisted that what overthrew Mubarak 'was quite clearly a conservative coup'.[9] There had been an impressive popular protest movement which did not overthrow Mubarak and then a military coup which did.* Where, then, was there a revolution for the Brothers to betray?

---

* In addition to ICG, which described the overthrow of Mubarak as a coup in the report it published on 24 February 2011, the coup thesis has also been firmly supported by Tamir Moustafa, 'Law in the Egyptian revolt', *Middle East Law and Government*, 3, 2011, 181–91, at 189.

The answer appears to be that, for Achcar, a revolution, in the sense of a radical social as well as political change that would have not only superseded authoritarian government but also challenged the prevailing neo-liberal economic order, was – or at any rate ought to have been – still, somehow or other, in the making, irrespective of what had actually happened in general and the SCAF's decisive moves in particular. That is, that the making of the revolution had its being in the realms of his and others' wishful thoughts and nowhere else, as an immanent act that existed within the mind without producing external effects.

The immanent social as well as political revolution is indispensable to his argument about Egypt as the allegedly imminent Benghazi massacre is indispensable to his argument about Libya. Achcar reinforces this desperate case for the betrayal thesis with his insistence that the Muslim Brothers, as Islamic fundamentalists, were *ipso facto* reactionary and therefore inherently counter-revolutionary, subjectively and objectively; as inveterate counter-revolutionaries *ex hypothesi*, they *must* have betrayed a revolution somewhere along the line. Thus his thesis relies heavily on a cluster of deductions from left-secularist dogma (with which, we should note, adherents of at least some other varieties of Marxism would disagree).

A more reasonable answer to this question would be that the complex process begun on 25 January and punctuated by a military coup on 11 February did not end there but continued, if in a messy fashion, and had or could at least be reasonably believed to have the potential to amount to what might deserve the name of revolution to the extent that a significant measure of democracy superseded the authoritarian *ancien regime*. But, in that case, when the democratically elected Muslim Brother president – the first president of Egypt ever to be elected in a genuinely contested pluralist election – was deposed *manu militari*, it was not only the SCAF but also those forces calling for, facilitating and then celebrating this violation of the new democratic norm (that is, the liberals and the Left) who were the counter-revolutionaries. But this is not the answer Achcar wishes to give us.

III

The outlook of the Muslim Brothers was neither revolutionary nor counter-revolutionary; it was reformist. Sunni doctrine enjoins submission to a Muslim ruler, even an unjust or incompetent one; rebellion against a Muslim ruler is *fitna*, sedition, division of the *umma* (the community of believers), the supreme evil to be avoided at all costs. Sunni Islamists can adopt a revolutionary stance only if they first convincingly judge a professedly Muslim ruler to be a fraud, that is if they engage in *takfir*, the procedure of judging and condemning something – such as a regime – as impious (*kufr*), and its nominally Muslim ruler as in reality an infidel (*kāfir*). The Brothers had flirted with *takfir* under the influence of the theorist Sayyid Qutb in the particular circumstances that obtained after they had been crushed by Nasser in the 1950s, but explicitly disavowed the *takfiri* line when their Supreme Guide, Hassan al-Hodeibi, wrote a crucial text, *Du'āt, lā Qudāt* (Missionaries, Not Judges), in 1969. Although this was published only in 1977, it had undoubtedly circulated among senior Brothers long before then, since the reversion to the earlier, non-*takfiri* line was an accomplished fact by the early 1970s and an indispensable condition of Sadat's allowing the Brothers to resume their missionary activity in 1973.

The Brothers were reformists in practice as well as principle, in that they had long actively pursued a gradualist strategy of promoting their Islamic vision by peaceful propaganda and accepted the Egyptian state and its constitution as the framework within which they sought to operate, while criticising the dictatorial and repressive aspects of Mubarak's regime and calling for political liberalisation through constitutional reform. They were conservative in important respects, in accepting the (capitalist) nature of the economy as a given, and above all in their promotion of what they considered to be Islamic precepts and values with respect to cultural issues, public and private morality and the family. But their agitation for political liberalisation and in particular for the repeal of the Emergency Law, free elections, an independent judiciary and an enhanced role for the Egyptian

Parliament meant that a substantial measure of common ground existed, or should have existed, between the Brothers and secular democratic forces. Why, then, did they fail to secure a stable place for themselves in the post-Mubarak political landscape and go down to a catastrophic defeat at the hands of an alliance of Egypt's liberals and leftists and the army commanders?

The answer which Hazem Kandil offers is that they brought this entirely upon themselves through their own incompetence, and that this was rooted in a fundamentally deficient political outlook, which he calls 'religious determinism'.[10] There is a degree of ambiguity in his argument here. At times he appears to be suggesting, as I myself have argued,[11] that the change in the Brothers' public platform and leadership between 2007 and 2010 was a key factor that disabled the Brothers politically, when the most conservative and politically inexperienced elements, men who had spent their lives inside the organisation, running the specifically religious mission and the network of charitable associations, took over at the expense of those who had up until then led the Brothers' expanding presence in the wider public sphere.[12] At others, he suggests that this 'religious determinism' was a congenital flaw from the outset and inherent not only in the Brothers' outlook but in Islamism in general:

> In Hegelian and Marxian thought, when certain historical conditions materialize, change inevitably follows. Islamism maintains, quite similarly, that realizing certain religious conditions prompts historical change – specifically, that producing a godly community triggers a divinely ordained transformation of that community's material situation.[13]

Drawing on interviews with individual Brothers or former Brothers, Kandil is able to show that some at least had elements of this outlook: as one of them told him, 'If I perform the manageable duties, God will deal with the difficult ones.'[14] He interprets this to mean that the Brothers in general relied on divine intervention to give them victory; political competence was surplus to requirements. 'But, in the summer of 2013, God did not intervene – at least not on the Brothers' side.'[15]

There are numerous problems with this version of the logic of events. First, Kandil does not establish that the attitude, found in individual Brothers, that he classifies as 'religious determinism' has been the outlook of the movement's leadership. Yet, as his description of the internal workings of the movement clearly shows, the organisation was an extremely hierarchical one, with several degrees of initiation into the membership and a tight structure of command and discipline that might be called 'Islamic centralism', by analogy with Communist Parties' 'democratic centralism', except that it was considerably more elitist and undemocratic than the latter.

Second, Kandil does not describe individual instances of the Muslim Brothers' alleged incompetence, let alone document them. To establish incompetence as the explanation of questionable choices would require him to consider the context of particular decisions and especially the behaviour of other political forces, but Kandil makes no mention of these. Moreover, his account of the Brothers' political behaviour before 2011 and in fact before the leadership changes of 2009–10 seriously misrepresents this. His claim that the Brothers' tally of eighty-eight National Assembly seats in 2005 was not their own achievement but that 'the security forces engineered it from start to finish' is very misleading. The phrase quoted is Kandil's, but he attributes it to Mohamed Mahdi Akef, the Brothers' General Guide. This is putting words in Akef's mouth; it is not what Akef said in the interview he gave to journalists cited by Kandil as his source.[16] As already noted in Chapter 2, it was because the Brothers' polling far exceeded what the regime had expected that the interior ministry mobilised its security forces to prevent electors from voting in many places in the second and third rounds; had they not done this, the Brothers' tally of seats would have exceeded 100.

Kandil's next step is to dismiss the Brothers' performance in Parliament:

After managing to form the largest opposition bloc since 1952, the Brotherhood's members of parliament simply sat on their hands. Not a single memorable proposal, let alone legislation, came from their quarter. Inaction in parliament was made worse by their perceived mediocrity in the media after the elections.[17]

None of this is documented; it is all mere assertion and quite untrue. With no more than 20 per cent of the seats the Brothers could not hope to get their legislative proposals passed, but that did not mean that they were idle. It has been estimated that, between December 2005 and June 2006, 80 per cent of all parliamentary activity came from the Muslim Brothers' members of the National Assembly, and, far from sneering at them, the semi-official daily *Al-Ahram* acknowledged that 'the Islamic trend' was playing a 'noticeable and distinguished role that cannot be denied' in legislative sessions.[18] And it was because of the disturbing impact these eighty-eight MPs were having on the regime's National Democratic Party members in the Assembly, and the extent to which they were challenging the previously complacent officialdom and stirring public interest, that the regime embarked on a massive clampdown.[19] It not only arrested many hundreds of Brothers, including Deputy Guide Khairat al-Shater and the head of the Brothers' parliamentary department (a certain Mohamed Morsi), but also, among numerous other repressive measures, aggravated the Brothers' extremely vulnerable position as an organisation denied legal status and so exposed to arbitrary repression, with revisions to the Constitution (formally ratified, on a miniscule turnout, on 26 March 2007) that banned any political activity based on religion (Article 5), abolished the judicial supervision of elections (Article 88) and in other ways sought to ensure that the Brothers could never again enjoy significant electoral success.[20]

The regime would have had no reason to do all of this had the Brothers in Parliament 'simply sat on their hands'. Kandil's claim that the Brothers' failure to get anywhere in the 2010 legislative elections proved that their success in 2005 had merely been 'yet another regime manœuvre in its endless game with Washington' is reductionist in the extreme, casting the Brothers as nothing more than the regime's pawns and wholly denying their own agency.[21] The regime certainly wanted to frighten Western onlookers with an exhibition of the Brothers' potential strength in order to get Washington to stop meddling in Egyptian politics in the name of its 'democracy-promotion' agenda, as I argued in 2013, but it was banking on the Brothers merely doubling their 2000 tally of seventeen seats.[22] The outcome of the 2005 elections far exceeded what the regime had expected or wanted, because of the brilliant way the Brothers made the most of this opportunity; the regime accordingly took steps to prevent such an outcome from recurring five years later. Kandil's attempt to reinforce his depiction of the Brothers' performance in 2011–13 as a saga of incompetence and mediocrity by projecting it backwards in time does not work.

His account of the events of 2012–13 does not work either. This consists of several claims, by far the most important of which is the assertion that the Brothers 'were expected to stabilize the political arena, but they failed to deliver because of their ineptitude at political bargaining' and that it was because the SCAF was disappointed if not exasperated with the Brothers' unsatisfactory performance of this mission that it reluctantly deposed President Morsi on 3 July 2013.[23]

The presidential election which Mohamed Morsi, as the candidate of the Brothers' Freedom and Justice Party, eventually won was initially held under the terms of the Provisional Constitution of the Arab Republic of Egypt (also known as the Constitutional Declaration), concocted by the SCAF in February–March 2011 and ratified in a refendum on 19 March 2011, but then subjected to further arbitrary amendment by the SCAF before it was published on 30 March 2011. The provisions of this constitution furnished the basis on the which the National Assembly elections had been held between November 2011 and January 2012 and appeared to provide a reasonably stable constitutional basis for the presidential election to proceed in May–June. In the middle of this election, after the conclusion of the first round and before the second, the SCAF massively changed the constitutional ground rules by dissolving the People's Assembly, in which the FJP had a clear plurality, and issuing another 'constitutional declaration' drastically reducing the prerogatives of the presidency and allocating former presidential powers to the judiciary and to itself. In doing this, the SCAF deliberately destabilised the political arena: its actions gave the new president an interest in securing rapid agreement on a new constitution, as the precondition of holding fresh legislative elections in order to recover the support of his party in the People's Assembly, and crippled him, hugely reducing his powers and the authority he could bring to the task of securing agreement on the eventual constitution from the other principal political forces.

The procedure for agreeing a new constitution was already a shambles by this time in any case, and there can be little doubt that the SCAF, with its arbitrary but invariably self-serving behaviour, was responsible for this. Unlike Tunisia, where a genuine Constituent Assembly was elected democratically in October 2011, in Egypt elections had been held for the People's Assembly, the lower house of the national Parliament, and then for the Shura Council, the upper house, but not for a Constituent Assembly. The Tunisian body had the task both of agreeing a new constitution and providing, *pro tem.*, a mandate for the government, but the Egyptian People's Assembly, elected in cumbersome stages between 28 November 2011 and 11 January 2012, had neither function. Instead, it was required by the terms of the SCAF's Constitutional Declaration to meet in a joint session with the Shura Council 'to elect a provisional assembly composed of 100 members which will prepare a new draft constitution for the country'* rather than perform the function of a Constituent Assembly itself. A 100-member 'provisional assembly' (unthinkingly dubbed 'the Constituent Assembly' by the media) was elected on 24 March 2012.

This did not consist only of elected members of Parliament; it included no more than fifty of these (thirty-seven from the People's Assembly, thirteen from the Shura Council) in fairly exact proportion to the shares of seats won by the various political parties in the recent elections. The other fifty consisted

---

* Terms of Article 60 of the SCAF's Constitutional Declaration in late March 2011, which functioned as an interim constitution thereafter.

of a range of well-known personalities, experts, judges, scholars and representatives of civil society bodies (chambers of commerce, unions, the lawyers' and journalists' syndicates, and so on) and particular institutions (Al-Azhar, secular universities, the Ministry of Justice, the SCAF itself).* But the authority of the People's Assembly and Shura Council to determine the composition of this 'Constituent Assembly' was quickly contested, and on 10 April the Supreme Administrative Court declared this first 'Constituent Assembly' null and void on the grounds that the two houses of Parliament had elected fifty of their own members to serve on it – alongside, as we have seen, a judicious mixture of personalities from various walks of life and sectors of opinion – when, or so the court ruled, they had no right to do so.

This was an extraordinary, certainly questionable and arguably outrageous ruling by the court. In fact, the two houses of Parliament had not infringed in any way the terms of Article 60, which had left the matter of who might be 'elected' entirely open and thus for the Parliament to decide.† What had happened is that special interests – especially sections of the liberal elite, with privileged positions under the old regime but little or no political support in the wider public – had successfully lobbied against the principle that the democratically elected Parliament should have so much as a 50 per cent stake in determining the new constitution.

Parliament made a second attempt to 'elect a provisional assembly', as mandated, to 'prepare a draft constitution'. A revised formula, which reduced the number of parliamentarians from fifty to thirty-nine and correspondingly increased to sixty-one the number of prominent personalities, was agreed by

---

* The names, party affiliations where known and other professional or institutional connections of all 100 members of this first Provisional Assembly were published by *Al-Ahram* on 26 March 2012.

† Article 60 did not stipulate that the houses of Parliament could not elect any of their members to serve on this Provisional Assembly. Article 60's use of the term 'elect' arguably implied that they should do precisely that. If not electing their own members, they would have merely been appointing other persons.

twenty-two political parties and the head of the SCAF, Defence Minister Mohamed Hussein Tantawi. The sixty-one personalities now included six judges, nine 'legal experts', five representatives of the Al-Azhar establishment, four representatives of the Coptic Orthodox Church, about a dozen leaders of unions and syndicates, several leaders of smaller parties which had not done well in the legislative elections, several of the 'revolutionaries' of Tahrir Square (notably Ahmed Maher of the 6 April Youth Movement), and one representative each for the armed forces (Lieutenant-General Mamdouh Shahin, Tantawi's aide and a member of the SCAF), the police and the justice ministry.[24] The revised list of 100 members was published on 12 June.[25] In an analysis of these developments published the next day, Marina Ottaway observed:

> The battle over the new constitution, like many political battles in Egypt today, is moving fast from the electoral arena, dominated by the better-organized Islamists, to the realm of non-electoral politics, where the military and the courts, and thus the elements of the old regime, still hold sway . . .

> No matter what happens in the end, the hope that the constitution will be written through a democratic process is dwindling rapidly, if it has not vanished altogether. Far from being a process to develop consensus on a way forward, the writing of the constitution is at the center of the struggle for power between Islamists and secular political parties that, as in the days of Mubarak, are now openly counting on the military to thwart Islamists and allow secular parties to dominate despite their dismal electoral performance.[26]

The following day, 14 June, 48 hours after the announcement of the revised composition of the 'Provisional Assembly', the Supreme Constitutional Court invalidated *in toto* the legislative elections of November 2011–January 2012. Twenty-four hours later, by decree of the SCAF, the People's Assembly was dissolved. As Nathan J. Brown remarked: 'The overriding effect of the events of the past week has been to contain and sideline the role of elected institutions in Egypt's transition.'[27] And all this happened while a presidential election was taking place.

Nonetheless, the Provisional Assembly in its second, revised, incarnation ended up writing the new Constitution, despite the demise of the Parliament that gave birth to it. But it did so in a manner that made it child's play for the SCAF to delegitimate and eventually destroy the Morsi presidency. With the dissolution of the People's Assembly, the newly formed 'Constituent Assembly', containing – as its authors had been pressured to ensure – a wide spectrum of parties, particular interests and points of view, functioned inevitably as a surrogate for the People's Assembly *qua* arena of political competition, with the debates and disputes over the Constitution standing in for all the other reasons for division and hostile manœuvre. As Yasmine Farouk has explained:

> The lower chamber's dissolution turned the Constituent Assembly into an alternative space for parliamentary politics. The Constituent Assembly thus became an arena for *realpolitik* among different political currents ... The planned parliamentary election therefore became the main focus of all political actors, not only those from outside the Constituent Assembly but also those from within. Consequently, the performance of political parties in the constitutional process was seen as part of their parliamentary election campaigns. The ability of political parties and independent political actors to make concessions became limited out of fear of losing votes in the upcoming elections.[28]

This state of affairs owed nothing whatever to the alleged incompetence of the Muslim Brothers. It owed everything to the ruthless manœuvres of the SCAF and the by now self-evidently anti-democratic attitudes and impulses of Egypt's liberal, professional and administrative, as well as military, elites.

With the dissolution of the People's Assembly, the transition to a more democratic constitution of the Egyptian state was irremediably sabotaged. Morsi and his FJP would eventually get a draft constitution voted by the Provisional Assembly on 22

November, although with many of the latter's members boycotting the debates and abstaining in the final vote. The text was formally approved in the ensuing referendum by 63.8 per cent of those voting, but, with a turnout of 33 per cent, this was a Pyrrhic victory at best, in reality a defeat. It remained only for Mohamed ElBaradei to intensify, with the support of sundry liberals, secularists, Nasserists and leftists, the campaign his National Salvation Front had launched against the Morsi presidency on 24 November to pave the way for Tamarrud's eventual *entrée en scène* as the picadors in what increasingly resembled a bullfight, with the hapless Morsi the doomed bull, before General Sisi finally unsheathed his matador's sword.

The coup of 14–17 June 2012 was the decisive watershed event. The fat was in the fire again – where the protesters in Tahrir Square had originally thrown it in making it possible for the SCAF to depose Mubarak in violation of the Constitution – and no civilian political force would be allowed to rescue it.

IV

The outcome of the eighteen days of mass protests in Cairo and elsewhere across Egypt in January–February 2011 empowered the army commanders and precipitated a complex constitutional crisis which eclipsed the original concerns of the protesters and could not be resolved in their interest. The army's coup against Mubarak on 11 February 2011 spawned a constitutional problem, not merely because it was, in spirit, a violation of the Constitution, but because it was in effect a double coup: against Mubarak, but also against his vice president, Omar Suleiman, who could have succeeded Mubarak, as Anwar Sadat had succeeded Nasser in 1970 and Mubarak had succeeded Sadat in 1981, had the SCAF not acted unconstitutionally to prevent this and thereby created a vacuum at the level of the presidency which it had no constitutional right to fill. Thus it was that, on 11 February, the latent difference between Egypt and Tunisia rose to the surface and began to demonstrate the extent to which it was determining the flow of events.

The Tunisian revolution was an inspiration to the thousands and ultimately scores if not hundreds of thousands of Egyptian men and women who marched and demonstrated from 25 January onwards, and many of the ploys and tactics of the Tunisian revolutionaries were copied to great effect by the Egyptian protesters in their confrontations with the Interior Ministry's security forces. But, in attacking and setting on fire the headquarters of the National Democratic Party (NDP) on the Nile Corniche on the evening of 28 January, the protesters were imitating the Tunisians without emulating them. In Tunisia, the party – the Democratic Constitutional Rally (Rassemblement Constitutionnel Démocratique, RCD) – was the source of power, and so for the revolutionaries to break the RCD was to open the way towards genuine political pluralism, democratic elections and the rule of law. And because President Ben Ali controlled the RCD, overthrowing him was the indispensable preliminary to breaking the single-party regime. In Egypt, as we have seen, the NDP was a mere façade party; it was not the source of power, nor where policy was decided.[29] The source of power was the army, which delegated presidential power to one of its own, on certain undisclosed conditions. To attack the NDP was to attack a symbol of the regime; but destroying it did not open the way towards democracy and the rule of law, it merely damaged the regime's façade while leaving the substance of the power structure intact. And overthrowing Mubarak did not threaten the army's role as the source of power, it merely exposed it, which is why the SCAF needed to pretend that the unconstitutional overthrow of Mubarak (and Suleiman) was a revolutionary and so virtuous act which it had merely – and commendably – helped the Egyptian people to accomplish.

To get from Mubarak's version of the Free Officers' state to anything approaching a democracy required the Egyptian revolutionaries to forget about the Tunisian example and find their own way through the very different wood they were bustling about in. The protesters who occupied Tahrir Square on 25 January and then, in increased numbers, occupied it again on 28 January and held it thereafter were undoubtedly revolutionary in spirit, but in objective terms what they had achieved fell far short of a revolution. They had wrecked the NDP headquarters and numerous local police stations but they had seized not one building of strategic significance to the Egyptian state: neither the presidential palace, nor the Parliament, nor the state broadcasting centre, nor a single ministry, let alone an airport or a barracks. Wherever state power was now located, it was not in Tahrir Square. They could not overthrow Mubarak on their own but only with the help of the army and/or an external force. They had no acknowledged and authoritative leader, no agreed candidate of their own to replace Mubarak, and so to overthrow Mubarak was directly to empower the army commanders.

The operative choice was either to negotiate with Mubarak, the devil they knew, whom they had on the ropes, or negotiate with the army leaders, whose public standing and capacity for decisive action were intact and whose true outlook and ambitions were unknown, but, given the history of the Free Officers' state, could not realistically be assumed to be modest. The protesters did not have the measure of the army commanders and did not have the army commanders at a disadvantage in any way. The only hope of making headway lay in exploiting the temporary advantage they had over the Mubarak presidency to secure strategic concessions that opened up new possibilities for the future in exchange for allowing him a dignified exit at the end of his term seven months later, while keeping the generals at bay. But in the excitement of the moment the protesters were unable to see this, in part because they lacked an informed understanding of the Free Officers' state since 1952; in part because, lacking experience, they had no idea how to conduct a negotiation; but, above all, because they lacked leaders who had it in them 'to be cold and reasonable' when the situation required this if the uprising was to be kept on the right course and bear lasting fruit.

There was an element of schizophrenia in the Western media's coverage of this aspect of the story. The 'leaderless' character of the uprising was noted but, since the uprising was to be enthusiastically endorsed, its lack of leaders was presented as a virtue, in fact a major one. At the same time, the instinct to investigate combined with the impulse to personalise events induced many reporters to stress the role of particular individuals, notably Mohamed ElBaradei but also Ahmed Maher, the founder and leader of the 6 April Youth Movement, and eventually Wael Ghonim, the Dubai-based Google executive who had created the successful 'We Are All Khaled Sa'id' Facebook page. The extent to which Maher and Ghonim could be credited with spearheading the use of social media in mobilising the initial demonstrations further endeared them to many reporters, as the media narcissism Kirkpatrick highlights kicked in. The irony in this is that Ghonim and his Facebook page (which he ran as its anonymous 'administrator') and Maher and his 6 April Youth Movement were celebrated at the precise moment that their original perspectives had lost all purchase on events.

V

The campaign that Ghonim had launched on social media in 2010 had been very focused, making an issue of police violence and nothing else; as such it could naturally extend to demanding the resignation of the interior minister, but not much beyond this. Ghonim's gaze widened subsequently to embrace the objective of changing the system as a whole, but he continued to think in terms of specific ills and specific remedies in a strategic vision that might best be called revolutionary reformism. As he himself insisted, in a post on his Facebook page in the immediate run-up to 25 January:

> Jan25 is the beginning ... A beginning for what, exactly? A beginning for us to join forces and start to apply pressure ... And to have specific demands and a legitimacy that most Egyptians would agree about ... And for these demands to resonate, we will take to the streets in the form of sit-ins, protests, and marches in all of Egypt. The objective is not to overthrow the regime or to change the president overnight ... Because the

problem now is not the president ... The problem now is an
entire system that needs to change, and the chances of changing
it are tied to the necessity that we all change and demand change,
and apply pressure to reclaim our rights.[30]

The 6 April Youth Movement had been formed in 2008 in solidarity with the workers' strike at El-Mahalla el-Kubra in the
Nile Delta and, while later broadening its scope to a range of
democratic issues (human rights, freedom of speech, association
and the press), kept a slender link to its initial orientation to the
working class with the demand for a minimum wage. By late
2010, however, Maher's group had come under the influence of
Otpor!, the Serbian movement which had played a part in the
overthrow of Slobodan Miloşevic in 2000 on the basis of the
teachings of the American theorist of anti-authoritarian activism Gene Sharp, and, unlike Ghonim's campaign, had raised its
sights to target Mubarak and so played a part in prompting
Tahrir Square to reject all thought of negotiating.[31] And the
possibility that Ghonim might have injected a realistically
modest perspective into the protest movement was nipped in the
bud by his immediate arrest on his return to Cairo on 27 January,
a turn of events that made him a celebrity, as his family and
friends explained who he was in publicising his disappearance,
which was promptly blamed on Mubarak's police.[32]

The protesters derided Mubarak's concessions, but these were
not trivial, let alone risible. On 28 January he announced that he
was sacking the cabinet and would appoint a new one; this
disposed of the interior minister, Habib El-Adly, held responsible for the police violence denounced by Ghonim's Facebook
page. On 29 January he appointed former intelligence chief,
General Omar Suleiman as his vice president, which, as
Kirkpatrick notes, eliminated the prospect of Gamal Mubarak
succeeding his father and so signified the end of *tawrith al-sulta*,
the inheritance of power that had been denounced since 2004
by the Kefaya movement.[33] On 31 January he swore in a new
cabinet. On 1 February, he promised that he would not seek
re-election when his current term expired in September, and that
Parliament would discuss amending Articles 76 and 77 of the

Constitution to relax the previous severe restrictions on eligibility in presidential elections and to set term limits on the office of president. He also announced that he had instructed Suleiman to engage in dialogue 'with all the political forces and factions about all the issues that have been raised concerning political and democratic reform and the constitutional and legislative amendments required to realise these legitimate demands'.[34]

If the protesters refused to negotiate, it was not because the Mubarak presidency had denied them an opportunity to do so, nor was it solely because of their own lack of political experience and skills (although lacking these was certainly a source of inhibition), let alone because of the revolutionary stance that the 6 April Youth Movement had taken up. Three other forces were in play which acted to sabotage a negotiation when a negotiation was on offer and thereby, in concert, destroyed the possibility of political reform within the framework of the Constitution.

The first of these was Mohamed ElBaradei. While serving as the director-general of the International Atomic Energy Agency in Vienna between 1997 and 2009, he had won respect in Egypt for the way he defied London and Washington over their claims that Saddam Hussein still possessed weapons of mass destruction. In late 2009 his name began to circulate as a possible presidential candidate, and on 24 February 2010 he announced that he was forming his own movement, the National Association for Change (NAC), with an agenda which called for the end of the Emergency Law (long a priority of the Muslim Brothers) and six other reforms to allow for free elections.[35] His stance was that he was interested in the presidency on condition that the political and constitutional changes he was calling for were enacted but, apart from ending the Emergency Law and securing free elections, in which he had an evident interest, he had nothing to propose.

The NAC got off to a fast start but then faltered, primarily because ElBaradei spent so much of his time outside Egypt. This exposed the contradiction between his position and that of many of his initial followers, notably the NAC's general coordinator, Hassan Nafaa. Although a political science professor at

Cairo University, Nafaa had a strong sense of reality and his regular opinion columns in the Egyptian press, which were usually critical but always down to earth as well as carefully reasoned, had established him as one of Egypt's most influential public intellectuals, and as such a major catch for the NAC. But Nafaa became totally disillusioned with ElBaradei and left the NAC in late 2010. This was because ElBaradei's interest in political reform was limited, in practice, to an interest in the rules governing presidential elections. His interest in the presidency was premised on the assumption that the army commanders would block the Gamal succession because this deprived them of their historic right to choose the president, but would consider a civilian candidate as a possible president of their own choosing. This tacit wooing of the army's favour ruled out a vigorous agitation for democratic reform inside Egypt, whereas building support for his candidacy outside the country, attracting the support of Western governments and media and ex-patriate Egyptians, could enhance his appeal to the generals while causing no trouble at home.[36] When Nafaa realised what he had got into, he resigned. But other elements stayed in the NAC, notably the 6 April Youth Movement, which was inclined to look favourably on ElBaradei's presidential ambition, since overthrowing Mubarak had become its overriding objective.

On 27 January 2011, ElBaradei arrived in Cairo and promptly declared: 'If people, in particular the young people, if they want me to lead the transition, I will not let them down', repeating verbatim the statement he had prudently made that same day in Vienna before his flight.[37] This offer to 'lead' the protest movement quickly hardened. On 29 January, following Mubarak's first response to the protesters, he told Al-Jazeera television that the protests would continue until the president stepped down, dismissed Mubarak's speech as 'disappointing' and called on him to resign.[38] The next day, he criticised the stance of the United States, declaring that Washington was losing credibility by talking of democracy while still supporting Mubarak, and told the *Guardian* that he wanted 'to negotiate about a new government with the army', and that 'our essential demand is the departure of the regime'.[39] Following Mubarak's second speech offering more substantial concessions, ElBaradei immediately dismissed these, declaring that Mubarak's pledge not to stand again for the presidency was 'an act of deception'.[40] The next day, he called on the international community to withdraw support from 'a regime that is killing its people' and declared, 'we have no intention whatsoever – at least I speak for myself on this – in engaging in dialogue with this regime until the number one person responsible for this, Mubarak, leaves the country. He must get out.'[41]

ElBaradei's stance endeared him to the Western media, which wanted a revolution to cover, not something which fell short of this. When a rumour circulated on 28 January that he had been placed under house arrest, the London *Guardian* promptly offered support, insisting that 'Mohamed ElBaradei must be free to give political leadership'.[42] The rumour was untrue, as was the *Guardian*'s subsequent report that ElBaradei had emerged 'as the opposition candidate for a new government'.[*] A further claim that the Muslim Brothers had joined other opposition groups in calling on ElBaradei to represent them in negotiations with the Mubarak regime was vigorously refuted by the Brothers the next day.[43]

This dispute was not a trivial matter. In line with their adherence to classical Sunni doctrine and rejection of *takfiri* revolutionism, the Brothers had combined firm support for the protest movement with opposition to any unconstitutional move to overthrow Mubarak. In insisting that Mubarak must go at once, ElBaradei had radicalised his rhetoric since 27 January in a way which predictably precipitated a conflict with the Brothers that would continue all the way through to 3 July 2013, a conflict the Brothers had neither sought nor done anything to provoke.

---

[*] ElBaradei's 'emergence' was a figment of the *Guardian*'s imagination and illustrated the paper's relentless promotion of the man.

VI

The phrase 'a regime that is killing its people' alluded to the events of 2–3 February, the Battle of the Camel, which, in the wake of pro-Mubarak demonstrations, took place when the anti-Mubarak protesters in Tahrir Square were attacked, and fighting between them and their assailants lasted for about twelve hours, to 3 a.m. the next day, by when at least eleven people were dead and hundreds badly wounded.[44] This event appeared to vindicate beyond all possibility of argument ElBaradei's claim that Mubarak's offer of major concessions had been insincere. The damage it did to Mubarak's position was immense. How had this turn of events come about?

In approaching an answer to this challenging question, let us first look ahead.

Nineteen months later, on 11 September 2012, the trial, begun in July 2011, of twenty-four men and women accused of being the architects of the violence on 2–3 February 2011 neared its conclusion in Cairo. A twenty-fifth defendant had died in the meantime. Heading the list of the accused was Safwat El-Sherif, the former Speaker of the Shura Council (the upper house of the Parliament) and secretary-general of the NDP from 2002 to 2011, and Fathi Surour, the Speaker of the People's Assembly (the lower house). El-Sherif and Surour were the long-time bosses of the NDP machine. There is no doubt that it was they who organised the pro-Mubarak demonstrations and marches that took place shortly before the Battle of the Camel began on 2 February. But organising such loyalist demonstrations was a standard operating procedure for the Egyptian regime, as for other authoritarian regimes, and the demonstrations on 2 February were entirely non-violent at first.

Mubarak's speech the previous day had been an attempt to recover the political and moral initiative and there is evidence that he had succeeded. Recognition of this fact is almost entirely absent from the main academic as well as journalistic accounts, nearly all of which align their commentary with that of the anti-Mubarak protesters in Tahrir, who derided Mubarak's speeches as a matter of course.* A partial exception is Stacher; citing the Egyptian journalist Ahmed Kadry's perceptive report at the time that Mubarak's 'speech was very clever and it went much further than his earlier speech', Stacher acknowledges that 'Mubarak's performance revived the notion that he could wrestle the initiative from the protesters'.[45] But this still falls short of doing justice to the speech and its impact. Nobody can accuse Wael Ghonim of pro-Mubarak bias; let us therefore consider his account:

> Again the president appeared on television to address the nation. He asserted that he was not going to run in the next presidential elections, in September, and that he had no desire to remain in power. Yet this time he did one thing he hadn't done in his first speech. He made an emotional appeal: 'I cherish the time I spent in Egypt's service. I defended the soil of this homeland during peace and during war. Egypt is my home. In it I was born and in it I shall die. History will judge me, as it will judge others. And Egypt will remain a trust handed over from the arms of one generation to the next.'
>
> The speech was hugely divisive. One camp accepted Mubarak's pledges of reform and thought he should stay in power until the end of his term. Others rejected his speech, deeming it a manipulative attempt to stave off the end of his regime. In part the divide was generational. Many parents began to pressure their children, asking them to return home. Some protesters did indeed relent and leave Tahrir Square.[46]

It would be wrong, however to suppose that the Egyptians were evenly divided by the speech, for it is clear that a majority supported the president. Remarkably, one piece of evidence comes from Ghonim's own Facebook page, managed in his absence by a colleague:

---

* Achcar (*The People Want*) contrives not to mention the 1 February speech at all; nor – very oddly – does the interesting study by Amy Austin Holmes, *Coups and Revolutions: Mass Mobilization, the Egyptian Military and the United States, from Mubarak to Sisi* (New York: Oxford University Press, 2019).

On the *'Kullena Khaled Said'* Facebook page, Ahmed Salah, the new admin, continued to upload images of Tahrir ... At one point, when he criticized the president's most recent speech, a storm of angry comments flooded the page. It was clear that Mubarak had won many hearts. The page's event 'The Friday of Departure' had fewer confirmed attendees than another Facebook event called 'I will not protest on Friday'. That event had already attracted more than 140,000 supporters, while the one on *'Kullena Khaled Said'* only had 55,000 ...

The next morning, thousands of people began rallying in support of President Mubarak at Mostefa Mahmoud Square in Mohandiseen.[47]

Later, following his release from detention, Ghonim got some old comrades to brief him on what had happened in his absence:

The guys said that Tahrir Square was now experiencing its most trying days since the beginning of the revolution. The president had won the sympathy of millions of Egyptians with his second speech. Tens of thousands took to the streets to demand that the protesters evacuate the square ... One sentence from the president's speech in particular had struck home with many. Mubarak said he was born in Egypt and would die in Egypt, the Egypt he had fought for as a fighter pilot. He also said he would implement all of the people's legitimate demands. Outside Tahrir Square, in hundreds of thousands of homes, he had touched a lot of hearts.[48]

No matter how many protesters in Tahrir Square had thrown their shoes at the television screen as he spoke, public opinion in general, of which the protesters were heroically unrepresentative, seems to have been largely favourable to the president. He had made major concessions but intended to assume his responsibilities for the rest of his term to ensure that the changes in prospect could proceed in an orderly way that preserved the country's stability, and this came across as a reasonable position to much of the Egyptian public. The NDP bosses organised rallies in various places to demonstrate this, notably at the radio and television studios of the Ministry of Information; this particular rally, involving some 700 Mubarak supporters, was clearly intended to catch the attention of the international media. Moreover, by this time the number of protesters still in the Square had fallen dramatically; from their high point of around 250,000 they had dwindled by the morning of 2 February to between 20,000 and 30,000, which suggests that most protesters had accepted Mubarak's response as promising and as good as it was likely to get and saw no reason to stay on, unlike the hard core intent on overthrowing him for their own reasons.[49] The NDP bosses also sent individual party members into Tahrir Square to try to persuade the protesters who were still there to leave; these party members were able to gain admittance to the Square through the checkpoints manned by the army because they carried no weapons. Soon larger groups were mobilised. As ICG reported:

> In the morning, a crowd numbering in the thousands converged on the square. At the outset, it resembled its opposition counterpart, with men, women and children chatting, chanting, holding signs and displaying pictures.[50]

In fact it was not one crowd but a number of distinct marches in support of Mubarak that converged towards midday on Tahrir Square from several directions, led by prominent NDP dignatories, members of Parliament and ministers or former ministers, including a woman, the minister of manpower, Aïsha Abdel-Hadi. These marches were entirely peaceful and the decision to direct them towards Tahrir Square can be explained, once again, by the concern to impress the international media.

Up to this point the pro-Mubarak counter-mobilisation had been non-violent; it then abruptly ceased to be. Startling changes occurred in rapid succession. The NDP dignitaries and other ordinary party members melted away. What seemed to be the remaining elements of the NDP presence came forward and showed themselves to be *baltagīya* (thugs), supposedly members of the party's notorious stable of strong-arm men, brandishing sticks, knives and even machetes. The army withdrew its troops from the square and its perimeter; there was nobody to stop men carrying weapons from entering the square and no buffer between the two sides.[51] The counter-mobilisation immediately turned into a tense confrontation with the protesters, eyeball to eyeball. Within minutes a pitched battle was under way.* And then, to cap it all, eighteen men on horseback and two more mounted on camels suddenly appeared and tried to force their way through the mass of protesters in the square. Although most of them were quickly hauled off their mounts and badly beaten, their bizarre intrusion gave all the violence that occurred that day its name: the Battle of the Camel. The serious part of the battle took place after this colourful incident, when the protesters came under sustained attack on several sides, including from sniper fire. The fighting went on through the night, into the early hours of 3 February.

The unleashing of the *baltagīya* and the riders, and then further contingents of *baltagīya,* was widely condemned and has been universally blamed on Mubarak and taken as proof that his offer of concessions was a cynical ploy, as ElBaradei had claimed. Does this interpretation accord with cold reason? The incident of the riders made good copy and even better television, but it was also extraordinary in a way that ought to have given food for thought, a peculiarly Egyptian parody of a Cossack charge that fell farcically short of the way the Cossacks dealt with demonstrations in Tsarist Russia. Is it really to be supposed that Mubarak ordered this? Had he wanted Tahrir Square cleared, why go about it in this ludicrously melodramatic and ineffectual way? The riot police had not been dissolved; could they not be deployed? Had the Egyptian state run out of tear gas? Did it possess no water cannon? And, if, on reflection, we can indeed see strong reasons to doubt that either Mubarak or Suleiman could conceivably have ordered these bizarre and calamitously counter-productive moves, we should ask what was really going on and whose orders the NDP bosses were obeying.

Which brings us to the role of the army.

---

* Kirkpatrick states (*Into the Hands of the Soldiers*, 49) that the confrontation with the protesters turned into a violent attack on them at 2.30 pm.

VII

The army commanders started deploying troops in the streets of Cairo (and Suez and Alexandria), and especially in and around Tahrir Square, on the night of 28 January. They also imposed a curfew (which the troops did not enforce) and the next day sent a detail to secure the Egyptian Museum. On 31 January, the army's spokesman, Isma'il Etman, declared on state television that the army supported the protesters' 'legitimate demands' and promised not to use force against the people. Around the same time soldiers started distributing leaflets 'encouraging people to exercise their "right to express [their] opinions and demands in a civilised manner"'.[52]

But, on 2 February, the army commanders made two very curious moves. Early in the day, they banned foreigners and specifically foreign journalists from entering Tahrir Square, which explains why there was so little media coverage of the large pro-Mubarak marches and demonstrations.[53] Some time later, they suddenly withdrew their troops from around the Square and allowed the *baltagīya* into it, leaving the protesters entirely unprotected.[54] They then made no move whatever to stop the fighting until the next morning.

On 23 July 2011, General Hassan El-Roweini stated on Egyptian state television that he had repeatedly manipulated the protesters in Tahrir Square, in particular by spreading false rumours: 'I know the effects of rumours on revolutionary groups,' he said. 'I know how to calm things down in a square and how to make things rowdy.'[55] If this was a vainglorious boast (we may wonder what his military peers thought of it; surely *ars est celare artem*?), it was not an idle one. But I very much doubt that spreading rumours was the centrepiece of the manipulation; the centrepiece was the unleashing of the *baltagīya* on 2 February, and this appeared to have been done through the agency of their employers, the NDP bosses.

Safwat El-Sherif and Fathi Surour were the surviving members of the triumvirate that had run the NDP for years; the third triumvir, Kamel El-Shazli, had died in November 2010. Between them, El-Sherif and Surour managed the party's domination of

Parliament and El-Sherif also oversaw the party's apparatus across the country. Machine politicians with no charisma, they were eclipsed by the rise of Gamal Mubarak from 2002 onwards, but not displaced. In public, Gamal and his entourage upstaged them; but El-Sherif and Surour were needed to do the NDP's routine spade work because Gamal & co. lived in a bubble, remote from ordinary Egyptians, including ordinary party members, and did not know how to fix things, as their mismanagement of the 2010 elections demonstrated. On 2 February, El-Sherif and Surour knew that Mubarak would go by September at the latest and that the Gamal succession was off. What could they look forward to? If Mubarak could be persuaded to resign, the resulting vacancy would, according to Article 84 of the Constitution, propel Surour, as the Speaker of the People's Assembly, into the position of interim president and back in the spotlight at last – a rewarding *fin de carrière* for the seventy-eight-year-old workhorse – and Safwat could hope to benefit in some way from facilitating this. Their stage management of the counter-mobilisation with the deployment of the *baltagīya*, if this was indeed their doing, dovetailed perfectly with the army commanders' decision to withdraw their troops from their buffer role at the crucial moment. There is no evidence whatever that the *baltagīya* were deployed on Mubarak's instructions and clear evidence that they were deployed with the assent and complicity of the generals. And the resulting scenes of murderous attacks on the protesters served to vindicate ElBaradei's regular denunciations of Mubarak, which were taken at face value by the Western media, and all this suited the generals' purposes to a T.

But the generals had no intention of making Surour interim president, because to do so would commit them to holding early presidential elections, when they had no candidate for this except the minister of defence, Field Marshal Mohamed Hussein Tantawi, or Omar Suleiman or Mohamed ElBaradei. Tantawi was elderly (seventy-five), widely perceived as Mubarak's poodle, and would go down too badly in the immediate aftermath of Tahrir Square, while, for those senior officers who had been intent on deposing Mubarak, Suleiman, aged seventy-four, known to be exceptionally able and extremely well informed but also as Mubarak's man, was almost certainly regarded as an even worse proposition. He narrowly survived an assassination attempt on 30 January, and his candidacy for the presidency in 2012 would be disallowed by the SCAF.[56] ElBaradei had let it be known on 7 March that he was a candidate for the presidency and confirmed this on 10 March, but for the SCAF this option too had major drawbacks. The role played by the Muslim Brothers during Tahrir had demonstrated to the generals that the Brothers represented something very substantial in the society and had formidable organisational capacities, whereas ElBaradei represented little other than himself and his retinue of myrmidons. So the generals knew that, once Mubarak was gone, they had to make at least a temporary deal with the Brothers, who did not want early presidential elections since they had at that time no intention of fielding a candidate, and wanted early legislative elections instead, so that they might have a strong position in the Parliament and the country by the time a new president was in office.

The SCAF accordingly decided that it could not satisfy ElBaradei's ambition and had to let him wait, which is why the divergence between ElBaradei and the Brothers became an abiding and bitter rivalry. Although ElBaradei contrived not to run for the presidency when elections were finally held in May 2012 – most probably because he flinched from running against the Brothers' candidate – he was equal to the task of spearheading a protest movement, the National Salvation Front, against the presidency of Mohammed Morsi in late November 2012, and personally approved the military coup that deposed Morsi the following July. Always the bridesmaid, never the blushing bride, ElBaradei would be rewarded with only the vice presidency for his services and, when General Sisi required him to earn his keep by justifying the horrifying massacre of unarmed Morsi supporters in Rabaa al-Adawiya Square in August 2013, he found he had no stomach for it and resigned, and his self-seeking, deceitful and disastrous career in Egyptian politics came to an end.

The need to make a deal with the Brothers in March 2011 was also why the SCAF needed everyone to agree that the ousting of Mubarak had been a revolution. Only a revolution could legitimise its refusal to follow the Constitution and appoint Surour and then hold presidential elections at this juncture. So a revolution it had to be, and a revolution it was; the SCAF itself collectively assumed the functions of the presidency, with Tantawi playing the ceremonial role of interim head of state, and Surour and El-Sherif got little or nothing for their services. But at least they were not treated cynically as fall-guys to be hung out to dry. On 10 October 2012, the court trying them and the twenty-two other accused delivered its verdict: all twenty-four were acquitted, and some if not all of the prosecution's witnesses were convicted of perjury and jailed for their pains. A key witness whom the defence tried repeatedly to call was General Hassan El-Roweini.[57]

To understand the Battle of the Camel, it is necessary first to appreciate that the chain of command from Mubarak down was being massively interfered with, as is likely to happen when an ageing autocrat is seriously challenged and soon to abandon power in any case.* That Mubarak was unable to get the violence to stop for twelve hours, despite the public relations disaster it represented for him, is strong evidence for this. But I cannot affirm with certainty that El-Sherif and Surour and their colleagues were consciously acting as the tools of the army commanders. Another way of understanding events is that they were responsible only for the non-violent demonstrations by Mubarak supporters and they themselves had not mobilised the *baltagīya*, a different force had done so, interfering not so much with Mubarak's chain of command as with, specifically, the NDP's own, internal, chain of command. On that hypothesis, the verdict of the court on 10 October 2012, acquitting all the accused, would appear valid. But, in that case it must have been the army commanders themselves who suborned and then deployed the *baltagīya*, brazenly violating their promise not to use force against the protesters. And is

---

* Joshua Stacher comments: 'By this point it is unlikely that Mubarak was running the country' (*Watermelon Democracy*, 42), but this is a passing remark and he does not explore its implications.

that what General El-Roweini and his colleagues would have us believe?

A variant of the last hypothesis that may be still closer to the truth is that it was not a matter of a different force mobilising the NDP's thugs but of a different force deploying a different contingent of thugs while timing this well, so that the transition from non-violent NDP demonstrations to violent *baltagīya* attacks appeared seamless and thus the work of the same 'pro-Mubarak' forces. The assumption that it was the NDP that mobilised the thugs that day owes everything to the memory of the NDP doing this on previous occasions, notably in repressive responses to demonstrations in 2004 and 2005, such that the term *baltagīya* came to mean not simply 'thugs' but 'the NDP's thugs'. It was always assumed that the NDP's thugs were NDP members, a special reserve drawn from the poorer party members, who could use some additional income, and in some cases from blue-collar members of the corporatist labour organisation linked to the party. But few if any of the thugs in action on 2–3 February 2011, as described by witnesses, resembled the NDP's strong-arm men. The camel riders and horsemen were an exotic element, for a start. The testimony of witnesses identifies some thugs as policemen or State Security officers out of uniform.[58] Others were reported to have been recruited and paid by wealthy businessmen; yet others turned out simply to have been enlisted on the street in return for cash payments.[59] And then there was the sniper, who was responsible for several of the protesters' dead.[*] There was no precedent for the NDP's stable of thugs to include snipers. It is armies, not political parties, that train and deploy snipers.

---

[*] Khalil records 'at least one sniper', and that twenty-six protesters were killed, as opposed to Worth's or Kirkpatrick's figures (eleven and thirteen respectively). The claim that there were several snipers is supported by Austin Holmes and by Brownlee. Ashraf Khalil, *Liberation Square: Inside the Egyptian Revolution and the Rebirth of a Nation* (New York: St Martin's Press, 2011), 233; Amy Austin Holmes, *Coups and Revolutions*, 56; Jason Brownlee, *Democracy Prevention: the Politics of the US-Egyptian Alliance* (Cambridge: Cambridge University Press, 2012), 146.

That the army commanders could easily mobilise their own thugs is made clear by Kirkpatrick's eyewitness account of the treatment dealt out to a demonstration that the 6 April Youth Movement had the temerity to hold in Abbasiya Square near the Ministry of Defence on 23 July 2011:

> Soldiers started firing in the air almost as soon as I arrived. The voice of an imam crackled from the loudspeaker at the top of the mosque's minaret. 'Peacefully, peacefully!' But when I turned to retreat, men from the neighborhood threw down rocks and bottles from the building. Soon others came out to square off against the march. Some of them brandished machetes and kitchen knives – 'white weapons', as Egyptians call them. They closed off the road in the other direction, back to Tahrir. Many of the neighbors earned their livings directly or indirectly off the nearby Defense Ministry headquarters, and they had heeded Roweini's warning to arm and protect themselves. (I heard secondhand reports that soldiers had gone door-to-door to help spread the message.)[60]

There is no evidence that directly implicates either Mubarak or Suleiman in the violent attack on Tahrir Square on 2–3 February, and they were unquestionably the principal political victims of it. And there is a great deal of evidence that this was a false flag operation, in which the army commanders were implicated from start to finish.

VIII

Although Mubarak's strategy – of negotiating his survival, until he could make a dignified exit in September, by offering substantial concessions – was holed below the water line on 2–3 February, he and Suleiman tried tenaciously to keep it afloat. On 3 February, Prime Minister Ahmed Shafiq publicly apologised on state television and radio for the violence, and a range of distinguished Egyptian personalities were contacted and invited to act as intermediaries with the protesters. The resulting formation of an eighteen-strong 'Group of Wise Men' was announced the following day, and this group began to explore how a compromise might be agreed. On 5 February, it was announced that the entire leadership of the NDP (including Gamal Mubarak) had been sacked, and Hossam Badrawi, well known and respected as an advocate of liberal political reform, appointed as the party's new secretary-general. And on 6 February, Suleiman held extended talks with representatives of a range of political viewpoints, including the Muslim Brothers. Suleiman offered further concessions at this meeting, including the eventual lifting of the Emergency Law and the formation of a committee of judiciary and political figures to study constitutional reforms, especially those concerning presidential elections and term limits and the freedom of the press; as Tamir Moustafa has pointed out, '10 of the 14 concessions detailed by Suleiman related to the Constitution or other legal reforms'.[61] He also promised to release all those detained since 25 January. Moreover, the membership of the committee to amend the Constitution promised on 6 February was announced two days later. There are grounds for thinking that these moves deserved to be taken seriously. As Moustafa has noted:

> The committee included independent legal personalities and outspoken reformist judges, such as Ahmed Mekki – who himself had faced disciplinary actions for his outspoken criticism of legal manipulation in the 2005 elections. The committee was charged with rolling back some of the illiberal constitutional amendments adopted in 2007.[62]

It looked as if a package of major reform measures might be agreed that Tahrir Square could be persuaded to accept. In the meantime, however, on 7 February, the army commanders had released Wael Ghonim.

It is widely if not universally assumed that Ghonim's arrest on 27 January had been ordered by the Mubarak presidency or by the Interior Ministry acting on the presidency's behalf. If that were the case, one would have expected Ghonim to be released on condition that, in line with his original profile as a single-issue campaigner whose recent statements had criticised the system rather than Mubarak personally, he call for calm and for the Mubarak–Suleiman offer of negotiations on political and constitutional reform to be taken up. That is not what Ghonim did; instead, on 8 February he made an impassioned speech to the crowds in Tahrir Square which diverted them from considering the compromise that was on offer and stiffened their resolution to see Mubarak gone. Before doing that, and as preparation for it, he had first appeared, on the evening of 7 February, on the Egyptian Dream TV channel's *10:00 PM* programme hosted by Mona El-Shazly, who allowed him to give an extraordinarily emotional interview, culminating in Ghonim in floods of tears at the sight of photographs of some of those killed by the police. This helped greatly to establish his name and personality in the public mind and undoubtedly encouraged many thousands of protesters who had gone home to return to Tahrir Square the next day; as Ghonim himself records, when he got there: 'The square was packed.'[63]

Ghonim tells us that the men who arrested him on 27 January claimed to be 'State Security'. In fact, he says that they repeatedly insisted to him that they were State Security, which is curious.[64] He later maintains that his release was ordered by Vice President Omar Suleiman, not because he knew this to be the case but because he was told so by Mostefa al-Nagar, ElBaradei's chief of staff, who claimed to have persuaded Suleiman to order Ghonim's release when he met him in the negotiation session with opposition forces that Suleiman hosted on 6 February. For Al-Nagar to make this claim had an obvious political dividend, but crediting Suleiman with ordering Ghonim's release can be read as a roundabout way of accusing Suleiman of ordering Ghonim's arrest and detention in the first place, and thereby discrediting him, which was a constant aim of ElBaradei and his followers from 29 January onwards. And later on Ghonim himself took aim at Suleiman, in an interview on Al Arabiya on 11 February following Mubarak's fall, in which he declared: 'Our tears are not tears of weakness but a sign of strength. Our tears are stronger than the bullets to our chests from Omar Soliman [*sic*] and his men. I am stronger than Omar Soliman [*sic*] and stronger than Hosni Mubarak.'[65] This outburst, blaming Suleiman for the violence used against the protesters and the numerous deaths this caused, was a farrago of nonsense; it was not Suleiman or 'his men' who used violence, including bullets, against the protesters. And nothing in Ghonim's personal political experience had given him reason to harbour such thoughts and feelings about Suleiman, who had never had anything to do with him.

Thus Ghonim's account implicated pillars of the Mubarak regime, in the form of State Security and Omar Suleiman, in his arrest and detention and in doing so closely echoed a claim published by the *Guardian* on 6 February 2011 and thus *before* Ghonim's release, citing an anonymous informant claiming to have spoken to 'a senior military figure', that asserted very much the same thing. There is no evidence for or independent testimony in support of this story, which appears to have been a plant by Egyptian military intelligence. And the fact that it was leaked to the *Guardian* on the day Suleiman was holding important talks with the opposition is very striking. Ghonim's account also implicates Suleiman specifically, via the service he ran, in the bloody repression of the protesters.

It is widely understood that the security forces which tried to prevent the protesters reaching Tahrir Square on 25 and 28 January were the riot police, who are part of the security service known as Quwwāt al-Amn wa Quwwāt al-Amn al-Markazi (The General Security and Central Security Forces), generally referred to as Al-Amn al-Markazi (Central Security) for short. Omar Suleiman had nothing to do with Central Security or its riot police, and Ghonim had no reason of his own to suppose that he had. Charged with various missions, including protection of government buildings and embassies as well as crowd control, Central Security should not be confused with the State Security Investigation Service (Mabāḥith Amn al-Dawla), widely known as State Security (or SSI) for short. Both Central Security and State Security have always been run out of the Interior Ministry; Suleiman never served in either of them. He served briefly (1991–3) as the director of the Office of Military Intelligence Services and Reconnaisance (Idārat al-Mukhābarāt al-Harbīya wa 'l-Istitla'), which comes under the Defence Ministry, and then from 1993 onwards as director of the General Intelligence Directorate (Gihāz al-Mukhābarāt al-'Amma), right up until his appointment as vice president on 28 January.* The wholly false claim that Suleiman was responsible for the killing of the protesters had clearly been suggested to Ghonim and, in his ignorance of Egypt's complicated police and intelligence milieux and of what had really gone on between 27 January and 7 February, and his distress at the numbers of protesters killed, he had yielded to prompting and gave voice to it.

It does not make sense to suppose that Mubarak's people had released Ghonim to do what he did. Clearly he had been in the custody of the military and released by them to make precisely the emotional and inflammatory speeches he then made on television and in the Square. The fact that, as he himself documents, key members of the new team appointed by Mubarak on 31 January (the new interior minister, Mahmoud Wagdy and information minister, Anas al-Fiqqi) and 5 February (the new head of the NDP, Hossam Badrawi) were unable to contact him until *after* his public appearance on the night of 7 February indicate that it had not been Mubarak's people who had the custody of him.[66] Moreover, later, in June 2011, by when the 'revolutionary' elements from Tahrir Square had long since become disenchanted with the SCAF and had grasped that it was no ally of theirs at all, Ghonim publicly declared his own faith in the army.[67] All of which indicates that it was certainly the army commanders and very probably the director of the Office of Military Intelligence Services and Reconnaissance, a certain General Abd al-Fattah al-Sisi – not State Security (let alone Suleiman's GID) – who ordered Ghonim's arrest and then kept him on ice for eleven days, until the time came to play him back into the protest movement.

But it is unlikely that the army commanders had Ghonim arrested solely or even primarily in order to make use of him eleven days later. Competent generals have a definite objective

---

*   The General Intelligence Directorate is also known in English as the General Intelligence Service (GIS).

and a view of their adversary and their allies or potential allies when they give battle, but, as Napoleon put it, *on s'engage, puis on voit* – that is, they then act and react depending on how matters develop, taking advantage of the opportunities that arise, some of which cannot be anticipated at all, let alone eleven days in advance. All of which prompts the question: why arrest Ghonim in the first place? To see the true point of this question we need to reformulate it as follows: why arrest Ghonim – *and not Ahmed Maher* – and why do this *on 27 January?*

Maher's 6 April Youth Movement had been going since 2008, and he himself had been arrested twice before, in May and July 2008. State Security undoubtedly knew all about him, and that he and his movement were by now linked to ElBaradei and had been in the van of the mobilisation on 25 January. But Maher was not arrested; Ghonim, who at this point was entirely unknown to the public, since his identity as the manager of the Facebook page *Kullena Khaled Sa'id* was veiled in anonymity, was arrested instead. The likely motive for this can be deduced from its most obvious effect. It precipitated the revelation of Ghonim's true identity as the man behind the Facebook page while silencing him for eleven crucial days, during which the thrust of the protests was focused entirely on forcing Mubarak out. It thereby made the Dubai-based Google executive an icon, especially in the eyes of the world's media enchanted by their own notion that social media had made a revolution, while wholly silencing him and leaving the field free to the one definite point of view within the uprising that suited the army commanders: ElBaradei's. Had Ghonim remained at large and able to play a part, this might have preserved the protest's original focus on specific issues and the objective – far wider and more important than ousting Mubarak – of changing the system, an objective the army commanders certainly did not share. And had a free Ghonim been available for interviews, this would also have qualified the Western media's interest in ElBaradei, diluted the latter's influence over events and complicated Western perceptions of these events.

If anything, Mubarak's people, including the Interior Ministry and the security services it controlled, may well be said to have had an interest in Ghonim remaining at liberty at this juncture; it was the faction within the power structure that was determined to bring Mubarak down but had no wider ends in view that needed to silence Ghonim on 27 January – *the day Mohamed ElBaradei arrived in Cairo* – while working to co-opt him when this served its purpose later. And what that means in turn is that the army commanders were intent on playing Tahrir Square against Mubarak from 27 January onwards, if not before. It is unrealistic to suppose that Mubarak and Omar Suleiman did not soon realise this and did not understand that what they were up against from early on, if not the outset, was a slow-motion army coup.

Is it seriously conceivable that Washington did not know this?

IX

The policy debate on Egypt inside Washington's beltway was a clash of dogmas: 'We must keep faith with a loyal client' vs 'We must make sure to be on the right side of history'. Neither of these positions embodied a democratic principle or a serious, realistic, conception of how a process of democratic development in Egypt might actually occur. Indeed, in themselves they bore no particular relation to Egypt or what was happening there; the clash between them could easily arise in numerous other countries where the US has made a point of having client rulers. In the particular context of Egypt in 2011, they translated into two equally simplistic notions: back Mubarak vs surf on Tahrir Square. No one in Washington seems to have proposed another. There seems to have been no idea that what was needed was neither of these but something else: to get the demonstrators to accept that Mubarak could finish his term in exchange for genuine constitutional reforms, and that it was essential to avoid a rupture with the existing Constitution, not because this was fine as it was, but because no one would be able to produce a new one that would both be an improvement and enjoy a consensus in its support.

The conflict between the 'back Mubarak' vs 'get on the right side of history' positions corresponded fairly neatly, at least at first, to the declarations of the State Department on the one hand and those of the White House on the other.

On 25 January, Secretary of State Hillary Clinton commented that 'our assessment is that the Egyptian government is stable and is looking for ways to respond to the legitimate needs and interests of the Egyptian people'. The same day, the White House press secretary, Robert Gibbs, declared that 'the Egyptian government has an important opportunity to be responsive to the aspirations of the Egyptian people and pursue political, economic and social reforms', but signally failed to echo Clinton's more positive assessment that the government was already seeking to be responsive. This slight difference widened appreciably over the next few days. On 26 January, Gibbs ducked a journalist's question, 'You still back Mubarak?' with the reply, 'Egypt is a strong ally', and evaded a similar question the next day. Vice President Joe Biden took a remarkably different line on 27 January when he said plainly that Mubarak should not step down, but this was a blip. Following Mubarak's initial response to Tahrir on 28–9 January (appointing a new government, sacking Interior Minister El-Adly and abandoning the Gamal succession scenario by appointing Suleiman as his vice president), Obama called on 30 January for 'an orderly transition to a government that is responsive to the aspirations of the Egyptian people', tacitly dismissing the moves Mubarak had just made – which had conceded two of the protesters' most prominent demands – as neither here nor there, as Clinton did the same day. This prompted CNN's Candy Crowley to comment in an interview with Clinton that 'the President's remarks . . . [have] been interpreted here by many, and some overseas, as a beginning to back away from President Mubarak. Do you agree with that translation?', a question that Clinton evaded while acknowledging that the necessary 'process of reaching out, of creating a dialogue . . .' by the Egyptian government 'will take time'. This realistic perspective was soon abandoned by Washington under pressure from the White House and, when Robert Gibbs was asked on 31 January: 'Is the administration not admitting that President Mubarak should leave?', he signally failed to say 'no'.[68]

Initially implicit, this refusal to support Mubarak was made wholly explicit on 1 February, when Obama declared: 'What is clear – and what I indicated to President Mubarak – is my belief that an orderly transition must be meaningful, it must be peaceful, and it must begin now.' The point is that he said this hours *after* Mubarak's speech that day, generally acknowledged to have been Mubarak's most effective effort, in which he had proposed a wide range of substantial political and constitutional reforms and invited the protesters to engage in dialogue about these.[69] To insist that the transition 'must be meaningful . . . and must begin now' was to deny that it had already begun, to pretend that nothing of significance had happened. Obama was dismissing Mubarak's offer as inconsequential if not worthless, a non-event, endorsing ElBaradei's line that all that mattered was Mubarak's departure, and inciting the protesters to spurn Mubarak's invitation and demand that he resign as the precondition of everything else. And the tone of voice was peremptory, imperious, even contemptuous: the White House was shafting Mubarak and both Tahrir Square and the army commanders could see this.

By this point, the two positions discernible in Washington's discourse had converged in the proposal that, without formally resigning, Mubarak 'step down' informally and hand over the reins of power to his vice president, Omar Suleiman. Frank Wisner, a foreign service veteran and former US ambassador to Egypt (1986–91) who had got on well with Mubarak, was given the mission of talking Mubarak into accepting this. Wisner arrived in Cairo on 31 January but could not persuade Mubarak to do what Washington proposed. Instead, Mubarak persuaded Wisner that Washington's proposal was ridiculous, which of course it was. Mubarak was an aged president whose legitimacy was being challenged on the streets of Egypt and whose authority was being defied by the commanders of the army; moreover, he had already declared that he would not seek another term but would retire in a few months. If, in these extremely adverse circumstances, he was now seen to be really stepping down, what lasting practical authority could he seriously hope to transfer to Suleiman? And if he was not seen to be really stepping down, how could this patent and accordingly self-defeating exercise in sleight of hand possibly impress the protesters in Tahrir Square? That this was all that the US government had to propose to Mubarak at this juncture speaks volumes about Washington's seriousness as a self-promoting promoter of democracy. The recipe had nothing to do with promoting democracy or the rule of law, nothing to do with securing good government or even maintaining stability, and everything to do with Barack Obama's preoccupation with his own image. The problem it was intended to resolve was this: how to avoid Sarkozy's fate of ending up with a lot of egg on his face for having been 'on the wrong side of history' (in supporting Tunisia's President Ben Ali), while taking formally on board the State Department's concern that the US should try to avoid betraying longstanding faithful friends in broad daylight because that would look bad too. Whether we attribute it to deep cynicism or crackpot realism, two time-honoured features of Beltway thought, as a policy it was a non-starter and as a proposal to Mubarak an insult.

When we take into account the assassination attempt on Suleiman on 30 January, which appears to have presupposed the kind of high-level knowledge of his movements that only a professional intelligence service could possess, we need to ask: was the White House unaware of this?[70] Surely it must have been aware of it. And if it knew about it, who did the White House think had been behind this attack? It could not have been Mubarak's people, or the Israelis (who were pro-Mubarak and had long appreciated Suleiman as a reliable interlocutor), and it presumably was not the CIA. So whom does that leave? And if the White House had a realistic view of the likely authors of this attack, why on earth did they think that, with Mubarak out of the picture, Suleiman's merely delegated authority would not be immediately and very seriously contested? There is reason to believe that they did not really think anything of the kind, and that the political-legerdemain solution was nothing more than a public relations gimmick, designed to enable the White House, if things went south, to deny any responsibility with the claim that it had urged Mubarak to stand down in good time and that it was not Barack Obama's fault if Egypt's president had refused to do so.

Wisner cabled Washington 'no sale', and flew out of Cairo on the morning of 2 February. His failure to get Mubarak to step down was a watershed event in that, from this point onwards, Washington was unquestionably conniving wholeheartedly at Mubarak's overthrow. But it must also have been a turning point for the army commanders in Cairo: can it seriously be supposed that they were not in the loop? Wisner's failure was accordingly a key premise of the violence visited on Tahrir Square a few hours later that so effectively sabotaged Mubarak's position when he had finally been winning over Egyptian public opinion. And when the dust of 2–3 February had had time to settle and Omar Suleiman was at last able to engage a range of parties and personalities in talks on 6 February, with the Muslim Brothers, very significantly, participating in these, US diplomatic cables from 2005, 2006, 2007 and 2008 were abruptly leaked to the Western media. As Reuters reported:

> Egypt's new vice-president, Omar Suleiman, has long sought to demonize the opposition Muslim Brotherhood in his contacts with skeptical U.S. officials, leaked diplomatic cables show, raising questions whether he can act as an honest broker in the country's political crisis.[71]

The *Guardian* made a point of reporting this story at length the same day.[72] That the purpose of these leaks and the press attention given them was to sabotage Suleiman's talks with opposition forces is self-evident.

On 8 February, following the release of Wael Ghonim and the flocking of scores of thousands of protesters back to Tahrir Square to hear his insistence that 'we won't give up', Vice President Biden, who had long since been whipped into line, contacted Suleiman to insist very publicly that the lifting of the Emergency Law, which Suleiman had broached, be enacted *immediately*, short-circuiting Suleiman's dialogue with opposition figures with an impossible demand given the continuing turmoil, as Washington must have known. The next day a wave of strikes got under way, adding to the perception that the Mubarak regime had lost control of events, and on 10 February the army commanders finally identified themselves as the Supreme Council of the Armed Forces, a body that had always previously met under the chairmanship of the president of the republic. Now the SCAF met with neither Mubarak nor Suleiman present, and issued its 'Communiqué Number 1'. This was the *coup de grâce*, and Mubarak and Suleiman gave up the ghost the next day.

Mubarak's fall was welcomed by Obama, who insisted that 'Egypt's transition' had at last begun, while also remarking that 'the military has served patriotically and responsibly as a caretaker to the state, and will now have to ensure a transition that is credible in the eyes of the Egyptian people'.[73] How well the military accomplished their mission has been clear since July 2013. But it was possible to anticipate this in outline long before. On 17 February 2011, an Egyptian diplomat interviewed by the International Crisis Group observed:

> The military's consultations so far have been far less open and transparent than those initiated by Omar Suleiman in the waning days of the Mubarak presidency. Dealing with the opposition, with protesters and with dissent is not in the military's culture. The tragedy of the current process is that it is in the hands of the institution least well equipped to conduct it.[74]

Lynch remarks that 'Obama could not have saved Mubarak.'[75] The implication is that the army commanders would have overthrown him anyway. There is strong reason to doubt this. The way in which the army commanders advertised their sympathy for the demonstrators made clear the generals' concern to have civilian cover for their own moves and tacitly expressed the inhibition that prevented them from openly mounting a coup. And the point about Obama's policy was that it encouraged the army commanders to do what they did to destabilise Mubarak; it facilitated this and legitimised it and so has its own crucial share of responsibility for it. In doing so the White House not only wasted but in fact deliberately sabotaged an opportunity for precisely what Obama claimed to want – a negotiated, orderly, transition to a more democratic form of government – by enabling the army commanders to violate the Constitution and precipitate Egypt into a period of turmoil it took another military coup and the advent of the most repressive regime in modern Egyptian history to bring to an end.

X

The destabilising and overthrow of Mubarak and the incipient re-militarisation of Egyptian politics are how the Arab Spring began. And the role of America in conniving at this, and so positioning itself to surf on, harness, divert, limit and ultimately frustrate Arab unrest from that point on, was clear on 1 February 2011 to those with eyes to see and even clearer ten days later. It is also how what Lynch calls 'the Arab Wars' began.

Washington's betrayal of Mubarak caused apprehension in Israel but outrage in Riyadh, especially since King Abdullah had made clear early on that he expected Washington to keep faith with its Egyptian partner.[76] Mubarak had been an important ally of the Saudis in regional affairs (notably regarding Iran) and in respect of his attitude towards the Muslim Brothers. The legalisation of the Brothers after Mubarak's fall was viewed with intense concern by the Saudis and also by the Emiratis, since both of these states refuse to allow any political parties at all and have long been especially hostile to the Brothers in this connection, given the Brothers' pretension to represent Islamic beliefs and precepts. The Saudis accordingly mobilised that element of Egyptian Islamism that was closest to them, the Salafis, and encouraged them to form a political party, Hizb al-Nour, in rivalry with the Brothers, who enjoyed Qatar's explicit support. This move entailed departing from, or at least putting into abeyance, a major feature of Salafi dogma, namely their explicit opposition to political parties – and especially political parties claiming to speak for Islam – as divisive of the community of the faithful and perpetrators of *fitna*.[77]

From then on the Salafis were a permanent bugbear to the Brothers on their Islamic flank, massively constraining Mohamed Morsi's ability to make concessions to the liberal-secularist parties and so making impossible the achievement of consensus on a new constitution in late 2012. And when General Abd el-Fattah Al-Sisi overthrew Morsi on 3 July 2013, Hizb al-Nour supported this, as their Saudi paymasters relied on them to do.[78] In this way, the rivalry between two Gulf monarchies became a major feature of the dynamics of party-political competition in Egypt before it had become a feature of the dynamics of civil war in Libya, and helped to sabotage the possibility of a democratic development in both cases.

None of this need have happened if Egypt's political crisis had not been turned, by American meddling, into an insoluble constitutional crisis in the first place. In the process, the events in Egypt saw what would prove to be a defining feature of the template of the action elsewhere established as a fundamental aspect of the Arab Spring: the refusal of the Western powers to allow the crises in question to be resolved in the way they pretended to want – in an orderly manner, politically, through negotiation between the principal parties in dispute in the country in question – and their insistence instead that the crisis should unfold in a chaotic fashion, given the disintegration of constitutional procedures following the extra-constitutional overthrow of the head of state, and at the expense of all serious prospect of movement towards democracy.

This is what was accomplished on 11 February 2011.

Appendix 1

Thoughts on the Libya Crisis

1. Yesterday was my first day back in harness as North Africa Project director. I have had a lot to do, hence my slowness to react to the Libyan situation. I now feel as if I am looking at a runaway train. It may be too late for me to persuade ICG to pause before it acts, but I am going to try.

2. With the news of the violence in Libya, and especially the regime's repressive response to the protests, colleagues seem to have got very excited, naturally enough. But excitement – and horror is of course a form of excitement – is not a good state of mind in which to take wise policy decisions. I sympathise with Rob's complaint about the 'cacophony'.

3. There seems to be a groundswell of support inside as well as outside ICG for a serious form of international intervention of the more heavy-handed variety, involving quite explicit violation of Libyan national sovereignty (e.g. no-fly zones) for essentially (or at least avowedly) humanitarian reasons. Before ICG nails its own prestigious colours to this mast, I suggest we take a moment to consider what outcome we wish to see that is a possibility of practical politics, as far as this can be gauged from the reliable – as distinct from unreliable – information available.

4. In addition, I think we ought to consider and decide what our responsibility is in this situation, and what our interest is. ICG has never been able to do any work in or on Libya. We have no established analytical or policy positions on Libya that we can or need to defend or assert. We do have an interest in being able to do work there in future. I agree

with Joost's earlier point that we should bear this in mind. Regarding the current drama, I think we have an interest in adding, and being seen to add, value to international discussion of the position, as distinct from joining a chorus.

5. The wave of protests in Libya can certainly be attributed in part to the contagion effect emanating from the protests in Tunisia and Egypt, as well as the unrest elsewhere (Algeria, Yemen, Bahrain, etc.). But this wave has been dashing against a very different kind of rock. The Qadhafi regime and the state–society relationship in Libya are very unlike what obtained in Tunisia under Ben Ali or in Egypt under Mubarak, or still obtains in Algeria under Bouteflika.

6. Apart from its first few years (roughly 1969–73), when Qadhafi & co. aped Nasser's Egypt and set up their own version of the 'Arab Socialist Union' as a façade party, there have never been any political parties in Libya. The Libyan public has had no experience of anything even pretending to party politics since the mid-1970s. The Tunisians were profoundly shaped by the experience of being mobilised and governed by the ruling party, which was a real party (Destour, then Neo-Destour, then Parti Socialiste Destourien, then RCD) and the later experience of futile, because tame or relentlessly hobbled, opposition parties. Ditto for the Egyptians and for the Algerians. In all of these cases, the regimes have always admitted the principle of political representation, and their failure to deliver or allow the reality of genuinely democratic political representation has been both a source of frustration to public opinion and a stimulus to the political reflexes of the society at large. None of this applies to Qadhafi's Libya.

7. In his *Green Book*, Qadhafi frankly and explicitly rejected the very concept of political representation. A key principle of the Jamahiriyya – the 'State of the Masses' – was that of direct participation in government at every level via the 'Revolutionary Committees'. This idea had a lot in common with the fanciful notions of 'direct democracy' once fashionable with the European *soixante-huitard* left, which similarly despised and rejected representative politics. But

in the Libyan case it linked up with and in effect translated and recycled traditional Beduin notions of self-government – what in Libya was popularly known as 'Arab government' (*al-hukuma al-'arabiyya* – 'Arab' here having no ethnic content but meaning 'belonging to the people', 'people's government'). Eventually, of course, the appeal of direct involvement in 'government' via participation in revolutionary committees palled and proved a failure, and the process of incremental alienation of public opinion from the regime set in. It appears that Qadhafi and his colleagues were unwilling or at any rate unable to draw the lesson of this and introduce a new formula in time. It is likely that the protracted emergency under which the regime operated throughout the long period of Western-imposed quarantine was a major factor inhibiting it from engaging in the necessary fresh thinking and experimentation.

8. Lacking any experience whatever of party politics and the routines of political representation, even inadequate ones, Libyan society has also largely lacked the experience of voluntary associations and anything approaching what we understand as civil society. Tunisians and Egyptians, by contrast, have had a substantial experience of these things, and this experience has been of enormous importance in forming the capacity for organisation and disciplined, purposeful, behaviour that the protest movements in both countries have displayed.

9. Qadhafi's regime came out of the army in the military coup of 1969, but he has long been wary of the regular army and has relied as much if not more on tribal alliances and a praetorian republican guard recruited from an inner circle of trusted tribes. In this respect, his regime has resembled those of the Gulf monarchies as much if not more than the other Arab 'republics'. From the outset, moreover, it has existed in a tense relationship of underlying antagonism to the political tradition of Cyrenaica – the home of the Sanussi order and the monarchy based on this that Qadhafi's coup overthrew – but also to the outlook and traditions of the long-established urban classes of Tripoli in the west. Qadhafi

himself is from the Qadhadhfa tribe around Sebha and Sirte, roughly in the centre of the country. A likely if naturally unstated rationale of his refusal of political representation and parties of any kind and his reluctance to allow much in the way of civil society to develop has been his awareness that these things would empower and rearm the urban elites of Tripoli and Benghazi. It is striking that the revolt achieved a critical mass in Benghazi first.

10. A crucial consequence of these historical realities is that the regime Qadhafi has constructed and presided over has fallen short of being a real state. It is a rather precarious, jerry-built power structure, rather than a state in the modern sense. A reason why the Egyptian army could strike an attitude of understanding towards the protest movement in Egypt and neutrality in the conflict between this movement and the Mubarak regime is that the Egyptian state had an existence independent of Mubarak & co. This cannot be said with any confidence at all of Libya. Mubarak's threat of 'me or chaos' could be treated as a bluff to be called. But there is a very real danger that Libya will collapse into real, prolonged and extremely violent chaos if the Qadhafi regime falls at this juncture. Moreover, the distinction which both Tunisians and Egyptians have made – between a particular president and his associates (whom they have come to detest) on the one hand and the state (to which they have remained loyal) on the other – is not one which the Libyan protestors have made because they cannot make it. There has accordingly been a raw, elemental if not primitive as well as volcanic aspect to their revolt which has arguably made it exceptionally difficult for the regime to engage in any kind of negotiation with it.

11. The most interesting reports that I have seen are those which claim that several senior army commanders as well as at least one major tribe have sided with the revolt. If this is true, it means that Qadhafi's son Saif al-Islam was not talking nonsense when he warned of civil war. But the threat of genuine civil war – with two rival power centres confronting one another – is not only bad news. It also has a hopeful

aspect. If senior generals are siding with the revolt, they may well be able to give it a degree of politically coherent and purposeful direction and leadership that could sooner or later make a negotiation between the regime and the rebellion a possibility. Such a negotiation could allow for a politically controlled evolution away from the Qadhafi formula.

12. The great danger in immediate, not to say gung-ho, intervention by the 'international community' is that it could precipitate the fall of the Qadhafi regime and the disintegration of the entire power structure before any politically viable alternative to it has had time to cohere. The consequences of that could be immensely more costly in human lives than what we have seen so far. It would also threaten to destabilise the whole of North Africa. If Libya becomes a power vacuum, it will also become a vortex which sucks other forces in. We cannot expect Egypt or Tunisia or Algeria to remain indifferent to such a vacuum on their borders.

13. I think that we should discuss these aspects of the position fairly thoroughly before concluding that we know what should be done for the best by outside actors. I also think that we should base our decision on clearly verified reports, not simply initial and uncorroborated reports, on what is actually happening. It turns out that Qadhafi has not flown to Caracas after all, for instance. We really should beware of the way vested interests invariably seek to manipulate international -perceptions in order to trigger international reactions.

Hugh Roberts
Director, North Africa Project

Cairo,
22 February 2011
00.30–03.00 a.m.

Appendix 2

How a Ceasefire Could Lead to a New, Democratic Libya

General considerations

1. Only a serious political negotiation can secure a good political outcome to the present conflict. Having rebuffed several initiatives made either by the Qadhafi regime or third parties such as Turkey and the African Union, it would be a very good move if the TNC were now to make its own serious proposal of negotiations. Arguably it has a definite responsibility to do so.
2. In doing so, it needs to have a clear conception of where this proposal fits into its overall strategy for achieving a new Libyan state that all Libyans can accept as legitimate.
3. It also needs to ensure that in making its proposal it seizes the high moral ground. This requires its proposal to be serious, realistic, carefully thought through and worked out, and to embody the principles of law-bound and representative government that ensure international and especially Western sympathy as well as domestic popular support.
4. If the TNC is to seize the high moral ground in this respect, it is essential that it be seen to be the independent author of the proposal and that it is acting on its own account on behalf of its Libyan constituency and not as the agent of any external force.

The strategic conception

1. If the TNC is genuinely seeking negotiations in the near future, it will have to propose these when the military position falls short of victory. It will therefore be inappropriate to propose negotiations for a ceasefire (let alone longer-term political purposes) on conditions that the other side will refuse to accept. Only clear-cut military victory enables one side to demand surrender (let alone unconditional surrender). To propose to negotiate is tacitly to acknowledge that a clear military victory has not been achieved. It makes sense to do this when the anticipated cost of continuing to pursue total military victory is excessively high.

2. The main basis of the TNC's military advantage is NATO's intervention, without which Qadhafi would have won the military confrontation in March. But NATO's continuing campaign and support has political costs as well as benefits for the TNC. It gives at least ideological and sentimental arguments to the Qadhafi side. The TNC therefore has an interest in using the military advantage external help has given it to secure an enduring political advantage internally as soon as it can do so.

3. *The key strategic idea in making a serious proposal for negotiations at this point must be to convert the present military advantage enjoyed by the TNC and its supporters into definitive and irreversible political gains.*

4. Before proposing negotiations and a ceasefire, the TNC will need to have thought through in detail the terms it wants for the ceasefire:
   - where peace lines are to be drawn;
   - what kind of peace-keeping forces can be deployed under what (UN?) auspices, etc.;
   - what arrangements are to be made for humanitarian aid; etc.

5. But the TNC needs first of all to have worked out what it wants the subsequent negotiations on the transition to lead to. It must have a clear idea of the political end result it is seeking, and it should work out its precise ceasefire terms as a function of this longer-term objective.

6. If the rising against the Qadhafi regime was not motivated simply by hostility to Qadhafi personally and was not based on the ideology of radical Islamism (e.g. al-Qaeda) nor on the objective of restoring the pre-1969 monarchy, but expressed hostility to the Jamahiriyya and a positive demand for democracy as this is generally understood, it follows that the post-Qadhafi state must be based on the principles of political freedom, pluralism, political representation and accountability and the rule of law. It follows that a strategic aim of the TNC must be to secure a democratic republican constitution for the Libyan state after Qadhafi.

7. The function of the ceasefire should be not only to stop the fighting and save lives, but to enable politics to resume its rightful place and a new, constructive, political process to get under way. If this political process is correctly conceived and launched it will in itself lead to an irreversible change in Libya.

Conceiving the ceasefire as both compromise and stepping-stone

1. The ceasefire should not only stop the fighting, it should also lead directly to political negotiations between the TNC and the Qadhafi regime with a view to agreeing four fundamental points:
   - the basic principles of the post-Jamahiriyya state as a democratic, law-bound, sovereign republic and nation-state;
   - the institutions of a provisional government during the transitional phase, their functions and their personnel;
   - the political road-map for taking Libya out of the transitional phase into the post-Jamahiriyya state;
   - the personal futures of Qadhafi and his family.

2. These negotiations will be complex and will take time. Two things follow from this.
   - The organisational arrangements for maintaining the ceasefire – especially the deployment of mutually acceptable peacekeeping forces to monitor the ceasefire and guarantee

it by acting as buffers between the two sides – must be solid and lasting. The peacekeeping force may need to remain in place for months. The delivery of effective humanitarian assistance will also be necessary to the maintenance of the ceasefire.

- The *political* arrangement for maintaining the ceasefire must also be solid. This means that the TNC must face the fact that to get a ceasefire it needs someone to deliver the Qadhafi regime's acceptance of and commitment to the ceasefire. An agreement to a ceasefire is a deal. Who will deliver the regime's side of the deal if not Qadhafi himself? The TNC must start thinking through the implications of this stark fact.

3. Given the complexity of the political considerations involved, it may be wise to think of the ceasefire as itself occurring in two phases:
   - phase I: mutual declaration of a truce, to allow talks on securing a definitive ceasefire (these will address and agree peace lines, deployment of peacekeeping forces, delivery of humanitarian assistance, etc.);
   - phase II: mutual declaration of a cessation of fighting and announcement of talks on the shape and modalities of the transition to a new Libyan state.

4. An advantage of conceiving the ceasefire in two phases is that it gives both sides the time to adjust their political attitudes and expectations and those of their respective supporters.

5. A fundamental matter that the TNC must address and come to a decision about concerns its conception of Mu'ammar Qadhafi's role in this process. The question of his role in the process leading to a ceasefire has to be considered in connection with the question of his eventual role and fate.

Handling the Qadhafi issue

1. If the TNC genuinely wants a ceasefire, it needs someone on the other side to deliver the regime's agreement to a ceasefire and guarantee this. No one else in the regime has the authority

that Mu'ammar Qadhafi himself has. It follows that the TNC
has an interest in a deal with Qadhafi.

2. For such a deal to be possible it is essential to make a distinction
between Qadhafi *going* – ceasing to have any political role or
power – as a key element of *the desired political end result* and
his going *immediately*, as the precondition of everything else.

To insist that Qadhafi goes now, as a precondition of a
ceasefire, is to make a ceasefire extremely difficult, if not
impossible. Another figure in the regime might be able to
deliver a verbal or written agreement to a ceasefire, but more
than this is needed. It is necessary that all of the regime's fighting forces respect the ceasefire terms. This means that discipline must be kept. With Qadhafi gone, the regime and its
security forces could fall apart in political chaos, which could
lead to endless security problems and a collapse into a kind of
warlordism. An orderly transition to a post-Jamahiriyya state
requires an orderly ceasefire and this requires a commanding
authority on the regime's side. This means that the TNC has
an interest in Qadhafi retaining the authority to deliver a
ceasefire for the time being.

3. For Qadhafi to be able to play this role, at least two conditions must be met:
   - The TNC cannot agree to Qadhafi playing this constructive role in the short term unless it is made quite clear that
   he will have no role in the post-Jamahiriyya state (that is,
   the TNC must be able to promise and convince its supporters and NATO allies that Qadhafi will indeed go eventually, as part of the end result);
   - Qadhafi cannot be expected to play this constructive role
   in delivering a ceasefire unless he gets something in return.
   The TNC must therefore work out what it is prepared and
   able to offer Qadhafi.

4. Qadhafi has no formal position to step down from. His position is radically unlike that of President Ben Ali and President
Mubarak. He is not president. This is of course a reason for
wanting him to leave the country and go into exile, but the
ICC arrest warrants mean that he is almost certain to refuse
to do that. His own pride also is likely to forbid this, as is his

concern to protect his family and his closest circle within his tribe and the alliance that underpins his regime. But the ICC warrants are actually cards in the TNC's hands, in that they enable the TNC to offer Qadhafi & co. immunity as part of any deal, in the spirit of a national reconciliation process that will need to be part of any definitive political settlement.

5. Given the degree of personal hostility towards Qadhafi from many Libyans, and especially those whose relatives have been killed or wounded by the regime's repression, this will be politically difficult. It will be essential:

- to make clear that neither Qadhafi nor any of his sons will hold any positions in either the government of the post-Jamahiriyya state or the interim administration put in place for the duration of the transition period;
- to secure from Qadhafi and his sons a declaration, as part of the deal leading to phase II of the ceasefire (complete cessation of combat) that they recognise and accept that Libya will have a new constitution, and that they will have no role in Libya's government in the post-Jamahiriyya state.

6. At the same time, if Qadhafi is to retain the authority to deliver and maintain the ceasefire, he has to retain some influence with his supporters, which means that he has to be able to promise them something. While it will be essential that he and his sons accept and publicly acknowledge that they will have no governing role in the future, it is equally essential that their supporters are able to look forward to being represented – and so having a political stake – in the post-Jamahiriyya state. If they cannot look forward to anything like this, there will be a danger of a situation developing similar to Iraq after the fall of Saddam and the dissolution of both the Ba'th Party and the army, when the Sunnis felt entirely excluded from the new regime and went into violent rebellion against it.

7. To avoid this, the TNC should be prepared to announce that it recognises that *all* Libyans will have a right to representation within the new Libyan state, including those Libyans who continued to serve the old regime up until now. It should also be prepared to agree, at an appropriate point in what will be complex negotiations, to Qadhafi's supporters having at least

some representation within the interim administration of Libya during the transition period. If the TNC can be prepared to agree to these things, it will have something it can offer Qadhafi in return for his playing a constructive role in delivering and guaranteeing his side of a ceasefire.

8. The main danger in making these concessions to Qadhafi and his regime is that this will be misunderstood by sections of the TNC's own supporters and allies and lead to divisions within the TNC's own camp. It will accordingly be important to be able to convince these supporters and allies that the concessions do not compromise the prospect of a future, Qadhafi-free, post-Jamahiriyya state – in short, that these tactical concessions do not in any way endanger the central objective of establishing a free Libya as a democratic republic.

9. The way to do this is to secure guarantees in the shape of the terms of the agreement to be negotiated with the Qadhafi regime concerning the transition phase and the institutions of the interim administration.

Key features of the transition phase and interim administration

1. Once phase II of the ceasefire is in place, with agreed peace-keeping forces deployed and agreed delivery of humanitarian assistance under way, the TNC will need to proceed directly to secure three strategic objectives:
   - formation of an interim administration for the transition period;
   - establishment of conditions for resumption of national political life;
   - agreement on the road-map – that is, the time-frame and modalities – towards the establishment of a definitive, law-bound, democratic republic.

2. In approaching the formation of an interim administration for the transitional period, the TNC has two main options:
   - it can put itself forward as the interim authority;

- it can agree on the formation of an interim authority that is distinct from itself.

3. If it puts itself forward as the interim authority, there will be dilemmas and drawbacks.
   - the main dilemma will be whether it enlarges itself to include at least some representatives of the Qadhafi regime, which it cannot do except at the expense of its original identity and role as the political leadership of the popular anti-Qadhafi revolt and so, possibly, at the expense of its own coherence and unity;
   - the main drawback is that the interim administration by definition is something that will have a temporary role, whereas the TNC may well see itself as having a major political role to play beyond the transition period and should certainly keep its options open in this respect;
   - a secondary drawback is that the TNC will find it hard to combine the task of providing an interim administration of the country as a whole with the political objective of extending its own political constituency and organisation across the country.

   There is therefore a case for the TNC at this stage to aim for the setting up of an entirely new body as interim administration, while it itself assumes a new name – the Libyan National Union, or the National Democratic Alliance, or something of the kind – in order to underline the distinction between itself, as the political leadership of the popular democratic movement, and the caretaker administration during the transition period.

4. A formula which could work is that which was adopted at the end of the Algerian war of liberation in 1962. The FLN and France had agreed a political settlement, but the military outcome was inconclusive and, although the colonial regime was clearly finished, the FLN had to take on the task of establishing a new state in a country where there were many European settlers, and of course continuing French links and interests (as well as French troops and bases), and where the FLN's own organisation was far from fully developed (in part because of the severe French repression).

What was agreed as a first phase was the setting up of what was called L'Executif Provisoire – the Provisional Executive, which included people appointed by the French authorities as well as people appointed by the FLN's leadership. It was the Executif Provisoire which administered the country over the summer of 1962, maintaining essential services and doing its best to maintain security and order, until the FLN had had time to establish itself fully inside Algeria, and organise elections to a National Assembly in September 1962, and then presidential elections and the formation of a government.

I would recommend that the TNC adopt this basic formula: that it propose the setting up of an interim executive body distinct from itself, but on which it will of course be strongly represented, while also agreeing to some representation on this body for the Qadhafi regime and its supporters plus a third, neutral element (composed perhaps of technocrats and one or two respected independent figures).

5. Once the interim executive body is in place, the TNC (or whatever it may call itself by this stage) should be concerned to extend the range of its own effective political presence to all regions of the country. The aim would be to enable those Libyans in Tripoli and elsewhere, in the until now regime-controlled towns and districts, who support the TNC's basic objectives of establishing a democratic post-Jamahiriyya state to join and take part in its activities and discussions.

6. To this end the TNC should seek to secure agreement, in negotiations with the Qadhafi regime, that one of the interim executive's first acts should be to issue a decree guaranteeing freedom of movement and freedom of association and assembly throughout the country, (subject to the necessary conditions of the maintenance of the ceasefire and the operations to guarantee this of the peacekeeping forces).

7. It would be a mistake to work out and commit to a detailed roadmap of the transition to a definitive post-Jamahiriyya state at this point. However, if this state is to differ fundamentally from the Jamahiriyya:
   • it must have real and properly functioning institutions;
   • it must have the rule of law;

- it must have a real constitution that is its fundamental law;
- it must explicitly guarantee the key principle that the Jamahiriyya explicitly rejected, namely the principle of political representation, which implies the right to choose your political representatives and thus implies political pluralism.

8. This means that the culmination of the transition phase must be the framing of a new constitution. For this to be consistent with democratic norms, and nationally as well as internationally legitimate, this constitution should be debated and approved by a democratically elected representative assembly.

9. It follows that there is a very strong case for a key point in the transition process being the holding of elections to a Constituent Assembly. This consideration in turn means that the TNC should face and determine its position on the following issues:
   - what specific kind of democratic constitution does it want (it may already have set up a working group to examine this question – if not, it would be well advised to do so)?;
   - how will nationwide democratic elections to a Constituent Assembly be held and organised, and their fairness guaranteed?;
   - specifically, what kind of independent monitoring or supervision will be appropriate?;
   - will *all* strands of political opinion in Libya be allowed to participate in the election process and, through elected representatives, the subsequent deliberations of the Constituent Assembly? Specifically, will the TNC be willing to agree that former supporters of the regime will retain their political rights as Libyan citizens, including the right to form political parties and advocate their views and stand for election?

Conclusions

1. The TNC needs to work out its positions on most if not all of these numerous questions.

2. It may be politically unrealistic to expect it to be able to offer much in the way of attractive terms to its adversaries in a civil war while the fighting is still going on. But the more it can bring itself to offer as inducements in any negotiations, the more cards it will have to play in the negotiations that may take place. These might include:
   - recognising a constructive if temporary role for Qadhafi in securing a ceasefire;
   - offering immunity for him and his family thereafter;
   - conceding a measure of representation for the former regime on the interim executive authority;
   - guaranteeing former regime supporters and personnel the right to participate as equal citizens in the political processes that establish and thereafter regulate the new, post-Jamahiriyya, Libyan state.

3. In this context, the TNC might bear in mind that, however brutal the regime's repression has been, it bears no comparison with the French army's operations during the Algerian war, in which hundreds of thousands of Algerians were killed. If the FLN could negotiate, and allow some concessions, to its French adversary as a way of getting what it wanted most, an independent Algerian state, the TNC might recognise that it can do something comparable in the Libyan context, and that it would gain in the Libyan popular perceptions of its own national legitimacy in acting in this spirit and making – on its own, democratic terms – the peace between the Libyans.

Hugh Roberts
Cairo
27 May 2011

Notes

Preface

1 That is, the Parti du Front de Libération Nationale (PFLN) and the Rassemblement National Démocratique (RND) in Algeria, and the National Democratic Party (NDP) in Egypt.

2 Ben Ali's Democratic Constitutional Rally (Rassemblement Constitutionnel Démocratique, RCD; al-Tajammuʻ al-Dustūrī al-Dīmuqrātī) was an evolution of Habib Bourguiba's New Constitutional Liberal Party (al-Ḥizb al-Ḥurr al-Dustūrī al-Jadīd; usually called the Parti Néo-Destour in French and renamed the Parti Socialiste Destourien – al-Ḥizb al-Ishtirāki al-Dustūrī – in 1964. In reality these different labels named phases in the life of the same political animal and masked substantial continuity of political outlook and behaviour.

3 Joel Beinin, 'Egypt's workers rise up', *Nation*, 7–14 March 2011, and Joel Beinin, 'Political economy and social movement theory perspectives on the Tunisian and Egyptian popular uprisings of 2011', London School of Economics, Middle East Centre Paper Series, 14, January 2016. See also Robert Bianchi, 'The corporatization of the Egyptian Labor movement', *The Middle East Journal*, 40, 3, Summer 1986, 429–44.

4 Volker Perthes, *The Political Economy of Syria under Asad* (London and New York, I. B. Tauris, 1995), 173–80.

5 Beinin, 'Political economy and social movement theory perspectives', 2016, 14.

6 The founding in Cairo of a newspaper called *Al-Dustour* in 1995 did not materially affect the situation. During the years I lived in Cairo (April 2001 to January 2012), I never heard constitutionalist arguments or proposals being advanced by any of the numerous Egyptian intellectuals and political actors I met.

7 Rusha Latif, *Tahrir's Youth: Leaders of a leaderless revolution*, (Cairo, American University in Cairo Press), 2022, 61.

8 See my briefing of Scott Carpenter, US Deputy Assistant Secretary for Near East Affairs, on 10 March 2007, as reported by Carpenter: Cable Reference ID: #07CAIRO748 and published by Wikileaks.

1 Delivering Libya

1 Patrick Seale and Maureen McConville, *The Hilton Assignment* (London: Maurice Temple Smith, 1973).

2 According to an Egyptian doctor's statement reported by Agence France Presse; see the AFP report reproduced in the Algerian daily *El Watan*, 19 February 2011; see also 'L'Insurrection gagne du terrain en Libye', *El Watan*, 21 February 2011; 'Violent protests paralyse Tripoli', Sky News, 21 February 2011; *Daily Telegraph*, 20 February 2011; see also Donatella Rovera, 'Revenge killings and reckless firing in opposition-held eastern Libya', Amnesty International, 13 May, 2011.

3 *Haaretz*, 21 February 2011; 'Libya's "exiled Prince" says Gaddafi must go: prince praises the flag carried by the protesters', Alarabiya News, 26 February 2011.

4 John Davis, *Libyan Politics: Tribe and Revolution. An Account of the Zuwaya and Their Government* (London: I. B. Tauris, 1987).

5 See Samir Amin's article in *El Watan*, 6 September 2011.

6 *Echorouq*, 11 March 2011; Egyptian Chronicles blogspot, 13 March 2001.

7 Mu'ammar Al-Qadhafi, *The Green Book* (London: Martin, Brian and O'Keefe, 1976); see also John Davis, 'Qaddafi's theory and practice of non-representative government', *Government and Opposition*, 17, 1, 1982, 61–79.

8 Davis, *Libyan Politics*, 141–53, 274–8; see also Davis, 'Qaddafi's theory and practice', 66–74.

9 Davis, *Libyan Politics*, 43, 185, 211, 213.

10 Dirk Vandewalle (ed.), *Qadhafi's Libya, 1969 to 1994* (New York: St Martin's Press, 1995), *Libya since Independence: Oil and State-Building* (London: I. B. Tauris, 1998), and *A History of Modern Libya* (Cambridge: Cambridge University Press, 2006); see also John Wright, *Libya: A Modern History* (London and Canberra: Croom Helm, 1981); Hervé Bleuchot, *Chroniques et documents libyens, 1969–1980* (Paris: Éditions du CNRS, 1983); Lisa Anderson, *The State and Social Transformation in Libya and Tunisia, 1830–1980* (Princeton, NJ: Princeton University Press, 1986).

11 Davis, *Libyan Politics*, 217ff., 259.

12 Ruth First, *Libya: The Elusive Revolution* (Harmondsworth: Penguin African Library, 1974).

13 'Le but du gouvernement constitutionnel est de conserver la République, celui du gouvernement révolutionnaire est de la fonder.' Maximilien Robespierre, *Rapport sur les principes du gouvernement révolutionnaire* (report to Committee of Public Safety, Paris, Year II, 5 Nivôse (25 December 1793)), 3.

14 Vandewalle, *Libya since Independence*, 146–53; Ali Abdullatif Ahmida, *Forgotten Voices: Power and Agency in Colonial and Postcolonial Libya* (New York and London: Routledge, 2005), 82; Hanspeter Mattes, 'The rise and fall of the revolutionary committees', in Vandewalle (ed.), *Qadhafi's Libya*, 89–112; Vandewalle, *History of Modern Libya*, 140–3.

15 Donald Macintyre, 'Western leaders looking for an exit should be wary of the obvious quick fix', *Independent*, 5 April 2011; 'Ex-Islamists walk free from Libyan jail', Reuters, 1 September 2010; Kim Sengupta, 'Rebels concede Tripoli may be out of reach after 100-mile retreat', *Independent*, 30 March 2011; George Joffé, 'Saif al-Islam: the whole (Libyan) world in his hands?', *Arab Reform Bulletin*, December/January 2010; Bruce Maddy-Weitzmann, *The Berber Identity Movement and the Challenge to North African States* (Austin: University of Texas Press, 2011), 139–43.

16 See 'Jim Swire: my hopes', BBC News, 17 April 2000; Dr Jim Swire, 'Should we doubt the Zeist verdicts? A personal view', *UK Families Flight 103*, 27 March 2002; 'UN monitor decries Lockerbie judgement', BBC News, 14 March 2002; Dr Hans Köchler, *Statement*, August 2003; Dr Hans Köchler, *Statement*, October 2005; 'Lockerbie campaigner collapses at verdict', *Guardian*, 31 January 2001. See also the petition Swire started, 'PE01370: Justice for Megrahi', on the Scottish Parliament website, 1 November 2010.

17 Libyan Government's Letter to UN Security Council, 15 August 2003 (English text available at BBC, 16 August 2003); House of Commons Debate, 5 January 2004, *Hansard*, vol. 416, cc.21–33: 21 and 29; 'Dismay over Libyan PM's claims', BBC News, 24 February 2004.

18 When this chapter was originally written in September–October 2011, I was unaware of the powerful article on the Lockerbie affair by Hugh Miles, 'Inconvenient Truths', *London Review of Books*, 29, 12, 21 June 2007. I strongly recommend it, and would certainly have cited it had I known about it.

19 'A Ceasefire and Negotiations the Right Way to Resolve the Libya Crisis', ICG Media Release, Brussels, 10 March 2011; African

Union, *Communiqué of the 265th Meeting of the Peace and Security Council*, PSC/PR/COM.2 (CCLXV), 10 March 2011; Louise Arbour (president and CEO, International Crisis Group), 'Open Letter to the UN Security Council on the Situation in Libya', 16 March 2011.

20 *Convention (IV) respecting the Laws and Customs of War on Land and Its Annex: Regulations concerning the Laws and Customs of War on Land*, The Hague, 18 October 1907.

21 'Egypt said to arm Libyan rebels', *Wall Street Journal*, 17 March 2011.

22 UN Security Council Resolution 1973 (2011).

23 Tom Chivers and Barney Henderson, 'Libya as it happened: March 18', *Daily Telegraph*, 19 March 2011; 'Ceasefire as Tornados Head to Libya', Sky News, 18 March 2011, 02.42 GMT; Ewen MacAskill and others, 'Libya: Obama tells Gaddafi to withdraw or face UN-backed air strikes', *Guardian*, 18 March 2011, 20.38 GMT.

24 'New Libya ceasefire as jets zero in', Press Association, 20 March 2011; 'L'UA tente de trouver une solution négociée à la crise', *L'Expression* (Algiers daily), 26 March 2011; 'Turkey offers to broker Libya ceasefire as rebels advance on Sirte', *Guardian*, 27 March 2011; Nabila Ramdani, 'Libya: is negotiation the answer?', *Guardian*, 28 March 2011; Imed Lamloum, 'African leaders fly in to seek end to Libya conflict', Agence France Presse, 10 April 2011; 'Col. Gaddafi Accepts African Union Peace Plan', Sky News, 11 April 2011; Joseph Krauss, 'African leaders in Benghazi to meet Libya rebels', Agence France Presse, 11 April 2011; 'Libya: opposition rejects African Union peace plan', *Daily Telegraph*, 11 April 2011; 'Libya: Benghazi rebels reject African Union peace plan', BBC News, 11 April 2011.

25 As ICG pointed out in its second media release, 'Libya: Achieving a Ceasefire, Moving toward Legitimate Government', Brussels, 13 May 2011.

26 See Appendix 2. This paper was not an official ICG publication and so was signed by its author but was circulated with the approval of senior ICG staff as a contribution to the ceasefire debate.

27 'Libya: rebels and NATO dismiss Gaddafi ceasefire offer', BBC News, 30 April 2011; 'Libya approaches Spain for NATO ceasefire', Al Jazeera, 26 May 2011; Martin Chulov, 'Libyan regime makes peace offer that sidelines Gaddafi', *Guardian*, 26 May, 2011; 'Libyan prime minister proposes ceasefire, amnesty, reconciliation and constitutional reforms', Constitutionnet, 26 May 2011; Jonathan Steele, 'Why no mention of a ceasefire for

Libya, Obama?', *Guardian*, 27 May 2011; 'Going postal: purported Gaddafi letter to Congress urges ceasefire', RT, 11 June 2011.

28 'Libyan Rebels: "no talks with Gaddafi"', Sky News, 16 August 2011; 'Libye: confusion autour des négociations', *El Watan*, 17 August 2011; 'Calls for ceasefire as rebels advance', Sky News, 21 August 2011.

29 Larry Diamond, 'Obama's moment of truth', *New Republic*, 15 March 2011; Indira A. R. Lakhshmanan and Hans Nichols, 'Samantha Power brings activist role inside to help persuade Obama on Libya', Bloomberg.com, 25 March 2011; Marc Lynch, 'Why Obama had to act in Libya', *Foreign Policy*, 29 March 2011; Helene Cooper and Steven Lee Myers, 'Obama takes hard line with Libya after shift by Clinton', *New York Times*, 18 March 2011.

30 Yasmine Ryan, 'Reports: Libyan protesters fired on', Al Jazeera, 21 February 2011; 'Libya airforce bombs protesters heading for army base', *Haaretz*, 21 February 2011; 'Libya: violent protests paralyse Tripoli', Sky News, 21 February 2011; 'Libya protests: growing pressure on Gaddafi regime', BBC News, 21 February 2011; 'Gaddafi under pressure as death toll rises', ITN, 21 February 2011; 'Libye: répression sanglante des manifestations, première apparition de Kadhafi', *Le Monde*, 21 February (updated 22 February) 2011; 'Libya's Gaddafi: "I will die a martyr"', Sky News, 23 February 2011; *Informed Comment* (website), 24 February 2011; *Guardian*, 24 February 2011.

31 The analysis in this paragraph is based on information from the following news sources: *El Watan* (Algiers daily), 19 February 2011; *Daily Telegraph*, 20 February 2011; *Guardian*, 20 February 2011; *El Watan*, 21 February 2011; BBC News, 21 February 2011; Sky News, 21 February 2011; ITN, 21 February 2011; *Haaretz*, 21 February 2011; *New York Times*, 21 February 2011; *Le Monde*, 22 February 2011; ITN, 22 February 2011; Sky News, 23 February 2011.

32 'Libya: Governments should demand end to unlawful killings', Human Rights Watch, 20 February 2011; 'Massacres in Libya: the African Commission on Human and People's Rights must refer the situation to the African Court on Human and People's Rights', FIDH, 21 February 2011; 'L'Insurrection gagne du terrain en Libye', *El Watan*, 21 February 2011; 'Libye: repression sanglante des manifestations, première apparition de Kadhafi', *Le Monde*, 21 February 2011.

33 Serge July, 'L'Embarras français', *Libération*, 12 October 1988; 'La France reste sur sa réserve', *Libération*, 13 October 1988;

André Mandouze, 'Sur un "silence"', *Le Monde*, 15 October 1988; 'M. Rocard: le silence peut avoir une lourde signification', *Le Monde*, 15 October 1988.

34 Craig Johnson, 'Libyan no-fly zone would be risky, provocative', CNN Politics, 2 March 2011.

35 Muhammad Al-Sanussi, quoted in 'Libya's "exiled prince" says Gaddafi must go', Alarabiya News, 26 February 2011; President Nicolas Sarkozy, on the occasion of the war conference in Paris, 19 March 2011, quoted in 'Factbox: key quotes from world leaders on Libya', Reuters, 19 March 2011.

36 'Readout of the President's Call to Chancellor Angela Merkel of Germany', The White House, Office of the Press Secretary, 26 February 2011; 'Remarks in explanation of vote on Resolution 1970 on Libya sanctions', US Mission to the United Nations, Susan Rice, US Permanent Representative to the United Nations, 26 February (evening) 2011.

2 Loved Egyptian Night

1 'The Egyptian army took their orders from us', *Observer*, 6 July 2013.

2 Patrick Kingsley, 'Protesters across Egypt call for Mohamed Morsi to go', *Guardian*, 30 June 2013; Shaimaa Fayed and Yasmine Saleh, 'Millions flood Egypt's streets to demand Mursi quit', Reuters, 30 June 2013; 'Egypte: manifestations massives contre le pouvoir', *Le Monde* (with AFP and Reuters), 30 June 2013. All three of these sources acknowledged that the figure of 14 million demonstrators was given their reporters by an Egyptian army officer; see also the propaganda video, accompanied by stirring martial music, on YouTube, entitled '33 Million protester [*sic*] in Egypt – 30 June 2013' (this video was shot from an Egyptian army helicopter flying over central Cairo on 30 June 2013); Sameh Naguib, 'Four days that shook the world', *Socialist Workers Party Bulletin*, 5 July 2013; Ruth Alexander, 'Counting crowds: was Egypt's uprising the biggest ever?', *BBC News Magazine*, 15 July 2013; Nawal al Saadawi, 'Not a crisis or a coup: the People's Revolution in Egypt', *Counterpunch*, 9 July 2013.

3 Jack Brown, 'Egypte: combien de millions étaient-ils, mon général?', *Maghreb Emergent*, 11 July 2013; republished as 'Exactly how many were we, my general?', *International Boulevard*, 17 July 2013. The British press gave currency to the notion that Tahrir Square could hold a much bigger figure, 'up to 500,000':

see Patrick Kingsley, 'Protesters across Egypt call for Mohamed Morsi to go', *Guardian*, 30 June 2013.

4 'Egypt's 6 April joins signature drive against President Morsi', *Ahram Online*, 12 May 2013; Tom Perry and Shadia Nasralla, 'As Egypt lionizes police, activists worry', Reuters, 16 August 2013; Dahlia Kholaif, 'Egypt army crackdown splits Morsi opponents', Al Jazeera, 19 August 2013; 'Ahmed Maher, leader of the Egyptian April 6 Movement, says revolution back at square one', *Pan-African News Wire*, 23 August 2013; 'Leading activist says Egypt revolution back at square one', *Egypt Independent*, 24 August 2013. See also Margaret Warner's interview with Ahmed Maher on *PBS News Hour*/YouTube, 10 September 2013; 'Egypt liberal group vows anti-regime rallies', Alarabiya News, 22 December 2013; 'Down with military rule! Down with Al-Sisi, the leader of the counter-revolution!', *Revolutionary Socialists*, 14 August 2013.

5 Ian Black and Patrick Kingsley, 'Egypt: resentment towards Brotherhood fuels crackdown support', *Guardian*, 16 August 2013.

6 Albrecht, *Raging against the Machine*, xxii and 73.

7 International Crisis Group, *Reforming Egypt: In Search of a Strategy*, Middle East/North Africa Report No. 46, 4 October 2005, 9–13, at 10.

8 ICG, *Reforming Egypt*, 11–12.

9 Wael Ghonim, *Revolution 2.0* (Boston and New York: Houghton Mifflin Harcourt, 2012), 58*ff*.

10 Dalenda Larguèche, 'La trajectoire politique tunisienne', *Journal of African History*, 46, 3 (November 2005); Mohsen Toumi, 'Le Parti Socialiste Destourien', *Revue Française d'Études Politiques Africaines*, 9, 107 (1974), 26–45; Rabeh Kraifi, *La Fin du Parti-État en Tunisie* (Tunis: Regroupement Larache des Livres Spécialisés, 2015).

11 Denis J. Sullivan and Sana Abed-Kotob, *Islam in Contemporary Egypt: Civil Society versus the State* (Boulder, CO and London: Lynne Riener, 1999), 63.

12 Interview with Mohammed Habib, first deputy to the Supreme Guide, Cairo, 20 April 2005.

13 For an English-language digest of the petition's shamelessly exaggerated, demagogic, claims, see 'Profile: Egypt's Tamarod Protest movement', BBC News, 1 July 2013.

14 'Brotherhood's candidate, Salafi, Mubarak ex-VP fail in election appeals', Alarabiya, 17 April 2012.

15 Decree No. 4991, published in the *Official Gazette* on 13 June but in fact issued by Judge Adel Abdel Hamid on 4 June; see

Human Rights Watch, 'Egypt: military power grab creates conditions for abuse', 21 June 2012.

16 HRW, 'Egypt: military power grab'.

17 'English text of SCAF amended Constitutional Declaration', *Ahram* Online, 18 June 2012.

18 Owen, *The Rise and Fall*, 9.

19 Anouar Abdel Malek, *Egypt, Military Society* (New York: Random House, 1968), first published as *L'Égypte, société militaire* (Paris: Le Seuil, 1962).

20 Anouar Abdel Malek (ed.), *La Pensée politique arabe contemporaine* (Paris: Le Seuil, 1970).

21 Gamal Essam El-Din, 'Brotherhood steps into the fray', *Al-Ahram Weekly*, 11–17 March 2004; Amr Elchoubaki, 'Brotherly gesture', *Al-Ahram Weekly*, 11–17 March 2004; Magid Fayez and Muhammad Mursi, 'Islamist initiative', *Cairo Times*, 11–17 March 2004.

22 Samir Shehata and Joshua Stacher, 'The Brotherhood goes to Parliament', *Middle East Report*, 240, Fall 2006.

23 International Crisis Group, *Egypt's Muslim Brothers: Confrontation or Integration*, Middle East/North Africa Report No. 76, 18 June 2008.

24 For an interesting account of the Brothers' election campaign, see Amr Elshobaki, *Les Frères musulmans des origines à nos jours* (Paris: Karthala, 2009), 266–72.

3 The Hijackers

1 Jean-Pierre Filiu, *From Deep State to Islamic State: The Arab Counter-Revolution and Its Jihadi Legacy* (London: Hurst, 2015), x, and ch. 3, 'The modern Mamluks', 45–82.

2 Filiu, *From Deep State to Islamic State*, xv, 194, 200–11.

3 Filiu, *From Deep State to Islamic State*, xv.

4 Filiu, *From Deep State to Islamic State*, 1–6.

5 Filiu, *From Deep State to Islamic State*, 17, 19–20.

6 Philip Williams, *Wars, Plots and Scandals in Post-War France* (Cambridge: Cambridge University Press, 1970), ch. 6, 'The Ben Barka affair', 78–128.

7 Halil Inalcik, *The Ottoman Empire: the Classical Period, 1300–1600* (New Rochelle, NY: Orpheus Publishing Co., 1989 (1973)), 78–80.

8 Fouad Ajami, *The Arab Predicament* (Cambridge: Cambridge University Press, 2nd edn, 1992), xiii–xiv, 50, 65, 94, 104.

9 Sami Al-Jundi, *Al-Ba'th* (Beirut: Dar al-Nahar, 1969), 10 (cited by Ajami, *Arab Predicament*, 50).

10 Muhammad Jalal Kishk, *Al-Qawmiyah wa 'l-Ghazw al-Fikri* (Nationalism and the Cultural Invasion) (Beirut, 1970), 67 (cited by Ajami, *Arab Predicament*, 65).

11 Ernest Gellner, 'The unknown Apollo of Biskra: the social base of Algerian puritanism', *Government and Opposition*, 9, 1974, 277–310; reprinted in Gellner, *Muslim Society* (Cambridge: Cambridge University Press, 1981), 149–73;

12 Filiu, *From Deep State to Islamic State*, x.

13 Filiu, *From Deep State to Islamic State*, x–xi, 46, 79–80.

14 Filiu, *From Deep State to Islamic State*, 32–9, 42–3, 48–53, 58–63*ff*.

15 Mohammed Harbi, *Aux Origines du FLN: le populisme révolutionnaire en Algérie* (Paris: Christian Bourgois, 1975), and *Le FLN, Mirage et réalité: des origines à la prise du pouvoir (1945–1962)* (Paris: Éditions J. A., 1980).

16 Hazem Kandil, *Soldiers, Spies and Statesmen: Egypt's Road to Revolt* (London and New York: Verso, 2012), 20–7.

17 For details of the CIA's important role, see Saïd K. Aburish, *A Brutal Friendship: the West and the Arab Elite* (London: Victor Gollancz, 1997; Indigo, 1998), 113, 124, 324–5.

18 Helena Cobban, *The Making of Modern Lebanon* (London: Hutchinson, 1985), 59, 61–4.

19 James Barr, *A Line in the Sand: Britain, France and the Struggle that Shaped the Middle East* (London and New York: Simon & Schuster, 2011), ch. 5.

20 This paragraph draws repeatedly on Patrick Seale's fine book *The Struggle for Syria: a Study of Post-war Arab Politics* (London, New York and Toronto: RIIA and Oxford University Press, 1965).

21 Patrick Seale, *Asad: the Struggle for the Middle East* (London: I. B. Tauris, 1988), 67–8.

22 Seale, *Asad*, 60–7.

23 Seale, *Asad*, 105*ff*.

24 Seale, *Asad*, 106, 120.

25 Seale, *Asad*, 173–7.

26 Peter Gaunt, 'Cromwell, Richard (1626–1712)', *Oxford Dictionary of National Biography*, online version 2008; Christopher Hill, *God's Englishman* (New York: Dial Press, 1970), 191, 248, 253.

27 As Joshua Stacher has argued; see my discussion of his book, *Adaptable Autocrats*, in Chapter 2.

28 Charles Glass, *Syria Burning: ISIS and the Death of the Arab Spring*, with a Foreword by Patrick Cockburn, (New York and London: OR Books, 2015), 65–6.

29 Quoted in Joshua Landis, 'Divisions within the Syrian Opposition

on Eve of Turkey Meeting', *Syria Comment*, posted 26 May 2011.

30 See Aron Lund, 'Divided They Stand: an Overview of Syria's Political Opposition Factions', Foundation for European Progressive Studies, Olaf Palme International Center, Uppsala, May 2012, 21; Samir Aita, 'Syria: aspirations and fragmentations' in I. William Zartman (ed.), *Arab Spring: Negotiations in the Shadow of the Intifadat* (Athens, GA: University of Georgia Press, 2015), 290–331, 300.

31 'Syrian activists form a "national council" ', CNN, 24 August 2011; see also 'Unified Syrian opposition hit by delay', Reuters, in 'Syria Comment', 25 August 2011, and Joshua Landis, 'Opposition disunity becomes the problem as the West gets its ducks in a row', 'Syria Comment', 29 August 2011.

32 'Sorbonne professor appointed head of Syrian opposition council', *Sputnik*, 29 August 2011.

33 Noah Blaser, 'In fight against Assad, Syrian opposition looks for its own model of revolution', *Today's Zaman*, 28 October 2011.

34 Joshua Landis, 'Free Syrian Army founded by seven officers to fight the Syrian army', *Syria Comment*, 29 July 2011; Joseph Holliday, 'Syria's Armed Opposition', Middle East Security Report 3, Institute for the Study of War, Washington DC, March 2012, 14.

35 Holliday, 'Syria's Armed Opposition', 15.

36 'Q&A: the Free Syrian Army', BBC News, 16 November 2011; 'Main base in Turkey, says rebel Free Syrian Army', *Hürriyet Daily News*, 30 August 2012.

37 'Profile: Syria's Burhan Ghalioun', Al Jazeera, 1 April 2012; Oliver Holmes, 'Facing dissent, Syrian exile leader changes tack', Reuters, 15 May 2012; 'Syrian opposition rift widens with resignation of Burhan Ghalioun', *Guardian*, 17 May 2012.

38 'Syria's opposition chooses president, formally signs coalition deal', Alarabiya News, 12 November 2012; Ignace Leverrier, 'Composition de la "Coalition Nationale des Forces de la Révolution et de l'Opposition syrienne"', *Le Monde* blog, 12 November 2012.

39 Quoted by Patrick Cockburn, 'How Syria became a more dangerous quagmire than Iraq', *Counterpunch*, 31 May 2013.

40 Littell, *Syrian Notebooks*, 3, 84, 111, 116, 155, 159.

41 Littell, *Syrian Notebooks*, 84, 130, 154–5.

42 Littell, *Syrian Notebooks*, 36.

43 Paul Harris, Martin Chulov, et al., 'Syrian resolution vetoed by

Russia and China at United Nations', *Guardian*, 4 February 2012; Ian Black, 'Syria crisis: Clinton lambasts China and Russia as Kofi Annan urges unity', *Guardian*, 6 July 2012; Adam Gabbat, 'Russia and China veto of Syria sanctions condemned as indefensible', *Guardian*, 19 July 2012; Ian Black, 'Russia and China veto UN move to refer Syria to international criminal court', *Guardian*, 22 May 2014.

44 'France, partners planning Syria crisis group: Sarkozy', Reuters, 4 February 2012; 'U.S., other "Friends of Syria" to call on Assad to step aside', National Public Radio, 24 February 2012; Media Note, 'Chairman's Conclusions of the International Conference of the Group of Friends of the Syrian People', US Department of State, 24 February 2012; Marc Daou, 'Friends of Syria push for tougher sanctions', France 24, 6 July 2012.

45 'Arab League votes to suspend Syria over crackdown', *New York Times*, 13 November 2011; 'Arab League votes on Syria sanctions', Al Jazeera, 27 November 2011; Ian Black, 'Syrian opposition takes Arab League seat', *Guardian*, 6 March 2013.

46 Karen Young, 'Syria conference fails to specify plans for Assad', *Washington Post*, 30 June 2012; 'Action Group for Syria: final communiqué (Geneva 1)', UN Drafts, 30 June 2012.

47 John Heilprin and Matthew Lee, 'Syria conference leaves open Assad question', Associated Press, 30 June 2012.

48 'Action Group for Syria: Final communiqué (Geneva 1)'.

49 US Mission to International Organizations in Geneva, 'Secretary of State John Kerry's intervention at the Geneva II international conference on Syria', 22 January 2014.

50 Susanne Koelbi, 'Interview with UN Peace Envoy Brahimi: "Syria will become another Somalia"', *Der Spiegel*, 7 June 2014.

51 Cockburn, 'How Syria became a more dangerous quagmire', 38.

52 David W. Lesch, 'Will Syria war mean end of Sykes-Picot?', Al-Monitor, 12 August 2013; Volker Perthes, 'The end of the Sykes-Picot system?', Qantara.de, 21 October 2013; Stratfor, 'The geopolitics of the Syrian civil war', Forbes, 21 January 2014; Owen Bennett-Jones, 'Middle East map carved up by caliphates, enclaves and fiefdoms', BBC News, 1 June 2015.

53 Mark Tran, 'Briton among dead in Tunisia museum attack', *Guardian*, 19 March 2015; 'Tunisia beach attack: British death toll "will top 30"', BBC News, 28 June 2015; 'Tunisia identifies all 38 victims of beach massacre; 30 British', Channel News Asia, 1 July 2015.

54 Cockburn, 'How Syria became a more dangerous quagmire', 92–3.

55 'Press briefing by Mr François Hollande, President of the Republic on the sale of Rafale combat aircraft to Qatar, in Doha on May 4, 2015', Élysée.fr, 4 May 2015.

4 What Was the Arab Spring?

1 Robert F. Worth, *A Rage for Order: The Middle East in Turmoil, from Tahrir Square to ISIS* (London: Picador, 2016), 12.

2 Gilbert Achcar, *The People Want: A Radical Exploration of the Arab Uprising* (London: Saqi, 2013), 244, 247.

3 Hugh Roberts, 'Algeria's national "protesta"', *Foreign Policy* (The Middle East Channel), 10 January 2011; see also Hugh Roberts, 'The negotiations that aren't', in I. William Zartman (ed.), *Arab Spring: Negotiating in the Shadow of the Intifadāt* (Athens and London: University of Georgia Press, 2015), 145–81.

4 David Ottoway, 'Morocco's Arab Spring', The Wilson Center, 22 June 2011; James N. Sater, 'Morocco's "Arab" Spring', Middle East Institute, 1 October 2011; Driss Maghraoui, 'Constitutional reforms in Morocco: between consensus and subaltern politics', *Journal of North African Studies*, 16, 4, 2011, 679–99; Abdellah Tourabi, 'Towards a cohabitation between the King and the Islamists?', Arab Reform Initiative, *Arab Reform Brief* 56, March 2012.

5 Lynch, *New Arab Wars*, 4.

6 Hugh Roberts, 'Face aux nouveaux défis, la politique arabe de la France au Maghreb selon des perceptions américaines et britanniques': presentation to a conference on 'La Politique arabe de la France' at the Institut Français des Relations Internationales (IFRI), Paris, 28 February 2011; my presentation at a public event on the Arab Spring organised by the *London Review of Books*, London, 3 March 2011; Hugh Roberts, 'Protest on the rocks', *The Middle East in London*, 7, 9, June–July 2011.

7 Achcar, *The People Want*, 206.

8 Achcar, *The People Want*, 208.

9 Achcar, *The People Want*, 323, n. 36. This claims that I was the main author of the report the ICG published on Libya in June 2011, and that I would be publishing a book on Libya; neither claim was correct.

10 'A Ceasefire and Negotiations: the Right Way to Resolve the Libya Crisis', ICG media release, Brussels, 10 March 2011; 'Libya: achieving a ceasefire, moving toward legitimate government', ICG media release, Brussels, 13 May 2011; Louise Arbour (President and CEO, ICG), *Open Letter to the UN Security Council on the Situation in Libya*, Brussels, 16 March 2011; *Popular Protest in*

the Middle East and North Africa, IV: Making Sense of Libya, ICG Middle East/ North Africa report No. 107, 6 June 2010. As Director of ICG's North Africa project, I commissioned a Libya specialist to research and write the report and edited the resulting draft.

11 'A Ceasefire and Negotiations', 1.
12 Achcar, *The People Want*, 223.
13 Achcar *The People Want*, 222.
14 Achcar, *Morbid Symptoms*, 51.
15 'Syria's endless nightmare: humanitarian and political consequences', podcast of public event with a panel of speakers organised by the Middle East Initiative of the Belfer Center of Science and International Affairs, Harvard Kennedy School, 6 May 2013, available on YouTube from 10 May 2013.
16 'Syrian death toll: UN envoy estimates 400,000 killed', Al Jazeera, 23 April 2016. The UN put the death toll as 'at least 350,209' in 2021; see 'Syria war: UN calculates new death toll', BBC News, 24 September 2021. Unofficial sources have given much higher figures: 400,000, even 600,000.
17 Lynch, *New Arab Wars*, 10.
18 Lynch, *New Arab Wars*, xiii, xviii
19 Lynch, *New Arab Wars*, xvi.
20 Lynch, *New Arab Wars*, xv, 8.
21 Lynch, *New Arab Wars*, 166.

5 The Reconstruction of Statelessness in Libya

1 Jeffrey Goldberg, 'The Obama Doctrine', *Atlantic*, April 2016.
2 House of Commons Foreign Affairs Committee, Third Report of Session 2016–17, *Libya: Examination of Intervention and Collapse and the UK's Future Policy Options*', 14 September 2016, 3.
3 Lynch, *New Arab Wars*, 85.
4 Mark Phillips, 'The ground offensive: the role of Special Forces', in *Accidental Heroes: Britain, France and the Libya Operation*, 'The ground offensive', 11.
5 Phillips, 'The ground offensive', 11–12.
6 Phillips, 'The ground offensive', 11–12.
7 General Sir David Richards, Annual Chief of the Defence Staff Lecture, 2011, RUSI, 14 December 2011.
8 Phillips, 'The ground offensive', 11–12.
9 International Crisis Group, *Holding Libya Together: Security Challenges after Qadhafi*, Middle East/North Africa Report No.

115, 14 December 2011; Amnesty International, 'Libya: "out of control" militias commit widespread abuses, a year on from uprising', 16 February 2012; Amanda Kadlec, 'Disarming Libya's militias', *Sada Journal* (Carnegie), 16 February 2012; 'Libya: job done?' (editorial), *Guardian*, 17 February 2012; 'Hundreds of Libyans protest against militias', *Guardian*, 7 April 2012; Chris Stephen, 'After Gaddafi, Libya splits into disparate militia zones', *Observer*, 9 June 2012; Frederic Wehrey, 'Libya's militia menace', *Foreign Affairs*, 15 July 2012; Reuters, 'Libya militias clash in central Tripoli', *Guardian*, 4 November 2012.

10 Worth, 'Revenge', in *A Rage for Order*, 36–60.

11 Worth, 'Revenge', 37–8, 54.

12 Worth, 'Revenge', 38.

13 Sir Richard Dalton, *Libya's New Era and UK Engagement*, Chatham House, 21 October 2011.

14 Ian Black, 'Libyan PM's top job: tackle power of regional militias', *Guardian*, 13 September 2012; David D. Kirkpatrick, Suliman Ali Zway and Kareem Fahim, 'Attack by fringe group highlights the problem of Libya's militias', *New York Times/ International Herald Tribune*, 15 September 2012; Olivier Talles, 'La Libye veut en finir avec les milices', *La Croix*, 23 September 2012; Elizabeth Palmer, 'Libya gov't tries to woo militias into subordination, but militias still hold all the cards', CBS World Watch, 25 September 2012; Patrick Haimzadeh, 'La Libye aux mains des milices', *Le Monde Diplomatique*, October 2012.

15 Worth, 'Revenge', 55–6.

16 Testimony of former UK ambassador to Libya, Sir Dominic Asquith KCMG, HoC/FAC, Oral Evidence: *Libya: Examination of Intervention and Collapse and the UK's Future Policy Options*, 27 October 2014, Q104.

17 See Kadlec, 'Disarming Libya's militias'; 'Libya: turning the page', Chatham House, September 2012, 10.

18 'Libya's NTC names interim prime minister', Al Jazeera, 1 November 2011; testimony of Sir Dominic Asquith, Oral Evidence, Q108, Q128.

19 Wolfram Lacher, 'Fault Lines of the Revolution: political actors, camps and conflicts in the new Libya', Stiftung Wissenschaft und Politik, Research Paper 4, Berlin, May 2013, 14.

20 'UN envoy praises Libyan election, highlights challenges faced by new government', UN News, 9 July 2012; European Union Election Assessment Team, Preliminary Statement: 'Historic elections lay foundation for democratic development of Libya', Tripoli, 9 July 2012; 'Elections in Libya on 7 July "Extraordinary Accomplishment", demonstrate how far country has come in

practice, spirit of democracy, Security Council told', United Nations Security Council, 18 July 2012; Jomana Karadsheh, 'Liberal coalition makes strides in historic Libyan election', CNN, 18 July 2012; 'Libya: turning the page', Chatham House, 11.

21 'Libya's Jibril in election landslide over Islamists', Reuters, 12 July 2012.

22 The Interim National Transitional Council, Law No. 4 for the Year 2012 for Election of the General National Congress, Tripoli, 28 January 2012; Law No. 4, ch. 3: 'The Electoral System', Articles 5, 6 and 7.

23 Law No. 4, ch. 3, Articles 5 and 6.

24 Interim Transitional National Council, 'Constitutional Declaration', Benghazi, 3 August 2011, Article 30, point 5; 'Libya's transitional rulers hand over power to elected assembly', *Guardian*, 9 August 2012.

25 'Constitutional Declaration', Article 30 point 5: section 1, clauses 1 and 2; section 2; sections 4 and 6.

26 'Constitutional Declaration', Article 30, point 5.

27 Jason Pack and Haley Cook, 'The July 2012 Libyan election and the origin of post-Qadhafi appeasement', *Middle East Journal*, 69, 2, Spring 2015, 171–98: 186.

28 Sami Zaptia, 'We changed the way the "Committee of 60" is to be chosen for the sake of unity – Mustafa Abdul Jalil', *Libya Herald*, 22 July 2012; Pack and Cook, 'July 2012 Libyan election', 180.

29 George Grant, 'National Congress passes raft of new measures regulating selection of PM', *Libya Herald*, 3 September 2012.

30 Michel Cousins, 'Zidan [*sic*] to resign from Congress to run for premiership', *Libya Herald*, 11 October 2012.

31 Karim Mezran and Alice Alunni, 'Libya: negotiations for transition', in I. William Zartman (ed.), *Arab Spring: Negotiating in the Shadow of the Intifadat* (Athens, GA: University of Georgia Press, 2015), 249–90: 261.

32 Mezran and Alunni, 'Libya: negotiations for transition', 254, 260, 263–6; Bell and Witter, *The Libyan Revolution*, Part 1, Institute for the Study of War, September 2011, 28.

33 Worth, 'Revenge', 43.

34 Bernard-Henri Lévy, *La Guerre, sans l'aimer: journal d'un écrivain au cœur du printemps libyen* (Paris: Grasset, 2011), 74–82, 104–18.

35 Lynch, *New Arab Wars*, 83.

36 Lynch, *New Arab Wars*, 28.

37 Lynch, *New Arab Wars*, 82–6.

38 Lulu Garcia-Navarro, 'Provisional government forming in eastern

Libya', National Public Radio, 23 February 2011; 'Discussions under way for provisional government in Libya', *Malta Star*, 25 February 2011; 'Anti-Gaddafi figures say form national council', Reuters, 27 February 2011; 'Libya opposition launches council', Al Jazeera, 27 February 2011.

39 The Interim Transitional National Council, *Founding Statement of the Interim Transitional National Council*, Benghazi, 5 March 2011; 'Libyan rebels form "interim government"', Al-Jazeera, 22 March 2011.

40 Patrick Wintour and Nicolas Watt, 'David Cameron's Libyan war: why the PM felt Gaddafi had to be stopped', *Guardian*, 2 October 2011.

41 International Crisis Group, *Holding Libya Together: Security Challenges after Qadhafi*, Middle East/North Africa Report No. 115, Tripoli/Brussels, 14 December 2011, 2–3, 8.

42 Lynch, *New Arab Wars*.

43 Bell and Witter, *Libyan Revolution*, pt 1: 'Roots of rebellion', 14.

44 Lévy, *La Guerre sans l'aimer*, 104–8.

45 Lévy, *La Guerre sans l'aimer*, 118–19.

46 Lévy, *La Guerre sans l'aimer*, 149–52.

47 Lévy, *La Guerre sans l'aimer*, 104–62; 163*ff*.

48 Lévy, *La Guerre sans l'aimer*, 176–82.

49 Lévy, *La Guerre sans l'aimer*, 191–2.

50 Lévy, *La Guerre sans l'aimer*, 236–40.

51 Lévy, *La Guerre sans l'aimer*, 269.

52 ICG, *Holding Libya Together*, 7.

53 John Davis, *Libyan Politics* (London: I. B. Tauris, 1988), 40–4, 179*ff*., 182*ff*., 255–7.

54 Davis, *Libyan Politics*, 15–19, 40–4, 250–2.

55 For an informative discussion of several key military councils, see ICG, *Holding Libya Together*, 19–23.

56 Lynch, *New Arab Wars*, 80-8.

57 Hugh Roberts, 'Thoughts on the Libya Crisis', 22 February 2011 (see Appendix 1).

58 Lynch, *New Arab Wars*, 79.

59 Lynch, *New Arab Wars*, x.

60 House of Commons Foreign Affairs Committee, *Libya: Examination of Intervention and Collapse*, para. 32.

61 Bernard-Henri Lévy, 'Intervening in Libya was the right thing to do', *Guardian*, 21 September 2016.

62 Lynch, *New Arab Wars*, 80.

63 Achcar, *The People Want*, 242.

64 Achcar, *The People Want*, 242.

65 Patrick Seale, 'The Hama uprising', in Seale, *Asad: the Struggle*

for the Middle East (London: I. B. Tauris, 1988), 332–4; Nikolaos Van Dam, *The Struggle for Power in Syria: Politics and Society under Asad and the Ba'th Party* (London: I. B. Tauris, 2011), 111–17.

66 Seale, *Asad*, 333.

67 Seale, *Asad*, 333.

68 Tom Chivers and Barney Henderson, 'Libya as it happened: March 18', *Daily Telegraph*, 19 March 2011.

69 Lynch, *New Arab Wars*, 80.

70 Transcript of Mu'ammar Qadhafi's speech on state TV, Tuesday 22 February 2011.

71 The online source for this quotation has disappeared. Wikipedia's entry on 'The First Libyan Civil War' includes the following extract, presumably derived from the same source: 'Gaddafi said in a speech addressed to Benghazi on 17 March 2011 that the rebels "can run away, they can go to Egypt . . . Those who would surrender their weapons and would join our side, we are the people of Libya. Those who surrender their weapons and would come without their arms, we would forgive them, and would have amnesty for those who put down their weapons. Anyone who throws his arms away and stays at home would be protected."' Corroboration of the basic point that Qadhafi made clear – that he was after only those who continued armed resistance and nobody else – is provided by, among others, David D. Kirkpatrick and Karim Fahim, 'Qaddafi warns of assault on Benghazi as U.N. vote nears', *New York Times*, 17 March 2011; see also Reuters, 'Gaddafi tells Benghazi his army is coming tonight', 17 March 2011.

72 *USA Today*, 17 March 2011.

73 Peter Beaumont, 'Muammar Gaddafi offers rebels an amnesty', *Guardian*, 2 March 2011.

74 Lord's Hague's testimony to HoC/FAC, Oral Evidence, *Libya: Examination of Intervention*, 19 January 2016, Q286.

75 Ethan Chorin, *Exit the Colonel: the Hidden History of the Libyan Revolution* (New York: Public Affairs, 2012), 211.

76 Lévy, *New Arab Wars*, 277.

77 House of Commons Foreign Affairs Committee, *Libya: Examination of Intervention and Collapse*, para. 49 (p. 18).

78 House of Commons Foreign Affairs Committee, *Libya: Examination of Intervention and Collapse*, Questions 314–407: Examination of Witness Lord Richards of Herstmonceaux: Questions 315, 319–22, Q340.

79 House of Commons Foreign Affairs Committee, *Libya: examination of intervention and collapse*, para. 23.

80 'Libyan demonstrators say they'll soldier on despite violent crackdowm', CNN, 19 February 2011, 21.07 EST.

81 Nick Meo, 'Libya protests: 140 "massacred" as Gaddafi sends in snipers to crush dissent', *Daily Telegraph*, 20 February 2011.

82 'Libya: Nicolas Sarkozy calls for Col Gaddafi to step down', *Telegraph*, 25 February 2011.

83 Interview with Patrice Paoli, directeur Afrique du Nord et Moyen Orient, Ministry of Foreign Affairs, Quai d'Orsay, Paris, 2 March 2011; my meetings with staff of the Délégation aux Affaires Stratégiques, Ministry of Defence, Paris, 2 March 2011, and with staff of the Department for International Development, London, 4 March 2011.

84 United Nations Security Council, Resolution 1970 (2011), 26 February 2011.

85 House of Commons Foreign Affairs Committee, *Libya: Examination of Intervention and Collapse*, para. 24; Anthony Bell and David Witter, *Libyan Revolution*, pt 2: 'Escalation and intervention', 16–20.

86 'RAF rescues 150 civilians from Libyan desert', Sky News, 26 February 2011; UK Parliament, 'Libya and the Middle East', *Hansard*, vol. 524, House of Commons, 28 February 2011.

87 'Readout of President Obama's Call with Chancellor Angela Merkel of Germany', The White House, 26 February 2011.

88 'Libya opposition launches council', Al Jazeera, 27 February 2011.

89 Ghaith Abdul-Ahad, 'Libya's Berbers join the revolution in fight to reclaim ancient identity', *Guardian*, 28 February 2011.

90 Ian Black, 'Libya: defections leave Muammar Gaddafi isolated in Tripoli bolthole', *Guardian*, 23 February 2011; Juan Cole, '90% of Libya in rebel hands', Informed Comment, 24 February 2011.

91 UK Parliament, 'Libya and the Middle East', *Hansard*, vol. 524; see also 'RAF Typhoons could enforce Libya no-fly zone', Sky News, 1 March 2011.

92 Peter Gooderham, 'UK at the UN Human Rights Council on Libya: "We are and will continue to take action [*sic*]"', Announcements, UK Government, 25 February 2011.

93 Maria Golovnina, 'U.S. warns of Libya civil war if Gaddafi stays', Reuters, 1 March 2011.

94 'Libya no-fly bid "legal without UN"', Press Association, 1 March 2011.

95 Golovnina, 'U.S. warns of Libya civil war'; see also Ewen MacAskill, Peter Beaumont and Nicholas Watt, 'Cameron backtracks on Libya no-fly zone as US distances itself', *Guardian*, 2 March 2011.

96 'Defense Department Fiscal Year 2012 Budget Request', C-Span., 2 March 2011; see also Craig Johnson's report of this hearing, 'Libya no-fly zone would be risky, provocative', CNN, 2 March 2011, in which he records: 'While testifying on Capitol Hill on Tuesday, Gates and Joint Chiefs Chairman Adm. Mike Mullen said they had no confirmation of reports of aircraft controlled by Gadhafi firing on citizens.'

97 'Libya: pro-Gaddafi forces check rebel advance', BBC News, 7 March 2011; 'Libya: Gaddafi forces push rebels from Ras Lanuf', BBC News, 10 March 2011; Peter Beaumont, 'Gaddafi takes key towns as NATO squabbles over Libya action', *Guardian*, 10 March, 2011; 'Libya: Gaddafi loyalists mount onslaught', BBC News, 11 March 2011; 'Gaddafi loyalists launch offensive', Al Jazeera, 11 March 2011.

98 Ewan MacAskill, 'NATO likely to reject Libya no-fly zone', *Guardian*, 9 March 2011; Ian Black, 'Libya's war intensifies but Nato shows no sign of intervening', *Guardian*, 9 March 2011; Ian Traynor and Nicholas Watt, 'Libya no-fly zone plan rejected by EU leaders', *Guardian*, 11 March 2011; Vanessa Mock and Nigel Morris, 'Britain and France alone as EU rejects no-fly zone', *Independent*, 12 March 2011.

99 Adrian Croft, 'Hague says Libya no-fly zone practical and realistic', Reuters, 8 March 2011.

100 Ewan MacAskill and Ian Traynor, 'Libya: NATO defence ministers agree on minimal intervention', *Guardian*, 10 March 2011.

101 Traynor and Watt, 'Libya no-fly zone plan rejected'.

102 Croft, 'Hague says Libya no-fly zone practical'.

103 'Cameron holds Libya no-fly talks', Press Association, 8 March 2011.

104 Julian Borger, Richard Norton-Taylor and Nicholas Watt, 'UN paves the way for no-fly zones as NATO steps up surveillance of Libya', *Guardian*, 9 March 2011.

105 MacAskill, 'NATO likely to reject'.

106 MacAskill and Traynor, 'Libya: NATO Defence Ministers'.

107 'Libyan rebels now retreating from Brega', *Times of Malta*, 13 March 2011; Mohammed Abbas, 'Gaddafi forces seize key town, G8 stalls on no-fly', Reuters, 15 March 2011.

108 Alex de Waal, 'The African Union ands the Libyan conflict of 2011', World Peace Foundation, 19 December 2012.

109 'World Powers mull moves after Libya declares cease-fire', Voice of America, 17 March 2011; Al-Shalchi and Ryan Lucas, 'Libya cease-fire aims to outflank no-fly zone', Associated Press and MPR News, 18 March 2011; Haroon Siddique, 'Libya calls cease-fire in response to UN resolution', *Guardian*, 18 March 2011.

110 Sara Sorcher, '"What the Frick": Panetta aides qualify off-the-cuff remarks', *Atlantic*, 12 July 2011.

111 Jeffrey Scott Shapiro and Kelly Riddell, 'Exclusive: secret tapes undermine Hillary Clinton on Libyan war', *Washington Times*, 28 January 2015; Shapiro and Riddell, 'Hillary Clinton's "WMD" moment: U.S. intelligence saw false narrative in Libya', *Washington Times*, 29 January 2015.

112 Lévy, *La Guerre sans l'aimer*, 80.

113 Lévy *La Guerre sans l'aimer*, 97.

114 'Interview exclusive – Saïf Al-Islam Kadhafi accuse Nicolas Sarkozy', Euronews, 16 March 2011.

115 See 'Quand Kadhafi assurait avoir financé la campagne de Sarkozy', *L'Observateur*, 28 January 2014.

116 Fabrice Arfi and Karl Laske, 'Présidentielle 2007: Kadhafi aurait financé Sarkozy', Médiapart, 12 March 2012.

117 Corbett Daly, 'Clinton on Qaddafi: "We came, we saw, he died"', CBS News, 20 October 2011.

6 The Playing of Tahrir Square

1 Worth, *A Rage for Order*, 4, 5.

2 Achcar, *The People Want*, 255.

3 Achcar, *The People Want*, 255.

4 Hazem Kandil, *Inside the Brotherhood* (London: Polity, 2015), 140.

5 David D. Kirkpatrick, *Into the Hands of the Soldiers: Freedom and Chaos in Egypt and the Middle East* (London: Bloomsbury, 2018), 41.

6 Worth, *A Rage for Order*, 23; Kirkpatrick, *Into the Hands of the Soldiers*, 31.

7 Kirkpatrick, *Into the Hands of the Soldiers*, 31.

8 Worth, *A Rage for Order*, 35.

9 Achcar, *The People Want*, 187.

10 Kandil, *Inside the Brotherhood*, 85–7, 88, 107, 175–8, 180–1.

11 See Chapter 2.

12 Kandil, *Inside the Brotherhood*, 136–7.

13 Kandil, *Inside the Brotherhood*, 85.

14 Kandil, *Inside the Brotherhood*, 87.

15 Kandil, *Inside the Brotherhood*, 87.

16 Kandil, *Inside the Brotherhood*, 135.

17 Kandil, *Inside the Brotherhood*, 135.

18 *Al-Ahram*, 4 August 2006.

19 Samer Shehata and Joshua Stacher, 'The Brotherhood goes to Parliament', *Middle East Report*, No. 240, Fall 2006.

20 Moustafa, 'Law in the Egyptian revolt', 184.

21 Kandil, *Inside the Brotherhood*, 137.

22 See Chapter 2, 64–5

23 Kandil, *Inside the Brotherhood*, 140.

24 'Egypt parties end deadlock over constitutional panel', BBC News, 8 June 2012.

25 'Official: the 100 members of Egypt's revamped Constituent Assembly', *Ahram* Online, 12 June 2012.

26 Marina Ottaway, 'Egypt: death of the Constituent Assembly?', Carnegie Endowment for International Peace, 13 June 2012.

27 Nathan J. Brown, 'The Egyptian political system in disarray', Carnegie Endowment for International Peace, 19 June 2012.

28 Yasmine Farouk, 'Writing the Constitution of the Egyptian revolution: between social contract and political contracting (March 2011 – July 2013)', Arab Reform Initiative, November 2013.

29 See Preface, xii, and Chapter 2, 52.

30 Wael Ghonim, *Revolution 2.0: the Power of the People is Greater than the People in Power. A Memoir* (Boston and New York: Houghton Mifflin Harcourt, 2012), 147.

31 Tina Rosenberg, 'Revolution U – what Egypt learned from the students who overthrew Milosevic', *Foreign Policy*, 17 February 2011.

32 Ghonim, *Revolution 2.0*, 197.

33 Kirkpatrick, *Into the Hands of the Soldiers*, 44.

34 'Hosni Mubarak's speech: full text', *Guardian*, 2 February 2011.

35 Ghonim, *Into the Hands of the Soldiers*, 44–5.

36 On ElBaradei's courting expatriate support, see Omar Ashour, 'ElBaradei and the mobilization of the Egyptian diaspora', *Arab Reform Bulletin*, 29 September 2010.

37 Peter Beaumont and Jack Schenker, 'Egypt braces itself for day of biggest protests yet', *Guardian*, 27 January 2011; Mark Memmott, 'ElBaradei back in Egypt; says it's time for a new government', NPR, 27 January 2011.

38 David Batty and Alex Olorenshaw, 'Egypt protests: as they happened', *Guardian*, 29 January 2011.

39 'Egypt protests: ElBaradei tells crowd "change coming"', BBC News, 30 January 2011; Jack Shenker and Ian Black, 'Egypt protests: change is coming says Mohamed ElBaradei', *Guardian*, 30 January 2011; see also 'ElBaradei: cut US Mubarak support', Al Jazeera, 30 January 2011.

40 'World reacts to Mubarak's announcement', CNN, 2 February 2011.

41 Jack Shenker, 'Mohamed ElBaradei urges world leaders to abandon Hosni Mubarak', *Guardian*, 2 February 2011.

42 'Egypt: a pivotal moment', *Guardian* (editorial), 29 January 2011.

43 Shenker and Black, 'Egypt protests'; 'Egypt protests', BBC News, 30 January 2011; 'Egypt protesters step up pressure on Hosni Mubarak', BBC News, 31 January 2011.

44 Worth, *A Rage for Order*, 30; Kirkpatrick gives the figure of at least thirteen killed (*Into the Hands of the Soldiers*, 49).

45 Ahmed Kadry, 'Egypt: the story so far', *Daily News Egypt*, 7 February 2011; Joshua Stacher, *Watermelon Democracy: Egypt's Turbulent Transition* (Syracuse, NY: Syracuse University Press, 2020), 41–2.

46 Ghonim, *Revolution 2.0*, 232–3.

47 Ghonim, *Revolution 2.0*, 232–3.

48 Ghonim, *Revolution 2.0*, 257–8.

49 See 'Egypt's "Battle of the Camel": the day the tride turned', *Ahram* Online, 2 February 2012.

50 International Crisis Group, *Popular Protest in North Africa and the Middle East, I: Egypt Victorious?*, Middle East and North Africa Report No. 101, 24 February 2011, 7. This report was researched and written by colleagues; I read and endorsed it on my first day back in my old job as ICG's North Africa Project director on 21 February 2011.

51 ICG, *Popular Protest in North Africa and the Middle East, I*, 8.

52 ICG, *Popular Protest in North Africa and the Middle East, I*, 7, n. 65.

53 Austin Holmes, *Coups and Revolutions*, 59 and 289, n. 61.

54 Kirkpatrick, *Into the Hands of the Soldiers*, 95–7; see also Ashraf Khalil, *Liberation Square: Inside the Egyptian Revolution and the Rebirth of a Nation* (New York: St Martin's Press, 2011), 222 (Chapter 11, 'The Battle of Tahrir', offers important testimony).

55 Kirkpatrick, *Into the Hands of the Soldiers*, 95–7.

56 The assassination attempt was initially reported on 4 February 2011, but the date of the attack was not made clear. See 'Egypt VP target of assassination attempt that killed two bodyguards, sources tell Fox News', Fox News, 4 February 2011; 'Two bodyguards killed in assassination attempt on new Egyptian vice president', *Daily Mail*, 5 February 2011; and 'Assassins took aim at Suleiman', *New York Post*, 5 February 2011. It was then denied altogether: see 'Source retracts statement on Suleiman assassination attempt', *Jerusalem Post*, 5 February 2011. On 24 February, after Suleiman was out of the game, the story was confirmed by Foreign Minister Ahmed Abul-Gheit: 'Assassination attempt on Omar Suleiman confirmed', *Ahram* Online, 24 February 2011; see also 'Egypt ex-VP survived "car shooting"', Al Jazeera, 24 February 2011; and

'Egypt confirms assassination attempt on Suleiman', *Haaretz*, 24 February 2011. Two years later, an article based on investigative reporting claimed that the attack took place on 30 January 2011, within hours of Suleiman's appointment as vice president: see Bradley Hope, 'Assassination attempt against Egypt's Suleiman a mystery two years later', *National*, 2 February 2013. For Suleiman's failed candidacy, see 'Brotherhood candidate, Salafi, Mubarak ex-VP fail in election appeals', Al Arabiya, 17 April 2012.

57 It is not certain that El-Roweini ever testified; he repeatedly failed to attend court sessions to which he had been summoned. See 'Update: Battle of the Camel trial defense team demands Shafiq be charged', *Egypt Independent*, 10 June 2012, 'Shafiq, SCAF member miss 'Battle of the Camel' trial session', *Egypt Independent*, 11 June 2012, and 'Shafiq, other witnesses skip Battle of the Camel trial', *Egypt Independent*, 14 June 2012.

58 Khalil, *Liberation Square*, 225–6, 233.

59 Austin Holmes, *Coups and Revolutions*, 54.

60 Kirkpatrick, *Into the Hands of the Soldiers*, 97–8.

61 Moustafa, 'Law in the Egyptian revolt', 186.

62 Moustafa, 'Law in the Egyptian revolt', 186.

63 Ghonim, *Revolution 2.0*, 263.

64 Ghonim, *Revolution 2.0*, 197, 198, 200.

65 Ghonim, *Revolution 2.0*, 288.

66 Ghonim, *Revolution 2.0*, 261, 265–6 and 275–6.

67 Khalil, *Liberation Square*, 270–1.

68 'Clinton, Remarks with Spanish Foreign Minister . . .', US Department of State, 25 January 2011, approx. 11 am EST; 'Statement by the Press Secretary on Egypt', White House, 25 January; Office of the Press Secretary Gibbs, White House, 26 January, 10.46 am EST; 'Readout of the President's calls to discuss Egypt', White House, written, 30 January; 'Interview with Candy Crowley of CNN's State of the Union', US Department of State, Clinton, spoken, 30 January; 'Press Briefing by Press Secretary Robert Gibbs', White House, 31 January, 2 pm EST.

69 'World reacts to Mubarak's announcement', CNN, 2 February 2011, 05.53 am EST; this report makes clear that Obama's remarks came after Mubarak's speech.

70 Hope, 'Assassination attempt'.

71 Matt Spetalnick and William Maclean, 'Exclusive: Egypt's Suleiman demonized Islamists: Wikileak cables', *Reuters*, 6 February 2011.

72 'News blog', *Guardian*, 6 February 2011.

73 'Remarks by the President on Egypt', The White House, Office of the Press Secretary, 11 February 2011, 15.09 EST.

74 ICG, *Popular Protest in North Africa and the Middle East, I*, 19. See also the acute observations on the SCAF's handling of these matters in Moustafa, 'Law in the Egyptian revolt', 187.

75 Lynch, *New Arab Wars*, xii.

76 'Update 1 – Saudi king expresses support for Mubarak', Reuters, 29 January 2011; see also 'Saudis told Obama not to humiliate Mubarak', *The Times*, 10 February 2011.

77 ICG, *Understanding Islamism*, Middle East and North Africa Report No. 37, Cairo/Brussels, 2 March 2005, 5, 12.

78 Jonathan A. C. Brown, 'The rise and fall of the Salafi al-Nour party in Egypt', *Jadaliyya*, 14 November 2013; see also Stéphane Lacroix, 'Egypt's pragmatic Salafis: the politics of Hizb al-Nour', Carnegie EIP, 1 November 2016.

Bibliography

Official communiqués, declarations, reports and resolutions

African Union, *Communiqué of the 265th Meeting of the Peace and Security Council*, PSC/PR/COM.2 (CCLXV), 10 March 2011

Amnesty International: 'Libya: "Out of control" militias commit widespread abuses, a year on from uprising', 16 February 2012

Convention (IV) Respecting the Laws and Customs of War on Land and Its Annex: Regulations Concerning the Laws and Customs of War on Land, The Hague, 18 October 1907

Sir Richard Dalton, *Libya's New Era and UK Engagement*, Chatham House, 21 October 2011

Sir Richard Dalton, *Libya: Turning the Page*, Chatham House, September 2012

Egypt Arab Republic Official Gazette

Hansard House of Commons Debates: UK Parliament, 'Libya and the Middle East', *Hansard*, vol. 524, House of Commons, 28 February 2011

Joseph Holiday, *Syria's Armed Opposition*, Middle East Security Report 3, Institute for the Study of War (Washington DC), March 2012

House of Commons Foreign Affairs Committee, *Oral Evidence: Libya: Examination of Intervention and Collapse and the UK's Future Policy Options*, Examination of Witness Lord Richards of Herstmonceaux, Questions 35, 319–22, 340

House of Commons Foreign Affairs Committee, Testimony of Former UK Ambassador to Libya, Sir Dominic Asquith KCMG, *Oral Evidence: Libya: Examination of Intervention and Collapse and the UK's Future Policy Options*, 27 October 2014, Q104

House of Commons Foreign Affairs Committee, Lord Hague's Testimony, *Oral Evidence: Libya: Examination of Intervention and Collapse and the UK's Future Policy Options*, 19 January 2016, Q286

Bibliography

Interim National Transitional Council (Libya), *Founding Statement of the Interim Transitional National Council*, Benghazi, 5 March 2011

Interim National Transitional Council (Libya), *The Constitutional Declaration*, Benghazi, 3 August 2011

Interim National Transitional Council (Libya), *Law No. 4 for the Year 2012 for Election of the General National Congress*, Tripoli, 28 January 2012

International Crisis Group, *Understanding Islamism*, Middle East/North Africa Report No. 37, Cairo/Brussels, 2 March 2005

International Crisis Group, *Reforming Egypt: in Search of a Strategy*, Middle East/North Africa Report No. 46, Cairo/Brussels, 4 October 2005

International Crisis Group, *Egypt's Muslim Brothers: Confrontation or Integration?*, Middle East/North Africa Report No. 76, Cairo/Brussels, 18 June 2008

International Crisis Group, *Popular Protest in North Africa and the Middle East, I: Egypt Victorious*, Middle East/North Africa Report No. 101, Cairo/Brussels, 24 February 2011

International Crisis Group, *A Ceasefire and Negotiations the Right Way to Resolve the Libya Crisis*, ICG Media Release, Brussels, 10 March 2011

International Crisis Group / Louise Arbour President and CEO, *Open Letter to the UN Security Council on the Situation in Libya*, 16 March 2011

International Crisis Group, *Libya: Achieving a Ceasefire, Moving toward Legitimate Government*, ICG Media Release, Brussels, 13 May 2011

International Crisis Group, *Popular Protest in the Middle East and North Africa, V: Making sense of Libya*, Middle East/North Africa Report No. 107, Cairo/Brussels, 6 June 2011

International Crisis Group, *Holding Libya Together: Security Challenges after Qadhafi*, Middle East/North Africa Report No. 115, 14 December 2011

Libyan Government's Letter to UN Security Council, 15 August 2003

North Atlantic Treaty Organization, *NATO Ready To Support International Efforts on Libya*, 10 March 2011

Mu'ammar Qadhafi, Transcript of his speech on state TV, Tuesday 22 February 2011

Royal United Services Institute (RUSI), *Accidental Heroes: Britain, France and the Libyan Operation*, September 2011

Supreme Council of the Armed Forces (SCAF), Egypt, *Constitutional Declaration*, March 2011

The White House, Office of the Press Secretary, 'Statement by the Press Secretary on Egypt', 25 January 2011.

The White House, Office of the Press Secretary, 26 January 2011, 10:46 am EST.

The White House, 'Readout of the President's Call to Discuss Egypt', 30 January 2011.

The White House, 'Press Briefing by Press Secretary Robert Gibbs', 31 January 2011, 2 pm EST.

United States Department of State, Hillary Clinton 'Remarks with Spanish Foreign Minister . . .', 25 January 2011, approx. 11 am EST.

United States Department of State, Clinton, spoken, 'Interview with Candy Crowley of CNN's State of the Union', 30 January 2011.

The White House, Office of the Press Secretary, 'Readout of President Obama's Call with Chancellor Angela Merkel of Germany', 26 February 2011

United Nations Security Council, *UNSC Resolution 1970*, February 2011

United Nations Security Council, *UNSC Resolution 1973*, 17 March 2011

Newspapers, news agencies and periodicals

Agence France Presse
Ahram Online
Al-Ahram (weekly)
Al Arabiya News
Al Jazeera
Associated Press
CBS World Watch
CNN
Daily News (Egypt)
Daily Telegraph
Der Spiegel
Echorouq (Cairo)
El Watan (Algiers daily)
Euronews
Guardian
Haaretz
Hürriyet
Independent
International Herald Tribune
La Croix
L'Expression (Algiers daily)
Le Monde

Bibliography

Le Monde Diplomatique
Libération
L'Observateur
London Review of Books
Malta Star
National
New York Times
Pan-African News Wire
Press Association
Reuters
Sky News
Today's Zaman
Wall Street Journal
Washington Times

Websites

Al-Monitor
Arab Reform Initiative
BBC News
Carnegie Endowment for International Peace
Counterpunch
Egyptian Chronicles blogspot
Médiapart
National Public Radio (NPR)
Sky News
The Revolutionary Socialists
UN News Centre
World Peace Foundation

Books

Anouar Abdel Malek, *L'Égypte, société militaire* (Paris: Le Seuil, 1962)
Anouar Abdel Malek, *Egypt, Military Society* (New York: Random House, 1968)
Anouar Abdel Malek (ed.), *La Pensée politique arabe contemporaine* (Paris: Le Seuil, 1970)
Saïd K. Aburish, *A Brutal Friendship: the West and the Arab Elite* (London: Victor Gollancz, 1997)
Gilbert Achcar, *The People Want: a Radical Exploration of the Arab Uprising* (London: Saqi, 2013)

Bibliography

Gilbert Achcar, *Morbid Symptoms: Relapse in the Arab Uprising* (Stanford, CA: Stanford University Press, 2016)

Ali Abdullatif Ahmida, *Forgotten Voices: Power and Agency in Colonial and Postcolonial Libya* (New York and London: Routledge, 2005)

Fouad Ajami, *The Arab Predicament* (Cambridge: Cambridge University Press, 2nd edn, 1992)

Holger Albrecht, *Raging Against the Machine: Political Opposition under Authoritarianism in Egypt* (Syracuse, NY: Syracuse University Press, 2013)

Sami Al-Jundi, *Al-Ba'th* (Beirut: Dar al-Nahar, 1969)

Lisa Anderson, *The State and Social Transformation in Libya and Tunisia, 1830–1980* (Princeton, NJ: Princeton University Press, 1986)

Amy Austin Holmes, *Coups and Revolutions: Mass Mobilization, the Egyptian Military and the United States from Mubarak to Sisi* (New York: Oxford University Press, 2019)

James Barr, *A Line in the Sand: Britain, France and the Struggle that Shaped the Middle East* (London and New York: Simon & Schuster, 2011)

Anthony Bell and David Witter, *The Libyan Revolution* (in four parts) (Washington DC: Institute for the Study of War, 2011)

Hervé Bleuchot, *Chroniques et document libyens, 1969–1980* (Paris: Éditions du CNRS, 1983)

Ethan Chorin, *Exit the Colonel: the Hidden History of the Libyan Revolution* (New York: Public Affairs, 2012)

Helena Cobban, *The Making of Modern Lebanon* (London: Hutchinson, 1985)

Patrick Cockburn, *The Rise of Islamic State: ISIS and the New Sunni Revolution* (London and New York: Verso, 2015)

John Davis, *Libyan Politics: Tribe and Revolution. An Account of the Zuwaya and Their Government* (London: I. B. Tauris, 1987)

Amr Elchoubaki, *Les Frères Musulmans des origines à nos jours* (Paris: Karthala, 2009)

Jean-Pierre Filiu, *The Arab Revolution: Ten Lessons from the Democratic Uprising* (London: Hurst, 2011)

Jean-Pierre Filiu, *From Deep State to Islamic State: the Arab Counter-Revolution and Its Jihadi Legacy* (London: Hurst, 2015)

Ruth First, *Libya: the Elusive Revolution* (Harmondsworth: Penguin African Library, 1974)

Ernest Gellner, *Muslim Society* (Cambridge: Cambridge University Press, 1981)

Wael Ghonim, *Revolution 2.0: the Power of the People is Greater than the People in Power. A Memoir* (Boston and New York: Houghton Mifflin Harcourt, 2012)

Charles Glass, *Syria Burning: ISIS and the Death of the Arab Spring* (with a foreword by Patrick Cockburn) (New York and London: OR Books, 2015)

Mohammed Harbi, *Aux Origines du FLN: le populisme révolutionnaire en Algérie* (Paris: Christian Bourgois, 1975)

Mohammed Harbi, *Le FLN: mirage et réalité: des origines à la prise du pouvoir (1945–1962)* (Paris: Éditions J. A., 1980)

Christopher Hill, *God's Englishman* (New York: The Dial Press, 1970)

Halil Inalcik, *The Ottoman Empire: the Classical Period, 1300-1600* (New York and Washington: Praeger Publishers, 1973; 2nd edn, New Rochelle, NY: Orpheus Publishing Co., 1989)

Hazem Kandil, *Soldiers, Spies and Statesmen: Egypt's Road to Revolt* (London and New York: Verso, 2012)

Hazem Kandil, *Inside the Brotherhood* (London: Polity, 2015)

Ashraf Khalil, *Liberation Square: Inside the Egyptian Revolution and the Rebirth of a Nation* (New York: St Martin's Press, 2011)

David D. Kirkpatrick, *Into the Hands of the Soldiers: Freedom and Chaos in Egypt and the Middle East* (London: Bloomsbury, 2018)

Muhammad Jalal Kishk, *Al-Qawmiyah wa 'l-Ghazw al-Fikri* (Nationalism and the Cultural Invasion) (Beirut: 1970)

Rabeh Kraifi, *La Fin du Parti-État en Tunisie* (Tunis: Regroupement Larache des Livres Spécialisés, 2015)

Bernard-Henri Lévy, *La Guerre sans l'aimer: journal d'un écrivain au cœur du printemps libyen* (Paris: Grasset, 2011)

Jonathan Littell, *Syrian Notebooks: Inside the Homs Uprising* (London and New York: Verso, 2015)

Marc Lynch, *The New Arab Wars: Uprisings and Anarchy in the Middle East* (New York: Public Affairs, 2016)

Bruce Maddy-Weitzmann, *The Berber Identity Movement and the Challenge to North African States* (Austin, TX: University of Texas Press, 2011)

Roger Owen, *The Rise and Fall of Arab President for Life* (Cambridge, MA: Harvard University Press, 2012)

Mu'ammar al-Qadhafi, *The Green Book* (London: Martin, Brian and O'Keefe, 1976)

Hugh Roberts, *The Battlefield: Algeria 1988–2002. Studies in a Broken Polity* (London and New York: Verso, 2003)

Patrick Seale, *The Struggle for Syria; a Study of Post-War Arab Politics* (London, New York and Toronto: RIIA and Oxford University Press, 1965)

Patrick Seale, *Asad: the Struggle for the Middle East* (London: I. B. Tauris, 1988)

Patrick Seale and Maureen McConville, *The Hilton Assignment* (London: Maurice Temple Smith, 1973)

Amira El-Azhary Sonbol, *The New Mamluks: Egyptian Society and*

Modern Feudalism (with a foreword by Robert Fernea) (Syracuse, NY: Syracuse University Press, 2000)

Joshua Stacher, *Adaptable Autocrats: Regime Power in Egypt and Syria* (Stanford, CA: Stanford University Press, 2012)

Joshua Stacher, *Watermelon Democracy: Egypt's Turbulent Transition* (Syracuse, NY: Syracuse University Press, 2020)

Denis J. Sullivan and Sana Abed-Kotob, *Islam in Contemporary Egypt: Civil Society versus the State* (Boulder, CO and London: Lynne Riener, 1999)

Nikolaos Van Dam, *The Struggle for Power in Syria: Politics and Society under Asad and the Ba'th Party* (London: I. B. Tauris, 4th edn, 2011)

Dirk Vandewalle (ed.), *Qadhafi's Libya, 1969 to 1994* (New York: St Martin's Press, 1995)

Dirk Vandewalle, *Libya since Independence: Oil and State-Building* (London: I. B. Tauris, 1998)

Dirk Vandewalle, *A History of Modern Libya* (Cambridge: Cambridge University Press, 2006, 2012)

Michael Weiss and Hassan Hassan, *ISIS: Inside the Army of Terror* (New York: Regan Arts, 2015)

Philip Williams, *Wars, Plots and Scandals in Post-war France* (Cambridge: Cambridge University Press, 1970)

Robert F. Worth, *A Rage for Order: the Middle East in Turmoil, from Tahrir Square to ISIS* (London: Picador, 2016)

John Wright, *Libya, a Modern History* (London and Canberra: Croom Helm, 1981)

I. William Zartman (ed.), *Arab Spring: Negotiations in the Shadow of the Intifadat* (Athens, GA: University of Georgia Press, 2015)

Journal articles and chapters in books

Samir Aita, 'Syria: aspirations and fragmentations', in I. William Zartman (ed.), *Arab Spring: Negotiations in the Shadow of the Intifadat* (Athens, GA: University of Georgia Press, 2015), 290–331

Hervé Bleuchot and Taoufik Monastiri, 'L'islam de M. El-Qaddhafi', in Ernest Gellner and Jean-Claude Vatin (eds), *Islam et Politique au Maghreb* (Paris: Éditions du CNRS, 1981)

Jonathan A. C. Brown, 'The rise and fall of the Salafi al-Nour party in Egypt', *Jadaliyya*, 14 November 2013

John Davis, 'Qadhafi's theory and practice of non-representative government', *Government and Opposition*, 17, 1, 1982, 61–9

Yasmine Farouk, 'Writing the Constitution of the Egyptian revolution:

between social contract and political contracting (March 2011 – July 2013)', Arab Reform Initiative, November 2013

Peter Gaunt, 'Cromwell, Richard (1626–1712)', *Oxford Dictionary of National Biography* (online version, 2008)

Ernest Gellner, 'The unknown Apollo of Biskra: the social base of Algerian puritanism', *Government and Opposition*, 9, 1974, 277–310; reprinted in Gellner, *Muslim Society* (Cambridge: Cambridge University Press, 1981), 149–73

George Joffé, 'Saif al-Islam: the whole (Libyan) world in his arms', *Arab Reform Bulletin*, December 2009/January 2010

Alan J. Kuperman, 'A model humanitarian intervention? Reassessing NATO's Libya campaign', *International Security*, 38, 1, Summer 2013, 105–36

Wolfram Lacher, 'Faultlines of the revolution: political actors, camps and conflicts in the new Libya', Stiftung Wissenschaft und Politik, Research Paper 4, Berlin, May 2013

Stéphane Lacroix, 'Egypt's pragmatic Salafis: the politics of Hizb al-Nour', Carnegie EIP, 1 November 2016

Joshua Landis, 'Divisions within the Syrian Opposition on the eve of the Turkey meeting', Syria Comment, posted 26 May 2011

Joshua Landis, 'Free Syrian Army founded by seven officers to fight the Syrian army', Syria Comment, 29 July 2011

Joshua Landis, 'Opposition disunity becomes the problem as the West gets its ducks in a row', Syria Comment, 29 August 2011

Dalenda Larguèche, 'La trajectoire politique tunisienne', *Journal of African History*, 46, 3, November 2005

Aron Lund, 'Divided they stand: an overview of Syria's political opposition factions', Foundation for European Progressive Studies, Olaf Palme International Center, Uppsala, May 2012

Marc Lynch, 'Why Obama had to act in Libya', *Foreign Policy*, 29 March 2011

Driss Maghraoui, 'Constitutional reforms in Morocco: between consensus and subaltern politics', *Journal of North African Studies*, 16, 4, 2011, 679–99

Hanspeter Mattes, 'The rise and fall of the revolutionary committees', in Vandewalle (ed.), *Qadhafi's Libya, 1969 to 1994* (New York: St Martin's Press, 1995), 89–112

Karim Mezran and Alice Alunni, 'Libya: negotiations for transition', in I. William Zartman (ed.), *Arab Spring: Negotiations in the Shadow of the Intifadat* (Athens, GA: University of Georgia Press, 2015), 249–90

Hugh Miles, 'Inconvenient truths', *London Review of Books*, 29, 12, 21 June 2007

Tamir Moustafa, 'Law in the Egyptian revolt', *Middle East Law and Government*, 3, 2011, 181–91

Jason Pack and Haley Cook, 'The July 2012 Libyan election and the origin of post-Qadhafi appeasement', *Middle East Journal*, 69, 2, Spring 2015, 171–98

Hugh Roberts, 'The politics of Algerian socialism', in R. I. Lawless and Allen Findlay (eds), *North Africa: Contemporary Politics and Economic Development* (London: Croom Helm, 1984), 5–49

Hugh Roberts, 'Algeria's ruinous impasse and the honourable way out', *International Affairs*, 71, 2, 1995, 247–67

Hugh Roberts, 'The struggle for constitutional rule in Algeria', *Journal of Algerian Studies*, 3, 1998, 19–30; reprinted in Hugh Roberts, *The Battlefield: Algeria 1988–2002. Studies in a Broken Polity* (London and New York: Verso, 2003), chapter 12

Hugh Roberts, 'Algeria's national "protesta"', *Foreign Policy: the Middle East Channel*, 10 January 2011

Hugh Roberts, 'Protest on the rocks', *Middle East in London*, 7, 9, June–July 2011

Hugh Roberts, 'The negotiations that aren't', in I. William Zartman (ed.), *Arab Spring: Negotiations in the Shadow of the Intifadat* (Athens, GA: University of Georgia Press, 2015), 145–81

Hugh Roberts, 'The Hirāk and the Ides of December', *Jadaliyya*, 19 November 2019

Jean-Louis Romanet-Perroux, 'Libya: the long way forward', World Peace Foundation, 3 January 2013

Maximilien Robespierre, *Rapport sur les principes du gouvernement révolutionnaire*, Paris, Year II, 5 Nivose (25 December 1793)

Tina Rosenberg, 'Revolution U – what Egypt learned from the students who overthrew Milosevic', *Foreign Policy*, 17 February 2011

Samer Shehata and Joshua Stacher, 'The Brotherhood goes to Parliament', *Middle East Report*, 240, Fall 2006

Mohsen Toumi, 'Le Parti Socialiste Destourien', *Revue Française d'Études Politiques Africaines*, 9, 107, 1974, 26–45

Alex de Waal, 'The African Union and the Libyan conflict of 2011', *World Peace Foundation*, 19 December 2012

Frederic Wehrey, 'Libya's Militia Menace', *Foreign Affairs*, 15 July 2012

Index